DOUBLE CROSS IN CAIRO

ALSO BY NIGEL WEST

DOUBLE CROSS IN CAIRO

THE TRUE STORY OF THE SPY WHO TURNED
THE TIDE OF WAR IN THE MIDDLE EAST

NIGEL WEST

Biteback Publishing

First published in Great Britain in 2015 by
Biteback Publishing Ltd
Westminster Tower
3 Albert Embankment
London SE1 7SP
Copyright © Nigel West 2015

ISBN 978-1-84954-796-3

10 9 8 7 6 5 4 3 2 1

A CIP catalogue record for this book is available from the British Library.

Set in Bulmer

Printed and bound in Great Britain by
CPI Group (UK) Ltd, Croydon CR0 4YY

Nicossof's a Russian name
And not what you might think,
A form of Oriental vice,
Or buggery, or drink.
A scion of this noble house,
An unattractive sod,
Was Stanislas P. Nicossof
Of Nizhni Novgorod.

COLONEL DUDLEY CLARKE

They call me Venal Vera
I'm a lovely from Gezira
The Fuhrer pays me well for what I do
The order of battle
I obtain from last night's rattle
On the golf course with the brigadier from GHQ.

ODE TO A GEZIRA LOVELY

Any trustworthy item of intelligence
is worth a dozen panzers.

ADMIRAL WILHELM CANARIS, FEBRUARY 1941

Chief among these masters of espionage was the
innocuously named agent CHEESE. This case
became one of the most successful of all the
double cross agents in the war.

TERRY CROWDY IN *DECEIVING HITLER*

CONTENTS

ACKNOWLEDGEMENTS

The author owes a debt of gratitude to the intelligence professionals who have assisted his research, among them Tommy Robertson, Rodney O. Dennys, David Mure and Bill Kenyon-Jones. He is also grateful for the assistance of the deception historian Thaddeus Holt, and Martin Levi and his family. In addition, the archivists at Winchester College and University College, Oxford, were generous with their time.

Renato Levi in 1949

GLOSSARY

18700	SIS Numerical code for Nicholas Elliott in Istanbul
89700	SIS Numerical code for Rodney Dennys in Cairo
ABEAM	Deception scheme
Abstelle	Abwehrstellen
Abwehr	German military intelligence service
AFU	Agentfunkgerät (Abwehr wireless)
ALADDIN	Abwehr officer in Istanbul
AMGOT	Allied Military Government for Occupied Territories
BGM	Blonde Gun Moll
BIJOU	Deception scheme involving HMS *Indefatigable*
CAMILLA	'A' Force deception scheme
CASCADE	'A' Force deception scheme in 1942
CBME	Combined Bureau Middle East
COMPASS	Allied attack at Sidi Barrani in 1940
CS	Commission Speziale
CSDIC	Combined Services Detailed Interrogation Centre
DAK	Deutsche Afrika Korps
DAKHLA	Abwehr agent in Egypt
D/F	Direction-Finding
DOWAGER	'A' Force deception scheme
DSO	Defence Security Officer

EAM	Greek National Liberation Front
ELAS	Greek Peoples Liberation Army
FABRIC	'A' Force deception scheme in 1942
FLESHPOTS	'A' Force deception scheme at El Alamein
GALVESTON	'A' Force deception scheme
GRANDIOSE	'A' Force deception scheme concerning the Prime Minister's travel itinerary in 1942
HARPOON	Unsuccessful Allied convoy to Malta
HATRY	Financial scheme to finance CHEESE
HERKULES	Axis plan for the invasion of Malta
HUSKY	Allied invasion of Sicily in 1943
IH	Einz Heer
IL	Einz Luft
IM	Einz Marine
ISLD	Inter-Services Liaison Department
ISOS	Signals intercepts
JACOBITE	Plan to establish CHEESE in Athens
KO	Kriegsorganisation
KONO	Kriegsorganisation Nahe Orient
LAMBERT	SIME codename for Paul Nicossof
LIGHTFOOT	Allied offensive in 1942
LLAMA	SIM agent in Tripoli run by the French as a double agent
LRDG	Long Range Desert Group
MIDAS	MI5 scheme to finance TATE
MI5	British Security Service
MI6	British Secret Intelligence Service
MI9	British Escape and Evasion Service
MI14	Combined Services Detailed Interrogation Centre
NCO	Non-Commissioned Officer
ODYSSEY	Plan to recover a wireless set in Athens
OETA	Occupied Enemy Territory Administration

GLOSSARY

OKW	Wehrmacht High Command
OSS	Office of Strategic Services
ONI	Office of Naval Intelligence
PAIC	Palestine and Iraq Command
PCO	Passport Control Officer
PEDESTAL	Allied relief convoy to Malta
RAYON	Deception scheme in 1942
RB	Rifle Brigade
RHSA	Reich Security Agency
RSS	Radio Security Service
SCU	Special Communications Unit
SENTINEL	Deception scheme in 1942
SIM	Servizio di Informazione Militare
SIME	Security Intelligence Middle East
STONEAGE	Allied relief convoy to Malta
TORCH	Allied invasion of North Africa in 1942
TREATMENT	Strategic deception scheme in 1942
TRIANGLE	Decrypts of Abwehr Signals traffic
TS	Tribunale Speziale
TURPITUDE	Deception scheme in 1944
VENDETTA	Deception scheme in 1944
VIGOROUS	Allied relief convoy for Malta
V-mann	Verbindungsmann
WANTAGE	Deception scheme in 1944
X-2	OSS counter-intelligence branch
ZEPPELIN	Deception scheme in 1944

DRAMATIS PERSONAE

Captain Alessi	Italian Air Force officer
Annabella	Abwehr assistant to Rossetti
APOLLO	Abwehr agent in Athens
ARMANDO	Abwehr agent in Athens
ARMAVIR	Unidentified Abwehr courier
ARTHUR	Abwehr codename for DOLEFUL
Bonzos	German agent codenamed RIO
Hamado Amin Bey	Member of the PYRAMIDS network
BLACKGUARD	SIS agent
Blonde Gun Moll	Evangeline Palidou
Cuthbert Bowlby	Head of ISLD
Max Brandl	Swiss watch salesman codenamed ODIOUS
Joseph Buchegger	Member of a criminal gang in Istanbul
Helene Cabri	Notional nominee for the receipt of money in Cairo
CARPELLASO	Abwehr agent in Sofia
Peter Chandos	SIS officer
CHARLES	Abwehr officer in Sofia
CHEESE	SIME codename for Renato Levi
Pat Clayton	Captured LRDG officer
Andrea Cohen	Notional recipient of funds in Switzerland
Henri Cohen	Corrupt merchant in Cairo

Costa	Swiss-Italian double agent codenamed PESSIMIST X
Geoffrey W. Courtney	SIS officer in Paris
Michael Crichton	SIME officer
CRUDE	ISLD double agent in Syria
G. R. C. Davis	SIME officer
DOLEFUL	SIME double agent, a wagon-lit attendant on the Taurus Express, known to the Abwehr as ARTHUR
Dudley Clarke	'A' Force director
Dr Delius	Abwehr officer in Sofia
Rodney Dennys	SIS officer
Desmond Doran	SIME officer
EFFIGY	SIS double agent in Athens
Otto Eisentrager	Abwehr officer in Sofia
Nicholas Elliott	SIS officer in Istanbul
Staff Sergeant Ellis	CHEESE's first wireless operator
EMILE	Abwehr codename for Clemens Rossetti
Johannes Eppler	Abwehr spy arrested in Cairo in July 1942
GALA	Double agent
GEORGE	Georges Khouri
GILBERT	Deuxième Bureau double agent in Tunis
GODSEND	Istanbul banker and SIS agent
GROWNUP	SIS agent
GULL	SIS agent
Rex Hamer	SIME officer
HAMLET	Abwehr codename for Jawad Hamadi
Kurt Hammer	Abwehr agent in Rome
HASSAN	Abwehr agent in Athens
Heilgendorf	Abwehr radio operator in Bari
Otto Helfferich	Abwehr chief in Rome
HELMUT	Notional sub-source of ARTHUR
Jack Hester	SCU 4

Major S. S. Hill-Dillon	SIS officer
Geoffrey Hinton	SIME officer
INFAMOUS	SIS double agent in Turkey
Michael Ionides	SIS officer
Giles Isham	SIME interrogator
JEAN	Abwehr agent in Paris
George Jenkins	DSO Egypt
Alec Kellar	MI5 officer
Bill Kenyon-Jones	'A' Force
Georges Khouri	Suspected spy in Cairo
KISS	SIS double agent
Klein	Abwehr agent in Palestine
Captain Knowles	SIS officer in Paris
Karl Kurt	Abwehr agent, alias Charles Masson
LAMBERT	SIME codename for the CHEESE network
Captain Lafontaine	SIS officer
Major Lethbridge	PCO in Belgrade
Renato Levi	Double agent, known as CHEESE to SIME and ROBERTO to the Abwehr
LUPO	Abwehr agent in Athens
Kenneth MacFarlan	Radio Security Service officer
Giovanni Magaracci	Real name of Fulvio Melcher
Alfred Major	British Consul in Genoa
MARIE	Abwehr codename for MISANTHROPE
Rolf von der Marwitz	German naval attaché in Turkey, codenamed DENNIS
Raymund Maunsell	Head of SIME
Captain McElwee	SIME officer
Fulvio Melcher	Alias of Giovanni Magaracci, Abwehr radio operator
MIMI	Abwehr agent known to SIME as PESSIMIST Y
MISANTHROPE	Notional Greek girlfriend of Renato Levi
MURAT	Abwehr codename for Erich Vermehren

NAHICHEVAN	Unidentified Abwehr courier
Paul Nicossof	Notional sub-agent of CHEESE
ODIOUS	Max Brandl
OTTO	Abwehr agent in Athens
PAPAS	Abwehr agent
Parker	OSS officer
PASCHA	Abwehr agent based in Istanbul
PEDANT	SIS double agent in Athens
PESSIMIST X	Swiss-Italian double agent run in Syria by SIME named Costa
PESSIMIST Y	Wireless operator and double agent codenamed Mimi by the Abwehr
PESSIMIST Z	Double agent and drug smuggler in Syria
Hans Piekenbrock	Deputy chief of the Abwehr
Eric Pope	SIME officer
PRECIOUS	Erich Vermehren
QUICKSILVER	George Liossis
RAM	French double agent
REALTER	Abwehr spy sent to Egypt
RIO	Codename of a Gestapo agent named Bonzos
ROBERTO	Abwehr codename for Renato Levi
Douglas Roberts	DSO in Beirut
James C. Robertson	SIME officer
Terence Robertson	SIME officer
Clemens Rossetti	Abwehr officer, codenamed EMILE
Gilbert Ryle	RSS analyst
John de Salis	SIS officer
SAVAGES	Double agent network in Cyprus
Count Scirombo	Italian intelligence officer in Rome
Walter Sensburg	Senior Abwehr officer in Athens
Rowley Shears	Royal Signals wireless operator

Harry Shergold	CSDIC interrogator
Evan Simpson	SIME officer
SMOOTH	ISLD double agent in Syria
Azeglia Socci	Cabaret artiste and Renato Levi's girlfriend
Blanshard Stamp	MI5 analyst
TATE	MI5 double agent in London
Hans Travaglio	Abwehr officer, alias Major Solms
Tschunscheff	Abwehr agent in Athens
Erich Vermehren	Abwehr defector codenamed PRECIOUS
WHISKERS	French double agent in Morocco
John Wills	SIS officer
Victor Whittal	SIS officer in Istanbul
WERNER	Abwehr agent
Kurt J. Zähringer	Abwehr officer, alias Zedow, at the German consulate-general in Istanbul.

INTRODUCTION

V ery little has ever been written about CHEESE because
almost nothing has been known about him for certain.
Even the declassification of MI5's wartime files in 2011
ensured that practically all references to his true identity had been
redacted, but it is now possible to tell his astonishing story in full
for the very first time since his death in 1954, with the support of
his surviving family.

As a double agent, CHEESE has few, if any, equals. He was an Italian Jew who was brought up in India, was educated in Switzerland,
and employed as a British agent while working for the French, Italian
and German intelligence services. During his extraordinary espionage career which spanned the entire length of the Second World
War, he worked for four intelligence agencies (sometimes simultaneously), and survived the experience. He was imprisoned in Turkey
and Italy, and his information, brilliantly fabricated in Cairo, had a
profound impact on the course of the war in North Africa and the
Eastern Mediterranean, and became the foundation upon which the
concept of strategic deception was constructed. He was fluent in
English, French, Italian and German, and his wireless traffic was transmitted in French. He was also entirely cosmopolitan, a womaniser,
and the legitimate holder of a British passport. Exceptionally brave,

he made a perilous journey to place himself back in the hands of the Abwehr in 1942 when his loyalties had come under German investigation. The huge quantities of misleading material that he conveyed to the Axis undermined the Afrika Korps's attempt to capture Cairo and the Suez Canal, and made a substantial contribution to the first defeat suffered by General Erwin Rommel. In particular, CHEESE is widely acknowledged as having played a pivotal role in the success of Operation CRUSADER, General Claude Auchinleck's offensive in November 1941 which took the enemy by surprise and successfully recaptured Tobruk.

In 1942 the British deception planners, known as 'A' Force, exploited the enemy's confidence in CHEESE's network by vastly exaggerating the Allied order-of-battle across the Middle East, and conveying bogus reports of deployments and intentions. According to Sir Michael Howard, the official historian of British strategic deception in the Second World War, CHEESE was 'the most successful channel at their disposal'. Best of all, TRIANGLE demonstrated that CHEESE's information was routinely circulated 'to the Admiral Aegean, Panzer Armee Afrika IC, and the Festungskommandant Crete'.

What makes CHEESE so remarkable, apart from the absence of any reference to him by the authorised historians of both MI5 and MI6 (Christopher Andrew in *The Defence of the Realm* and Keith Jeffery in *MI6*), is the entirely notional network of agents and casual contacts that he developed, among them the colourful, pipe-smoking Syrian Paul Nicossof, who eventually took over control of the organisation, and CHEESE's Greek girlfriend, codenamed MISANTHROPE. Although she was an invention, a very real woman, a fierce Cretan known as the Blonde Gun Moll, or BGM, acted her role when required.

As we shall see, CHEESE's spy-ring extended to informants of all types and ranged from an American general to cabaret artiste. Perhaps most importantly of all, CHEESE became the principal channel of ingeniously fabricated false intelligence which had been invented by a large team of case officers and analysts who effectively created the concept of military misdirection. As an agent of the British Secret Intelligence Service (MI6), he is unrivalled, and accomplished more, over a longer period, than any other. Quite simply, CHEESE became one of the most influential figures of the conflict, yet his role remains undisclosed until now.

Over the past forty years, since the first revelations about the XX Committee, which managed MI5's stable of double agents, and ULTRA, the signals intelligence product distributed from Bletchley Park, much has been published about the manipulation of the enemy's spy-rings, and the influence of Enigma and Geheimschreiber decrypts. Once highly classified, the concept of strategic deception is now acknowledged as yet another hidden dimension to the clandestine war, but few have stopped to ask how all this effort started. The extraordinary exploits of GARBO, SNOW, ZIGZAG and TRICYCLE have now been declassified, and much has been written about the D-Day deception campaign codenamed FORTITUDE and the highly imaginative schemes, such as MINCEMEAT and COPPERHEAD, designed to mislead the enemy. Such adventures have captured the public's imagination, and one can only marvel at the ingenuity of the British intelligence personnel who dreamed up a plan to drop the body of a dead courier on a Spanish beach in April 1943, or to send Monty's double to visit Gibraltar shortly before the invasion of Normandy. Schoolboy pranks or ruses designed with scientific precision to deceive the Abwehr and save thousands of Allied lives?

With the advantages of virtual control over the Axis intelligence collection system, access to the German High Command's internal communications, and the willingness to mount highly sophisticated deception campaigns, the Allies took significant gambles with the objective of misdirecting the enemy. The results certainly justified the risks. We know now that secret intelligence had a significant impact on the destruction of the Kriegsmarine's U-boat fleet during the Battle of the Atlantic, on the amphibious landings on the coast of France, and the defeat of the Afrika Korps in Libya. We have also learned much about the cryptographers who solved the most complex ciphers, the technicians who devised the machinery, such as Bombes and the Colossus computer, to assist their task, and the British agents and their case officers who worked in conditions of great secrecy to ensure victory. Some of these individuals have been recognised at exhibitions, with belated medals, biographies and even Hollywood movies. Much information has also been released about similar operations in the Far East theatre, where Peter Fleming ran double agents from India against the Japanese, and American cryptanalysts broke the PURPLE and other codes and circulated the results as MAGIC. However, all these triumphs owe their origins to a pioneering operation masterminded by a complete amateur, Evan Simpson, and his star, a playboy with the unprepossessing codename CHEESE.

CHAPTER ONE

RENATO'S TALE

A 38-year-old Italian Jew from a wealthy family whose mother, the actress Dolores Domenici, owned the Hotel Miramare in Rapallo and the Hotel Select in Genoa's Piazza delle Fontane Marose, Renato Levi was known to Security Intelligence Middle East (SIME) as CHEESE (later LAMBERT, and to his German controller as ROBERTO, later designated V-mann 7501). In MI5's opinion, as expressed in a report dated September 1942, he was motivated by his Jewish heritage, but not a dislike of either the Germans or the Italians. He enjoyed the adventure, and wished to settle in Australia after the war with a British passport. According to German documents, he was registered as an agent of the Athens Abstelle and an Abwehr officer named Heilgendorf acted as his radio control in Bari.

Born in Italy in 1902 of Jewish-Italian parents, Renato spent five years in Bombay, where the prosperous Levi family operated a ship-yard, until 1913 and then was educated at Zug in Switzerland until 1918. He remained in Italy until 1926 when he moved to Wentworth, and then East Sydney in Australia, but he returned to Italy in 1937 and settled in Genoa with his Australian wife Lina and son Luciano, who was born in 1925, together with his brother Paulo and step-father Alberico. Renato was good looking, with great charm and a penchant for nightclubs and beautiful women, but was a financial burden for his formidable mother. He was supposed to help her in the management of the hotels, but they often clashed and she occasionally banished him to a neighbouring pension, the Hotel Metropoli.

In 1939 Levi told the British consul in Genoa, Alfred G. Major, that he had been approached by the Germans to spy in Holland, and had been encouraged to accept the assignment. Subsequently, between December 1939 and June 1940, he had been in touch with the French Deuxième Bureau and the Secret Intelligence Service (SIS) in Paris where a former MI5 officer, Geoffrey W. Courtney headed the station. A former MI5 officer, Courtney had been transferred to Paris in 1938 from the Cairo station.

Upon his return to Genoa, his German contact, Hans Travaglio, had persuaded him to go to Egypt with a wireless transmitter to collect military information, and this scheme was approved by Count Scirombo, a senior Italian intelligence officer and formerly the Italian consul in Cairo. Levi was briefed in Bari and the plan changed. He would be sent a wireless after he had arrived in Cairo, probably through the Hungarian diplomatic bag, and he was required to send his encrypted messages in French. He was supplied with two questionnaires, one Italian and one German, and a list of contacts in Budapest and Belgrade, and given the address of two Abwehr officers, Otto Eisentrager and Dr Delius, in Sofia. He was warned to avoid any contact with German consulates in Turkey, for fear of attracting the attention of the British or Turkish authorities, but was told he could obtain assistance from any German consul in a neutral country simply by mentioning 'Emile from Genoa'.

SIS would later identify Hauptman Eisentrager as an Abwehr personality first identified in a report dated 12 June 1939 who used the alias 'Major Otto Wagner' and held a post in Ast III in Berlin. He later appeared in two ISOS decrypts, in October and November 1940, probably working in Sofia, responsible for the collection of economic and Air Force intelligence. Significantly, an ISOS intercept dated 9 November 1940 asked Eisentrager 'if and when the apparatus was leaving Sofia for Egypt and how long the transport was expected to take'. As SIME later commented, 'it seems not improbable that this message referred to the original arrangement for providing Levi with a transmitter'. After the war, MI5 learned that Wagner, an attorney from Mannheim fluent in Bulgarian, was Eisentrager's true name and that was his codename.

Levi's supervision was to fall to Sonderfuhrer Clemens Rossetti, an Abwehr personality who frequently appeared in Abwehr traffic handling agents across the Middle East. According to SIS, Rossetti had headed the Genoa Abstelle until the end of 1940 when he was replaced by Travaglio, whom SIME described as

Born in Munich, age about forty-five. Over 6ft in height, broad shoulders and stout build. Very large head – when buying hats always found difficulty in obtaining the correct size. Dark brown hair, very thin, particularly in the centre of the scalp. Ruddy fair complexion, fat cheeks. Clean shaven. Eyes dark brown (?). Large nose. Large mouth with full lips, three or four gold teeth. Rounded double chin. Large thick ears. Large very fleshy hands. Big feet. Speaks German with Bavarian accent. Walks ponderously. Large scar on left side of abdomen said to have been the result of a flying accident during the 1914–18 war, when he was a pilot.

Travaglio is very fond of music, particularly opera; plays the piano and sings himself. Jovial disposition and enjoys company. Has a fund of humorous stories about Hitler and Mussolini in particular. Generous, open-handed and romantic nature; professes to be deeply influenced by scenic beauty. Is an amateur antique collector, Levi considers Travaglio to be a very patriotic German but not a good Nazi. He confided to Levi on one occasion that he had been an agent in peacetime, travelling under cover of a guide for German tourist parties, particularly in Italy. He also stated (in strict confidence) that in 1936–39 he had succeeded in penetrating the British Secret Service in the Netherlands posing as an anti-Nazi. To support this cover he had had his name struck off the official list of Party members. Claimed to be responsible for the capture of the British agents on the Dutch-German frontier.

Holds German degree of Doctor of Philosophy. Languages: German, Italian, French, poor English. Has travelled Germany, Italy, France and the Netherlands. Private home address in 1940/41 was 10 Mariakirchenstrasse, Munich. May have moved his home since marriage in June 1941 with well-known German opera singer, age about thirty/thirty-five. Father dead, but mother still living, age about sixty-five. Has nervous trick of rubbing the tip of his nose, as though attempting to stifle a sneeze. Heavy cigarette smoker. Dresses smartly and expensively. Fond of motor-cars and women, in that order.

Thereafter Rossetti, codenamed EMILE, appeared in ISOS traffic as being engaged in Abwehr activity in Italy between January and May 1941, and in one intercept his address was given as 'care of the German consulate in Naples'. An ISOS decrypt dated 7 October 1941 suggested that Rossetti was then in Rome but had been 'Leiter I Luft' in the Munich Abstelle. After the war, when Count Scirombo was interrogated by Allied intelligence officers, he identified Rossetti's real name as 'Kurt Knabe'. A German defector, Wili Hamburger, would describe Rossetti as 'the most expensive member of the Abwehr in Turkey' and suggested that his status has been achieved because of his success in Holland where he had developed a relationship with Anton Mussert's pro-Nazi movement. His arrival in Istanbul had been sponsored by the former head of the local KO, Walter Schulze-Bernett.

ISOS disclosed that Rossetti

received frequent information from Helfferich in Rome, all of which were apparently concerned with the dispatch of agents. Thus on 3 February 1942 he was advised of Kurt Hammer's departure from Brindisi; on 5 March 1942 of the arrival of APOLLO and OTTO in Athens; on 13 April 1942 on the arrival of Emil Tisl, and on 6 May 1942 his presence was desired for a personal discussion in Rome with reference to the agent APOLLO. In addition to this Rossetti appears to have private connections of his own in Italy, of which are also productive of agents. On 13 January 1942 Ast Paris consulted him on the provision of a wireless set for WERNER of Rome's AFU man for Egypt; On 13 April 1942 they again consulted him on concerning the transfer of V-mann 7501, who had previously been working for I.I. Paris to 'Rome Annabella'. Further references to Rome Annabella occur in messages of Italy of September/October 1942 which seem to suggest that Annabella was a personal agent of Rossetti's in Italy, who was subsequently transferred to Athens in connection with the agent ARMANDO who set out from Turkey at the end of September. During the same period there were references to a visit paid by Rossetti to Rome to test two agents who were being considered as reserves for HAMLET in the Syrian undertaking; to the 'new V-mann PAPAS', who was to be vetted by Rossetti in Turkey; to one Hattenkorn, apparently an untrustworthy agent who had been dismissed; to two agents HASSAN and LUPO, who arrived in Athens in early October; to 'a Persian agent of CHARLES', who was to be visited by Rossetti in Sofia in January 1943; and finally to Rossetti's agent CARPELLASO who had reported at KO Bulgarien and asked for a German passport in the name of Hoffmann and a travelling allowance to Rome for the purpose of working in Cairo.

Rossetti also occupies himself with looking after the agents of other Stellen who are visiting Athens or are in the area in which Ast Athens works. Then on 13 December 1942 Berlin enquired whether he was in touch with the agent Hamado Amin Bey of IM Ast III whom it had become necessary to arrest; on 23 December 1942 he was asked to assist one Tschanscheff, apparently an agent who was arriving in Athens; on 7 December 1942 Rossetti, who was then in Istanbul, informed Berlin that he wished to speak with their agent T 400 when the latter was next in Istanbul, Sofia or Athens; in February 1943 Rossetti, who was still in Turkey, was announcing that he had been authorised by IM Ost to work upon a considerable scale in Turkey, and for that purpose wanted 20,000 Turkish pounds.

Even this does not reflect the full scale of Rossetti's activities, for it appears that he is also concerned with matters which usually fall outside the sphere of an Abt I officer. On 23 January 1943 he was provided with false information which he was to pass on to PARKER (presumably of OSS) from which we may assume that he is also concerned in the running of double agents. On 13 March 1942 he requested IH Ost to provide him with supplies of the drug Pervitin and a pistol with a silencer, reminding them that the former had been used with success by Ast Brussels. It is impossible to guess what was the reason for this request, but it suggests on the face of it Abt III rather than Abt I work.

There are two messages from which one can gather some idea of the attitude of Rossetti's superior officers to him. The first is the rebuke he received from Berlin at the beginning of September 1942, when he was instructed to curtail his endless journeyings about which had so far produced no visible result. This, however, seems to have been a temporary phase, for on 26 September, when Rossetti was in Italy, Sensburg informed him that he had interviewed the head of IH Ost and also the Chief Abt I, as a result of which they both now appreciated the work done by Rossetti in the past and, it was implied, would support his activities in the future. The circumstances of Sensburg having travelled to Berlin and taken up the question of Rossetti's work with Piekenbrock himself suggests that there must have been fairly serious trouble before. If this is fact, coupled with the general speciousness of the Abwehr, which suggests that Rossetti's constant activity may after all produce very little that is harmful, or of direct value to the enemy.

While still in Genoa, Levi and Travaglio manipulated the black market to exchange US dollars, which had been supplied by the Abwehr to pay agents, for Italian lira. This netted them almost double the official exchange rate, so the agents were paid in Italian currency, leaving Travaglio with a substantial profit. However, these activities led to Levi's arrest in Genoa in 1940 on black marketeering charges, although he was released after a few hours upon Rossetti's intervention with the spurious excuse that Levi had been participating in a clandestine operation. According to SIS, Travaglio was the alias of a Luftwaffe officer of Italian extraction who had been a pilot in the Great War. His dossier noted that he had been adopted by a wealthy widow and that although he claimed to have been an actor, had really earned a living by singing in cafés. SIS also identified him as the tall German officer with bushy eyebrows and a deep scar on his forehead who had used the alias Dr Hans Solms during the Venlo incident in November 1939.

The Venlo episode had cast a long shadow across all SIS operations since November 1939 when two SIS officers, Sigismund Payne Best and Richard Stevens, were abducted while attending what they thought was a rendezvous with anti-Nazi German officers on the Dutch frontier. The hapless pair, who were unarmed and unable to resist, were seized on Dutch territory and dragged across the border to face incarceration and interrogation, and the debacle had been a profound embarrassment for the supposedly neutral Netherlands government, forcing the resignation of the DMI. However, the impact on SIS was lasting, for the assumption was that the two SIS officers would inevitably compromise whatever they knew, and that amounted to the entire SIS structure, its operations and agents in Holland, and much else besides. Thereafter SIS exercised extreme caution in handling anyone claiming to possess anti-regime credentials, and took great care not to endanger other personnel in similar circumstances. The fact that Travaglio had participated in the Venlo affair must have been seen as ironic by Rodney Dennys and Nicholas Elliott, both of whom had served at the SIS station in The Hague under Stevens.

Once in Cairo, Levi was instructed that he would receive a message at the Carlton Hotel about how to acquire his transmitter, and he was given the names of George Khouri and Lina Vigoretti-Antoniada as two of Scirombo's local acquaintances.

Levi visited the British embassy in Belgrade on 12 September and 15 October 1940 to inform the SIS station commander, Major Lethbridge, of his plans, and this news was sent to Cairo which had been informed on 3 June 1940 by MI5 that he was likely to turn up in Egypt and require assistance. Actually, Levi then returned to Italy, visiting Eisentrager in Sofia, and did not reach Turkey, travelling on a German passport in the name of Ludovici, until 26 December 1940, where he was arrested on a charge of passport and currency fraud, together with his companion, Giovanni Magaracci. Alias Fulvio Melcher, Magaracci was to act as his wireless operator, but after three weeks in a Turkish jail Melcher abandoned his mission and returned to his native Italy. The other members of the gang, led by Joseph Buchegger, did not appear to have any links with the Abwehr or espionage.

Upon his release Levi was given a British passport by SIS and sailed to Haifa. He was interviewed by SIME in Jerusalem and finally reached Cairo on an RAF aircraft to establish himself in the famous National Hotel, on the corner of Talaat Harb and Abdel Khalek Sarwat Streets, on 10 February 1941. He did so, but was never provided with the promised transmitter. Instead, Levi claimed that he had been introduced in March in a bar in the Kharia Malika Farida to Paul Nicossof who had once been a ship's wireless operator. The meeting had been arranged by an Italian, Antonio Garbarino, who allegedly had access, for £200, to a radio provided by another Italian who had been hiding in his house. Of course, neither Nicossof nor

Garbarino ever really existed. Similarly, Levi was initially accommodated in the Abbassia Barracks, and not the National Hotel.

Levi's case, codenamed CHEESE, was handled by Rex Hamer, Rodney Dennys and John de Salis for ISLD's B Section, and Terence Robertson, Desmond Doran, Eric Pope and the novelist Evan J. Simpson, for SIME's Special Section. In one report dated 1 September 1942 Simpson said that 'Levi, as a result of his successful activities in France, Italy, Turkey and then in Egypt, has acquired an amazing self-confidence and complete belief in his own ability to travel anywhere and deceive anybody'. Simpson, who was only commissioned from the ranks in 1941, considered him

> a natural liar, capable of inventing any story on the spur of the moment to
> get himself out of a fix. He has very considerable intelligence and an inven
> tive mind. For example, he invented ciphers of his own, but immediately
> grasped the advantages of the one which was put up to him and mastered
> it in a very short time.

Simpson was born in London in April 1901, and was living in Surrey when he was sent away to school. He was educated at Winchester, where he went as a scholar in September 1914, and then from 1920 read history at University College, Oxford. As soon as he graduated he appeared at the Liverpool Playhouse as Mackenzie in *Abraham Lincoln* and in 1928 appeared in *Napoleon's Josephine* at the Fortune Theatre. He then managed the Festival Theatre in Cambridge before joining the Huddersfield Repertory Theatre. In 1929 he had married the actress Dorothy Holmes-Gore, the star of *Midshipman Easy*, and in October 1931 their son was born.

Simpson's first play, *The Dark Path*, about a pair of Englishmen in Japan, was performed at the Savoy Theatre in November 1928. Upon the outbreak of war he joined the Intelligence Corps and participated in

Operation CLAYMORE, the Commando raid on the Lofoten Islands on 3 March 1941, which led him to write *Lofoten Letter*. The true purpose of CLAYMORE was to capture one of the enemy's three Enigma cipher machines known to be there. In the event none were recovered because Lieutenant Hans Kupfinger, the commander of the unarmed trawler *Krebs*, threw his overboard moments before he was killed. However, the machine's rotors were seized, and so were cipher documents that disclosed the Kriegsmarine's Home Waters keys for February, allowing Bletchley Park to retrospectively read the traffic. Other material seized helped Allied cryptographers to solve much of the April traffic, compromising signals sent between 1 March and 10 May. Naturally, the raid's true purpose was known only to a handful of officers who undertook their special assignments while the rest of the troops engaged the enemy and destroyed economic targets, such as the local fish oil processing plant.

Originally intended as a letter written to his wife while sailing for enemy-occupied territory as a corporal in a Special Service Battalion, Simpson was obliged by the constraints of military security to cut large sections of the text from *Lofoten Letter*, and not even hint that the raid had an alternative, highly secret objective. The same considerations required him to identify the ship on which he sailed as HMS *Domino*, a non-existent warship, and certainly not part of the 6th Destroyer Flotilla. Nevertheless, *Lofoten Letter* was released, and probably stands as the first book of the conflict written by a participant in a clandestine operation undertaken on Nazi-held Europe. He was by then a published author under the nom-de-plume Evan John, and by the time he was transferred to SIME he had written *Plus ça change: An Historical Rhapsody in One Act* in verse in 1935, and *Kings Masque: Scenes from an historical tragedy* in 1941. The biographer of King Charles I, he would write five other one-act plays, some of which were performed on the London stage, and go on to publish historical novels such as *Crippled Splendour* and *Ride Home Tomorrow*.

Simpson was indeed an extraordinary intelligence officer, in a profession in which eccentricity is not a rare phenomenon, for while he was employed by SIME he also found the time to write a book, *Time in the East*, which described his travels to Jerusalem, Cyprus, Beirut, Aleppo and Persia, and included some unfashionable opinions about Charles I, psycho-analysis, literary criticism and blood-sports, not to mention some limericks in French, Latin and Greek. A 1946 review in *The Wykehamist* described Simpson's book as 'humourous and humane' while an earlier article drew attention to his versatility as a poet, actor, playwright and historian. He was also a frequent contributor to the *Spectator*.

Simpson was originally transferred to Cairo to run sabotage operations in the Caucasus to prevent oil being shipped to Germany, and to take over the work of a special bureau headed by Oliver Baldwin, son of the former prime minister. However, as Axis forces swept through the Balkans, the opportunities for sabotage diminished, and Simpson found himself posted to SIME.

Simpson gave some thought to Levi, reflecting that

> his motives for working for us are difficult to fathom. He is, of course, a Jew and says he wants to do something to help the Allied cause because it is fighting on behalf of the Jews. In addition, he obviously has considerable love of adventure, and enjoys the work for its own sake. He is very fond of women, and the work gives him opportunities of travel, and of handling large sums of money, which he would not otherwise get. He showed no particular dislike of the Germans or the Italians; in fact he often described the good times the Germans had given him, and how friendly he was with Travaglio.

Another SIME report, allegedly endorsed by Major Jones, observed that he appears to be a man of personality rather than character, quick-witted and resourceful, consciously proud of his role of his double agent (e.g. he was inclined to air his 'intimacy' with Helfferich and Travaglio) and highly imaginative (between Cairo and Istanbul he elaborated the man Paul he had met in a bar in Cairo into Paul Nicossof, born in Egypt, and believed to be a Syrian). He was fond of women and vain of his contact with them. It seems highly improbable that he acknowledged any loyalty, except to himself. His professed attitude towards the Germans was that he naturally resented their treatment of the Jews and he appears to have felt no antipathy.

Although he carried £500 in Sterling notes, there was no message for him at his Cairo hotel, and no wireless. Accordingly, Levi called on Lina Vigoretti-Antoniada, who was placed under surveillance by SIME, but she appeared 'unintelligent and quite unresponsive to his hints and suggestions' so she was put under discreet observation, with no result. Khouri, on the other hand, was a Syrian money-lender already known to SIME as being anti-British and involved in agitation in Palestine. An investigation by SIME revealed that Khouri had lent cash to several British personnel, among them officers named Chesterfield, Stirling, and Captains Massey and Soames.

Evidently the Abwehr believed that Khouri was the organiser of a network of low-level local spies, but his encounter with Levi, which was not monitored independently or recorded by SIME, proved to be unproductive. Khouri was interned and his network 'melted away' without Abwehr money. The relationship between Khouri and Levi presented some fundamental problems, not the least of which was the fact that Khouri 'was flesh and blood' so 'it was decided that Paul should not have any actual contact with him'. Instead of meeting, they corresponded through three addresses in Cairo, with Nicossof signing himself 'Willy' while Khouri wrote as 'Albert'.

Much later Evan Simpson recorded that he 'was very uncertain about how much of Levi's accounts of his conversations with Khouri could be believed'. Khouri, when arrested in 1941, denied ever having met Levi. While undoubtedly this was a lie it is considered possible that Levi met Khouri on one or perhaps two occasions, that Khouri refused to have anything to do with him and that the accounts given of subsequent conversations with Khouri were sheer invention on Levi's part. Before leaving Cairo, Levi told SIME that he had informed Khouri of the setting up of a wireless communication, arranged for him to supply the operator with reports for transmission by means of a post box and promised to send him more money, signing himself 'Willy Rogers'. In actual fact, no information was ever supplied through this post box.

Initially, Bill Kenyon-Jones's enthusiasm for promoting a wireless link with the Abwehr attracted some derision at GHQ, and in later life he would recall that the signals branch had explained to him that their principal function was to *prevent* illicit transmissions to the enemy, not to *assist* them.

CHEESE tried to communicate with the Abwehr on 17 May using a homemade transmitter constructed by a skilled Royal Signals technician, Staff Sergeant Ellis, whose role would later be taken by Sergeant Rowland ('Rowley') G. Shears, because of ill health. Shears held an amateur licence with the call sign G8KW and in 1956 started his own radio manufacturing business, KW Electronics, at his home at the Vanguard Works in Heath Street, Dartford, Kent. When he died in November 2009, at the age of ninety, none of his obituaries mentioned his connection with CHEESE.

Initially Ellis was unable to make contact and a technical study concluded that the agreed frequencies were unsuitable, so they were changed through a simple plain-language code over the commercial cable to Istanbul, as previously arranged for just such an eventuality, and his messages finally were relayed to Rome on 14, 17 and 21

July 1941 when the first radio link was established. For the first three months these signals were transmitted from a flat next to a military base in Heliopolis twice a week on most Mondays and Thursdays, but they contained little information of value as SIME's deception skills were then unsophisticated. During this same period the amateur transmitter was replaced with an army model, and illness required two changes in operators, none of which apparently attracted the enemy's attention.

SIME's case officer complained that 'the book-cipher code suggested by the Italians proved clumsy and unsuitable'; a SIME officer devised a new substitution cipher.

SIME also complained about the quality of Bari's substandard radio technique, observing that

> the organisation at Bari appeared to be very bad. The encoding was particularly careless (it has improved a little since but has never attained a reasonably good standard), and there was much repetition of questions, etc. The slipshod methods suggested that Levi himself was handling the job at the other end!

A survey conducted by SIME of the first 163 messages transmitted by Shears demonstrated that 'as many as twenty-four transmissions were unsuccessful due to four causes:

1. Bad atmospheric conditions – (particularly October – November).

2. Heavy interference.

3. Incompetence or laziness of enemy operator.

4. Enemy 'not on the air'.

14

The third cause became so bad that on 21 October he registered a complaint in no mean terms. This had the effect of bringing new operators into action. The enemy are now using six operators whom we call:

- The 'original' for whom CHEESE has a high regard.

- The 'goon' – a dull-witted and lazy operator.

- 'Curt' – so called from his style.

- 'Good' – an expert 'ham' operator.

- 'New Good' – first appeared late in December 1942.

- 'Square Morse' – a good operator who sends in Continental style.

    Wavelengths have been changed three times. We can now work two alternative frequencies. Callsigns have been changed five times and hours of transmission three times.

In April 1941 when Levi was scheduled to return home, he recruited Paul Nicossof, a notional agent, to replace him, and gave him £150. Thereafter, Nicossof became a valuable cog in the CHEESE deception machine, and at first was played by a SIME officer named Beddington. He was supposedly a Syrian of mixed Caucasian heritage, eager to work as a mercenary. In September 1941 'A' Force adopted CHEESE, and as a first step it was reported that he had acquired a South African source who, a few weeks later on 29 September, was replaced by PIET, a well-informed South African NCO with money and women trouble, but was employed as a confidential secretary to General John P. Whiteley at GHQ Middle East, and therefore 'in a position to acquire first-class information'. SIME noted that 'experience shows that the enemy is curiously unwary and eager to accept stories of the disloyalty of disgruntled Colonials, Irishmen, etc. and even of supposed ex-members of Fascist organisations in England.'

General Whiteley, a Woolwich graduate who was a willing participant in the scheme, had been commissioned in 1915 and had served in the First World War in the Royal Engineers at Salonika and across the Middle East, having won the Military Cross. He had been posted to Wavell's staff in Cairo in May 1940. In May 1941 he travelled to Washington, DC to negotiate delivery of Lend-Lease material to Egypt. Some sixteen ships arrived each month for the remainder of the year, bringing eighty-four M4 Stuart light 'Honey' tanks, 10,000 trucks and 174 aircraft. The arrival of the Stuart tanks, with their 37mm gun and high speed, ensured their participation in CRUSADER, although with a limited range they would be out-performed by Rommel's panzers which were equipped with better armour.

After Auchinleck replaced Wavell in July 1941 it was Whiteley who was selected by him to fly to London to brief Churchill in October 1941 on the delayed CRUSADER offensive. At the end of March 1942 Whiteley was appointed Chief of Staff for the 8th Army, but was replaced by General Freddie de Guingand in October, and in February 1943 Whiteley joined General Dwight Eisenhower as deputy Chief of Staff at Allied Forces Headquarters to plan the invasion of Sicily. In August 1943 he acted as Eisenhower's envoy to fly to London to brief Churchill again, and in January 1944 moved to SHAEF to plan the D-Day invasion.

Whiteley's senior staff posts enabled his notional clerk, PIET, to provide invaluable strategic information, as well as details of the Stuart tank to MISANTHROPE and, through her, to Nicossof.

As he reported to the Abwehr, Nicossof paid PIET 40 Egyptian pounds (E£), but was soon in debt to him to the tune of E£35, and when asked how much he needed, he replied E£1,000. By 4 July 1942, that figure had grown to E£1,400, and Nicossof claimed he was no longer in a position to borrow more. Indeed, CHEESE's chronic lack of cash led SIME to discuss the idea of inventing an alternative source of income for him, perhaps as the proprietor of a garage, but the idea was dropped. Another suggestion was that CHEESE should spend his afternoons giving lessons in Arabic and French, which would allow him to meet more officers, one of whom might be a construction expert from the Royal Engineers with a knowledge the Cyranaican and Tripolitanian railway systems.

As well as recruiting PIET, Nicossof from July had the benefit of a Greek girlfriend, codenamed MISANTHROPE, who he referred to as his '*petite amie*'. She is a fascinating character because, although she was mainly notional, SIME felt obliged to recruit a real person to act her role so she could, if the circumstances arose, act as an intermediary and receive Nicossof's money from the Abwehr. Accordingly, SIME went to considerable lengths to fabricate her background.

Codenamed MARIE by the Abwehr, she was

a Greek girl animated by her hatred of the British – well-educated, intelligent, witty and courageous sustaining him [CHEESE]when discouraged or disgruntled – she aided and abetted him by forming a series of friendships – and possibly 'alliances' – with British and American officers – military and Air Force. From these she extracted information of varying degree of reliability and importance. This enabled CHEESE to supplement information gleaned from his Greek military friends – and other acquaintances. Without funds he could no longer employ reliable agents. All information – whether high-level or low – true or false – he passed on to his Axis friends – leaving them to sift the chaff from the wheat. Those sources that misinformed him he discarded, and thus always had the requisite retort if and when accused of passing on false information. For instance – on 17 August 1942 he said that

he was sorry for having given false information but without money he had to
collect such information his friends told him and report what he saw himself.

SIME's decision to introduce MISANTHROPE turned out to be an
inspired one, and was probably taken by Evan Simpson in conjunction
with other Special Section colleagues and, of course, Dudley Clarke. It
may also have been influenced by Rowley Shears who had strong links
to the local expatriate Greek community and the Greek government-
in-exile's radio station in the suburb of Abu Zaabal which broadcast
bulletins twice a day on the medium wave in eleven languages under
the sponsorship of the Political Warfare Executive (PWE). The studios
belonged to Egyptian State Broadcasting but were largely managed
by British personnel, among them Shears's close friend Norman
Joly, and was the principal means for the coalition government to
maintain one-way contact with Greeks living under the Axis occupation. Among those who appeared regularly on the channel were
Crown Prince Paul and the leading politicians, among them Prime
Minister Emmanouil Tsouderos, his successor Eleftherios Venizelos,
the Minister for War, Panagiotis Kanellopoulos and Admiral Petros
Voulgaris. A conference in Beirut established George Papandreou as
the Prime Minister of a coalition government, and his administration
moved briefly to Naples before finally reaching Athens in October
1944. Whenever these individuals were allowed access to the micro-
phone a switch engineer was present who had the authority, under
the Chief Censor Professor Eric Sloman, to cut the transmission. Formerly the first director of Corfu's police academy, Sloman ensured
that no indiscretions were transmitted, fully aware that every broadcast was monitored by the enemy for any potential intelligence leads.

MISANTHROPE's Greek background allowed CHEESE access to a
complex world of political intrigue and competing groups who tried
to influence Allied policy and were anyway determined to exercise

18

power in Athens after the liberation. It was a maelstrom of personalities and military commanders who were, of themselves, of minimal consequence in terms of strategic importance, but they did represent a plausible milieu which SIME and 'A' Force could portray, to the Abwehr at least, as a constituency in Cairo that could shed light on Allied policy towards the Balkans. The dispossessed Greek forces would obviously be essential in any action taken in the eastern Mediterranean, and could be represented as a barometer of Allied plans in the region. At a time when there were no textbooks available on strategic deception, and little experience of the wholesale manipulation of double agents, not to mention the fabrication of notional sources, MISANTHROPE was a truly extraordinary development. Appropriately, Simpson created a narrative, complete with domestic details, to describe how she had gained CHEESE's confidence. They had met at a party with some Greek friends, and

he had attempted to obtain from her military information about the Greek forces, supposing her to have many officer friends. He had observed her air of indifference as to the military success of the Allies, and as they became more intimate she had revealed the full extent of her antagonism to the British.

Some time in May 1942 Paul had remarked to her half-seriously: 'Supposing that we were agents for the Axis. How easily we could obtain valuable information.' She had been skeptical; whereupon he had suggested that she should make the experiment of noting what she saw in the course of an hour's walk in the Cairo streets. She had agreed, and Paul had appeared much interested in the result of the experiment. A little later in the same month he had revealed to her (uncertainly and with much and anxious insistence on secrecy) that he was acting as an agent for the Axis. His manner had been at once vain and nervous. He had not at this stage told her that he was in wireless communication with the enemy. He had then asked her to continue systematically to keep her eyes open for badges and vehicle signs;

also for any other kind of military information obtainable visually; and to try and make the acquaintance of members of the Allied forces for the purpose of obtaining military information from them. She had hesitated, pointing out the risks and had asked for time to think the proposal over. But she has a natural disposition for the risk and had been finally convinced by Paul's assurance that there would be good money for them both in the venture.

She had noticed that Paul was always anxious that she should not be in or near his flat between about 7.30 and 10 o'clock in the evening. One night early in July, however, he had called her to look at his wireless receiver – on which they had been in the habit of listening to the radio programmes together and which she had never suspected to be anything but an ordinary domestic apparatus. Having locked the door of the room he had pulled back a false panel from the apparatus and shown her that it was a transmitter as well as a receiver. Unlocking a door, he had produced a Morse key; and then, to her further surprise, had suspended an aerial from nails already inserted in the walls near the ceiling.

All this had been done with an air of mysterious importance and great nervousness. At just after half past seven he had begun to tap out something that she could not understand on the Morse key. He had worn earphones and she could faintly hear the note of the signals. After about twenty minutes he had ceased tapping and had produced paper and pencil and began to write as he listened.

When the proceedings were finished he turned to her and remarked: 'Now you know exactly what I'm up to.' Then he told her the whole story of his nightly communication with the enemy and had proposed that they should work as partners. She had hesitated once more; but once more she had been persuaded by her own disposition for adventure and by Paul's assurance that it would make their joint fortune and assure their safety and honour when – he was certain, the genuine Rommel entered Cairo.

Paul had taught her to decipher the messages received from the German Intelligence Service and thereafter she had occasionally helped him in this;

she had found it very difficult however, and Paul had sometimes been impatient with her when she had made mistakes. She had also made some effort to learn Morse, but that had been a tedious business; Paul had given her a test a few days ago, and had been quite angry when he had found how little she knew. Since that time she had assisted Paul mainly in the collection of military information.

Following the collapse of Greece in April 1941 the level of political infighting and scheming among senior politicians and the senior military hierarchy rivalled any play, and the mutiny of April 1944 among the ratings at Alexandria and Port Said was a manifestation of the discontent felt within the Royal Hellenic Navy when activists among the sailors on the lower decks demanded the government-in-exile be reconstituted to allow the participation of the Communist-controlled National Liberation Front (EAM). Their intervention was opposed by the officers and NCOs, usually anti-Communist ELAS supporters, who were placed under arrest by so-called Revolutionary Committees aboard the destroyer *Terax* and the corvettes *Apostolis* and *Sachtouris*. The mutiny was eventually crushed by the expedient of denying the ships food and water, but the bitterness would re-emerge during the postwar civil war. One destroyer, the *Pindos*, threw their officers overboard and, after a voyage to Malta, reached Italy where it surrendered to the local Communist Party. Seven members of the Royal Hellenic Navy were killed in Alexandria as officers led 250 volunteers over HMS *Phoebe* to reach the mutineers. Among the vessels involved were the repair ship *Hyphaistos*, the destroyer *Criti*, together with some mine-sweepers and auxiliaries. The last to give up in Port Said were men aboard the battleship *Georgios Averof*, six destroyers and the submarine *Papanicolis*. Finally the rebels who had seized control of the recruitment office in central Alexandria surrendered, bringing the episode to a close in Egypt. Meanwhile, the trouble spread to Malta where three submarines, the submarine escort *Corinthia*, the destroyer *Spetses* and two auxiliary ships were taken over until the Royal Navy arrested the ringleaders, most of whom were concentrated on the destroyer *Navarinon*, and sent them back to a detention camp in Egypt.

These events demonstrated the volatility of Greek exile politics and the sensitivity of issues which were likely to be exploited by the Axis if the opportunity arose.

MISANTHROPE's SIME file identifies her as Mrs Evangeline Palidou, born in Canea, Crete on 25 July 1913. Five foot four inches tall, with brown hair and an oval face, her religion was Greek Orthodox. She had been issued with a Security Card, No. 615 on 28 May 1941 and had received a Red Card, No. 017002 on 25 May 1942. Educated at the Lycée in Canea, with a baccalauréat in French, she had been taken to visit Smyrna as a child in 1928. She had worked in the Anti-Fascist Movement in Crete from 1932 and been employed as a journalist on the anti-fascist newspaper *Literia* in 1933 before getting married and moving to Athens the following year. She returned to Crete in 1936, spent four months in exile on Naxos in 1938 after her arrest by the '4 August regime', and then worked first as a mannequin and secretary, and then for counter-espionage in Greece from November 1940. She was divorced from her 33-year-old husband, Evangelos Ktistakis in March 1942 and from July 1942 she worked for SIME's Greek Section and took up residence at the Metropolitan Hotel in Cairo.

Within SIME Evangeline was referred to as BGM, an acronym for 'Blonde Gun Moll', a name she acquired as a result of her reputation for packing a pistol. Some believed that she had shot one of her lovers dead, but others suggested this tale was something of an exaggeration, as she had simply thrown him off a roof.

The immense trouble taken by SIME to create MISANTHROPE extended to her entire family. He father, supposedly, was Nicholas

Palides, aged sixty-four, formerly the director of economic services in Crete's Ministry of Finance between 1910 and 1918. He then served in Athens for two years, then in Turkey for two years, returning to Crete where he still lived. His wife, Anastasia Kokytha, was aged fifty-eight, MISANTHROPE's infant son was still in Crete, and her brother Ionis worked in the port office at Canea.

Nicossof announced her recruitment in a transmission on 24 July but 'unfortunately uncertainty of livelihood – curtailment of his black bourse activities' and the non-arrival of funds from his Axis partners finally forced him to find regular employment. After trying from 7 December until 25 December 1942 he secured a post as an interpreter in the Occupied Enemy Territory Administration (OETA), an organisation created in the First World War to govern the Ottoman Empire, CHEESE commenced his duties on 1 January 1943, and on 27 January he announced that 'she could decode already and was learning to transmit'.

Nicossof's employment by EOTA followed a discussion in SIME, led by James Robertson, over the merits of planting an enemy spy in the organisation. A study of his duties for EOTA, and his contact with other EOTA personnel, would be a tremendous advantage and greatly expand his access to information that would be instantly attractive to the Abwehr. As Robertson noted,

> it would appear that in Eritrea OETA interpreters were also used as translators. While it is improbable that CHEESE's knowledge of English is sufficient to allow him to be employed in this latter capacity under normal circumstances, he might reasonably be employed to translate Italian into French for the convenience of his officers, or to translate simple English phrases into Italian. The publication entitled *Notes on the Military Government of Occupied Territories Part II* defines the duties of OETA and contains some points which might be of use to CHEESE for transmission to the enemy.

1. Air Raid Precautions. OETA is responsible for the maintenance and repair of civil ARP. Hence it is probable that reports of air raid damage of the territory would reach OETA Cairo.

2. Police. Civil security. Native raiding. Control of arms. Hence probable that CHEESE would hear of sabotage, attacks by Arabs on Italian settlers, desertions from Libyan Arab Force (Gendarmerie), sale of arms by native troops, concealed arms.

3. Collection of political intelligence. Morale of local population both European and native.

4. Hygiene. OETA is responsible for maintenance of civil hospitals and enforcement of hygiene regulations. Also for supply of drugs to civil hospitals and doctors.

5. Supplies and rationing.

6. Maintenance of roads, railways, and communications. (When taken over from HEs and HCS to relieve them for other duties.)

7. Propaganda.

8. Military security (in conjunction with the Corps of Military Police and the Field Security Wing).

9. Removal and installation of enemy officials.

Given OETA's very wide remit, and the breadth of its reach across the region, with a special emphasis on the former Italian colonies in East and North Africa, SIME was confident that CHEESE's new status would not only provide him with an income, but would also make him an increasingly attractive asset to his Abwehr controllers. The lengths to which Simpson and Robertson went to create scenarios for CHEESE to acquire apparently harmless pieces of gossip that, to an Abwenhr analyst, might have a rather more significant interpretation, was extraordinary, and much time was spent drafting scenes, in much the same way that a playwright would construct an episode, which gave CHEESE an interesting tidbit. For example, Simpson imagined that

CHEESE has had rather a trying day at OETA, where his habit of a cup of coffee from 10 a.m. to 11 a.m. does not meet with the full approval of his superiors. He drops into one of his favourite eating places, the Regent, just off the Kasr el Nil, the proprietor of which is a friend of his. (The Regent is patronised by British and Dominion NCOs and he has often gleaned titbits of information there.) On entering the place, he is pleased to see one of his Greek Army acquaintances. CHEESE joins him and they have dinner together. During dinner, the Greek tells him that they have returned from the desert and are back in Alexandria again. The Greek has taken the opportunity to pop down to Cairo to see a girlfriend of his. One may imagine his feelings on learning that this girl has decided to become a nurse; and so he finds himself at a loose end. He welcomes CHEESE and proceeds to drink more wine than is really good for him. CHEESE asks what he intends doing when he is back in Alexandria? The Greek gloomily replies that he doesn't know, but suspects that it will be more exercises again, adding that 'as if they hadn't done enough damned exercises already'. CHEESE discreetly guides the conversation into other channels adding that he, CHEESE, might be up in Alexandria soon, and that he would like to meet some of his aforetime friends and acquaintances, but supposes that they will not be so lucky as his friend, and still be up in the desert. The friend says that CHEESE needn't worry. For the whole of the 1st Greek Brigade are back, less those who were

unlucky enough to be bumped off, or wounded. Eventually CHEESE takes
his friend back to the latter's digs and then seeks his own flat.

This completely imaginary episode was created for the sole purpose of conveying the impression that the 1st Greek Brigade had
been withdrawn from operations in the Western Desert and was
now based in Alexandria. Similarly, another encounter, displaying
some humour and entitled CHEESE *Snoops Again*, was conjured
up in January 1943 to provide another piece of the Abwehr's intelligence jigsaw puzzle:

On Friday evening, 9 January 1943, CHEESE had been called in by his temporary boss, namely (War Substantive Lieutenant), (Temporary Captain),
Acting Major B. F. Cuselthwaite to translate some regulations into Italian
and Greek. At the end of this task the gallant major was summoned by telephone to go along to another office. As he was going out of the door he
said to CHEESE: 'When you have finished with that bumph, pin all the
papers together in their proper order and put them on the second shelf in
that cupboard. Lock up the cupboard and give the key to the sergeant next
door.' Cuselthwaite then went off to his colleague's office. CHEESE finished
sorting out the papers and in so doing caught sight of an engagement pad-
cum-diary, just alongside the blotting pad on the major's table. His first
glance was no more than cursory but as he was about to pick up the collected bumph, he recollected seeing the words '8th Army'. So he went to
look again and saw the following entries for Tuesday 12 January:

– 1000Hrs Conference GHQ. 8th Army War game. (S says Monty wants
full details re road and rail freight services? how soon get started, maintenance, reliability.

– 1315Hrs Lunch, Dick, Turf Club. ? Golf Gezira.

- Ring up Air Q Movements re seats Col S / Benghazi. Try BOAC if no can do. 2 seats 18th. ? how much.

- 1845Hrs Ring Angela re dinner Dolls 13th. Dick re. flat 13th. NAAFI re. whisky and gin. Any van der Rumm?

- Strickland – port facilities what naval personnel available – if any – whose responsibility? Not ours!

- 2100Hrs Joan, Continental.

- CHEESE noted other entries, the significance of which escaped him. However, on thinking things over on Friday evening, he came to the conclusion that he would verify the date as to the 8th Army, although he could not understand what 'War game' might mean. On Monday morning a colonel, whom he had not seen before, pushed his head round the major's office door (CHEESE was doing some translations) and said, 'B. F., don't forget those draft schedules for that bloody war game tomorrow.' The major replied: 'They're all OK, Sir. I don't think Monty will catch us out this time!'

In expanding CHEESE's circle of friends, SIME gave approval to another of Simpson's ideas, that he should cultivate a BOAC employee who would act as a conduit for information that, in one proposal, would identify the First Army at Tripoli:

Through his British Airways employee friend … [CHEESE] has met a pilot of the Airways run from Cairo to Cyrenaica. This pilot … call him James from Portsea, Hants. … was introduced to the *Amie*[1] a few weeks ago. Used by the RAF, has been lent to BOAC for a rest from operational

---

1   MISANTHROPE

duties, having had two years in the desert on bombers, now engaged upon flying freight planes. At a party this week he revealed to the *Amie* that he wanted to get back to work in the RAF again. Said that there was little or no fun in transporting supplies to Benghazi and bringing back staff officers. Didn't mind bringing back 'woundeds', they were only too glad to have a quiet life for a time; but the staff officers were so fussy and must have their silly little 'brief cases' with them; instead of putting the blasted bags with the rest of their kit. Best crowd that he carried were some 'commando wallahs and parachute blokes' who threw a terrific party on the way to Benghazi. They were full of fun and terrifically keen to get cracking with the preparations for what they referred to as the 'Triploli tea party'. Some of them were hoping to meet old friends whom they thought were now posted to the First Army.

A fourth tale dreamed up by SIME in January 1943 was intended to disclose inadvertently the supposed whereabouts of the aircraft carrier HMS *Indefatigable*, relying on CHEESE's friend who worked for BOAC.

CHEESE meets BOAC friend in January 1943. They speak of this and that, running the gamut of desultory topics. CHEESE says that he is kept fairly busy in his new job with the OETA, relating one or two amusing incidents connected with some of the 'officer personnel'.

BOAC … Mahmoud by name … tells CHEESE of an amusing episode, in his turn. A few days ago a couple of British naval officers with the letter 'A' in the curl of their golden rings upon their cuffs (CHEESE interrupts, wanting to know what the letter 'A' signifies. Mahmoud says that he has been told that it means the officers are naval aviators; and carries on with his tale.) One of these officers had changed in the plane … in which they were being flown to Cairo … and in changing had dropped a wallet. This wallet had, somehow, fallen into a crevice between the side of the machine and the flooring – and the officer to whom it had belonged had left word that he would call for it at the BOAC offices. Unfortunately, his name had been mislaid and to find out what was his name the wallet had been opened. The first things that came to light were several packets of French letters bearing the name of a Cape Town chemist, and some money (notes). The officer, on claiming the wallet, had opened it to check the notes, which were in South African currency, and out had dropped the rubber goods. The officer, good humouredly accepting the laughs against himself, had presented the three packets to the clerks, and had thrown out some pieces of paper, asking that they should be destroyed. The pieces of paper were nothing more than receipts for meals at various Cape Town restaurants and twelve pairs of silk stockings. CHEESE asked Mahmoud if he got one of the French letters, Mamoud produced a neat small envelope bearing the name Champion & Reads, Chemists, Alderney Street, Cape Town. This packet was in a larger envelope, on the top left-hand corner of which was printed the name 'Harvey Greenacres (Prpty Ltd)' in green and in the right-hand corner was a very small stamp, showing an airman in flying helmet and parachute harness. CHEESE shows interest in the stamp, so Mahmoud passes the envelope over to him to examine the stamp. While examining the stamp CHEESE sees that the envelope is addressed to: Lt. N. F. Ravenhead RN, HMS *Indefatigable*, c/o GPO Cape Town, A mild argument arises as to the pronunciation of the word 'Indefatigable'. During this discussion Mahmoud tells CHEESE that this was the envelope that had contained the receipt for the twelve pairs of silk stockings. The conversation wanders off via the subject of silk stockings, to various other things that are in short supply and profits to be made if only one could lay one's hands on the stuff. Later on, CHEESE considers whether there is any value in this information. He considers that it might be if he knew what sort of ship was HMS *Indefatigable*.

This apparently innocuous item obviously conveyed the impression that the Royal Navy's most modern aircraft carrier had been in South

Africa, the implication being that the warship, which carried seventy-three aircraft, had not only been commissioned, but was operational in the Indian Ocean, thereby doubling Admiral Sir James Somerville's cruiser strength, which actually consisted of HMS *Illustrious*. His concern was the threat from Japanese submarines off the coast of Kenya, and the illusion of another carrier in the area was considered a likely deterrent.

The reality, of course, was very different, for *Indefatigable* would remain under construction in the Clyde until she was commissioned in May 1944, and the bogus reports of the carrier's arrival in Simonstown, supported by fake radio traffic transmitted in the Atlantic for the benefit of the Funkbeobachterdienst or B-Dienst, the Kriegsmarine's signals interception branch, was intended to mislead both the Germans and the Japanese about British naval strength. Naturally, the problem for the deception planners was what to do with *Indefatigable* once the carrier had been established in the Indian Ocean, and the solution was to pretend that it had sailed to Addu, a very remote atoll in the even more remote Maldives. This scheme would become the source of some mirth, as no one in 'A' Force seemed to have a sufficient grasp of geography to know where precisely Addu was!

In December 1943 further measures were taken to support Plan BIJOU and tell the Abwehr that *Indefatigable* had returned to the Clyde for a refit, whereas the narrative simply reflected the carrier's authentic commissioning. Later study of Axis intelligence assessments contained in ULTRA intercepts, confirmed that the enemy was quite convinced that both the *Indefatigable* and the *Illustrious* were major components of Somerville's Far East command. However, the truth was that the carrier did not sail on her first patrol until July 1944, and did not reach the Far East until December.

In another example of Simpson's fertile imagination, SIME

developed a plausible narrative to explain the background to some
of his material.

CHEESE was sent for by his boss in OETA and told that the British Army were
looking for a number of Greek interpreters. All departments had been asked
if they had any to spare. The boss had been told by his boss that OETA is to
help if they can but he is loath to lose CHEESE. On the other hand CHEESE
could be dispensed with in an emergency. What does CHEESE think about
it? CHEESE thinks it is bloody awful. He will be parted from his precious set
and what price his money if he is in Suez or Kabrit? He says he would be very
sorry to leave OETA where he is so well looked after and that for private reasons he doesn't want to leave Cairo. Of course, if the war effort demands it he
will go but ... boss says that he quite understands and will do his best but...

That night CHEESE rushes on the air in a panic. What is he to do? He
won't be able to pass any more information – he won't get his money – it's
a disaster. Presumably the enemy will be a bit upset too.

A few days later CHEESE says – 'Here is a perfectly good channel and
a perfectly good set, can they send someone else to operate it? (NOTE: I
believe *Amie* was once trained to operate – this might be worked in).' As
and when necessary boss sends for CHEESE and says that he has worked
the miracle and that he is to remain with OETA. Panic subsides.

Comment:

1. We push the point that we have an interest in Greek-speaking countries.
(Admittedly this includes Crete but is a step in the right direction).

2. We get a very interesting reaction from the other side.

3. It is completely under our control and could be killed instantly if it gets
difficult.

Note: What about factually publishing in General Orders a demand for Greek interpreters. It would start a 'buzz' in the right direction.

Meanwhile, TRIANGLE revealed in August that Rossetti had applied for permission to travel to Rome, and had given one of his reasons 'to try again through Col S for the Italian War Ministry to send money to ROBERTO'. The analysts studying the traffic, who knew ROBERTO to be the enemy's codename for Levi, suggested that 'Colonel S' was probably Count Scirombo, but the important issue was that the Abwehr was still determined to send money to their agent in Cairo.

In operational terms, 'A' Force provided 'purely military information (this includes Naval and Air Force items and movements of highly important individuals). Special Section SIME provides domestic items, "build-up" of sources and deals with wireless problems.'

CHEESE's alleged employment at the Occupied Enemy Territory Administration gave him a salary which enabled him to 'pay his daily way but also benefit from the indiscretions of his employing officers who have a way of leaving their diaries about and discussing secret matters at the top of their voices'.

A review undertaken of the period 1 August 1942 to 16 February 1943 studied the work of the 'A' Force committee which was really what CHEESE actually was, concluded that it had 'passed over successfully no less than six major items. These, we believe, engendered six major headaches!' Despite these items, most secret sources inform us that CHEESE is still quoted as 'reliable' and 'authentic'. In addition, CHEESE maintains a steady stream of low-level information, of which a high proportion is true. The following analysis shows the volume of wireless traffic in which the Abwehr was involved:

Month	Messages Sent	Messages Received	Nights 'On the Air'
1942			
August	21	6	21
September	15	7	21
October	20	10	25
November	13	7	26
December	13	6	27
1943			
January	2	7	28
February (to date)	3	2	13
TOTAL	87	45	161

Levi was flown back to Palestine, and sailed on the SS *Talodi* from Haifa to Mersin on 19 April 1941. In Istanbul he was interviewed at the German consulate-general by an Abwehr officer identified only as 'the Admiral' and Kurt Zähringer, when he revealed only very vague details of Nicossof, and then submitted a report on the event to the local SIS station. According to MI5, 'the Admiral' was probably Kontor Admiral Buerkner, a senior personality responsible for liaison with the Abwehr's offices in Axis cities such as Rome and Budapest.

Levi was deliberately opaque about the non-existent Nicossof but suggested that he was in his mid-thirties and before the war had worked as a half-commission agent on the Alexandria Cotton Exchange. Later some of these details would be repeated when the Abwehr arranged in July for funds to be delivered to him by an intermediary named Fummo at his Cairo apartment at 20 Sharia Galal.

Levi's encounter with Zähringer was an opportunity to pass on some misleading information and to explain that Nicossof would begin transmissions on 25 May and continue twice a week. He accounted for his original £500 by saying that after he had paid £200 for the transmitter, incurred various incidental expenses, had made a payment to George Khouri and given the remainder, £150, to Nicossof.

On his visit to Turkey Levi had been accompanied by his girl-friend, Azeglia Socci, a cabaret artiste, who was to act as his motive for returning to Italy where supposedly he intended to get his wife Lina out of the country. This was the narrative that he told the Germans had been enough to persuade the British authorities to grant him the necessary travel documents. In reality, Levi's courage in going back to Italy placed him in extraordinary jeopardy, but also served to convince the Abwehr of his continued loyalty.

On 4 June 1941 Levi left Istanbul for Italy, travelling to Burgas, Sofia, Belgrade, Vienna and finally Munich where he reported to Major Hans Travaglio on 14 June at the Marien Teresienstrasse. His safe arrival was conveyed to Colonel Otto Helfferich, the Abwehr chief in Rome at his office in the Italian Ministry of War in the Via XX Settembre. Levi then went to Naples where he was met on 17 June by Major Clemens Rossetti who revealed that adverse reports had been received from Belgrade regarding Levi's relationship with British intelligence, and explained that the issue would be pursued the following week in Venice where they would be met on the Lido by Helfferich.

According to his SIME dossier, Helfferich was aged 'about fifty. Height 5ft 10in. Very well dressed. Autocratic Prussian personality, military bearing, a strict disciplinarian. Dark brown hair, greying slightly. Weather-beaten face. Clean-shaven. Thin nose. Thin mouth. Sharp pointed chin. Apaprently very strongly Nazi. Speaks German, Italian and French.'

Rossetti was identified by SIS as a German intelligence officer, fluent in Italian, who had served in the Great War and in 1912 had been expelled from Switzerland. He had also been arrested on 30 October 1928 when he had been acting as a courier for the Italian intelligence service on a route between Lyons and Geneva.

Age about thirty-eight. Height about 5ft 9in. Normal build. Well-dressed appearance. 'Prussian' type. Round head. Fair hair, very thin in front. Clean-shaven. Straight nose. Speaks German with Prussian accent. Calm, unruffled manner. Heavy cigarette smoker. Very ardent Nazi. In peacetime travelled extensively as a merchant in North Africa, Egypt, Palestine, Syria, Iran and Iraq, possibly on behalf of the Abwehr. Speaks German, French, Italian and Arabic. Married to a German, age about thirty. Has two daughters, the eldest being about sixteen. Is devoted to his family.

In Venice Levi was challenged that he had been linked to an agent known as JEAN who had been arrested in Paris after he had been discovered to have been working for the French Deuxième Bureau. Under interrogation, JEAN had denounced Levi as a British agent who had often visited the British embassy in Paris. Apparently JEAN had been employed by Travaglio in Holland before the war even though he had actually been working for the French, and Travaglio had later re-engaged him in Genoa. Somewhat embarrassed, Travaglio had been keen to have the accusations dismissed.

This subject had been a sensitive one for Levi because in February 1940, while in Genoa, he had been approached by a German or Polish Jew named Hermann who had expressed the wish to work for the British. Satisfying himself that Hermann was genuine, Levi had introduced him to Travaglio and persuaded him to send Hermann to Paris. There he had worked for Monsieur Petit of the Deuxième Bureau as a double agent. Levi recalled that he had later heard that Hermann had recruited two other Jews in Paris, including the drummer in a dance band in Paris, named Jacques, and that Hermann had been given a French passport in recognition of his work. Apparently, upon the fall of France, the trio had fled to Casablanca.

JEAN's second arrest had happened soon after the detention in 1938 of a German from Alsace, Karl Kurt (alias Charles Masson), who had been sentenced to death after a lengthy trial. Miraculously, Kurt had escaped from French custody as he had been escorted on a train into the unoccupied zone, and had been rescued by the Germans. When questioned Kurt claimed that he and fourteen of his network had been betrayed by an unnamed Frenchman, and later had gone to work for Travaglio in Italy. He was distinctive because he wrote his reports in characteristically microscopic handwriting, and in October 1940 in Rome Kurt and Travaglio had heard that JEAN had been arrested in Paris. Although Kurt had urged his execution for treason, Travaglio later mentioned that JEAN had been sent to a concentration camp.

According to Levi, he learned a week later in Rome that Kurt had been sent on a mission to Palestine via Syria to sabotage Allied oil pipelines. He was described as an experienced wireless operator and mechanic, of medium height, heavily built and with brown eyes. Levi encountered Kurt again in Rome in June or July 1941 when he learned that the original plan had been delayed because of his arrest, with another agent, in Tripoli while preparing for a mission behind enemy lines in Libya. Both men were then returned to Italy in handcuffs.

Radio contact with Cairo was finally established in July 1941 after a lengthy exchange of telegrams with Rome and Istanbul, and Helfferich urged Levi to return to Cairo to pay his agents and recruit another network in Egypt and Palestine and, feigning reluctance, Levi agreed to depart on 5 August. He underwent a briefing in Rome on 16 July, and was then granted leave so he could settle some family affairs in Genoa before his departure. He was given a new cipher, a radio schedule, a questionnaire and a large amount of British and American currency. He was also given a list of useful contacts in Haifa, Cairo and Alexandria, one of whom was alleged to be in touch with a high Egyptian government official. On 18 July the CHEESE wireless set received a signal that Levi 'leaves for Istanbul at the end of the present month with sufficient money'. This message was followed on

27 July by an instruction to CHEESE to 'tell GEORGE that Levi will arrive soon with funds'.

While in a hotel in Genoa awaiting his departure, Levi met Captain Alessi, a Regia Aeronautica Italiana pilot who claimed to have been sent by Major Rossetti's secretary, Annabella. During some long conversations with Levi, Alessi declared himself to be an anti-Fascist and anti-Nazi who had resigned from the air force after an incident with a Fascist official, stating that he had been friendly with an American, Charles A. Livengood, the economic counsellor, at that US embassy in Rome, and intended to stay away from Italy for the remainder of the war if the opportunity arose. He asked Levi to exercise his influence with Rossetti to have him sent abroad, and begged him not to reveal his disaffection. In a telephone conversation with Annabella on 1 August she urged Levi to consider taking Alessi on his mission, but he demurred, saying he preferred to operate alone. Then, on 2 August, Levi was arrested at his hotel, taken to the Regina Coeli prison in Rome and accused of collaborating with British intelligence. The evidence against him was the assertion that his network in Cairo was now operating under British control. Naturally, Levi denied the allegation, suggesting that perhaps his subordinates had sold out to the enemy. Although his girlfriend was also taken into custody briefly, she said nothing to incriminate him.

Levi was questioned for two and a half months, but not by the notorious Special Tribunal and, having concluded that a case of treason had not been proved, was sentenced on 17 October to five years' imprisonment on the island of Tremiti, a penal colony in the Adriatic, as a political prisoner, and a fine.

Meanwhile, of course, CHEESE had grown impatient about the Abwher's failure to pay him, and on 25 September he was asked to inform them 'if the money has arrived'. Then, on 16 October, he was assured that much money was '*en route ... sur un autre chemin*'.

On 20 October, Nicossof sent a critical signal:

> Very important message. PIET is desperate for money. He visited us yester-
> day. According to him Wavell visited Cairo secretly yesterday having come
> from Tiflis. Auchinlek under pressure from Churchill has consented against
> his better judgment to send one armoured division and three infantry divi-
> sions to help the Russians in the Caucasus. Wavell is going back to Iraq
> immediately to make the necessary plans for their reception.

This signal had a profound impact on the Germans who appeared to
accept the underlying implication that a weakened British army was in
no condition to launch an imminent offensive. On 11 November, just
a week before the CRUSADER campaign, the Akrika Korps advised
that there 'are no apparent signs of preparations for an attack on Cyrenaica' and in explanation directly referred to the Nicossof message:

> Abwehr reports state that there are also differences of opinion between
> Generals Wavell and Auchinleck concerning strategy in the Middle East.
> Wavell advocates an attack into the Caucasus, but Auchinleck does not wish
> to move any more troops or equipment out of Egypt.

In a later assessment dated 6 January 1942, SIME reported in a telegram to MI5's headquarters at Blenheim Palace, with the address
'Snuff-box, Oxford', that CHEESE/LAMBERT

> was the main source by which successful deception recently achieved, result-
> ing in complete strategic surprise at onset of Western Desert campaign.
> Without LAMBERT, main theme of the deception plan which was put over
> on 20/10 and 27/10 could not have reached enemy before 18/11. This very
> satisfactory and completely justifies care and trouble taken. LAMBERT still
> in touch but doubt further utility.

In November 1941 the network in Cairo appeared on the verge of collapse because of lack of promised funds and George Khouri's (authentic) internment. Nicossof protested that he was merely the radio operator, unable to recruit and pay for agents, and himself heavily in debt. SIME had anticipated that after CRUSADER his value to the enemy would diminish, but despite having been patently wrong, his standing appeared initially to be unaffected. This created a further opportunity to be exploited, but exacerbated the problem of Nicossof's finding. Without sufficient cash, it was hardly credible that the improvident spy would continue to put his life at risk for an ungrateful employer. This issue had been considered several times, but SIME had assumed that Nicossof would be abandoned after the full scale of the CRUSADER debacle emerged, and the general view was that this sacrifice was probably worthwhile. Now the priority was to support Nicossof by transferring any blame to Nicossof's unreliable informants (whom he had been unable to pay) and assist the enemy by providing a suitable channel for passing the money he demanded. One reassurance was a message sent on 18 December promising that more than enough money had been in a neutral country 'for a long time' although there was no explanation for what had happened to it.

One obstacle was some evidence which emerged in TRIANGLE traffic in November 1941 and again January 1942 that Nicossof had come under suspicion and the Abwehr had begun to lose confidence in an agent codenamed ROBERTO, an individual who strongly resembled CHEESE. The first sign of trouble was a text which included the ominous comment that 'the intrusion of the enemy Intelligence Service into the ROBERTO network is becoming clearer and clearer.'

As well as the TRIANGLE material, there was other evidence of German suspicions. SIME noted 'after the New Year message of good wishes, there was a marked change'.

The enemy frequently failed to reply to, or even acknowledge our signals, and contact was seldom established more than once a week. His messages showed far less interest in military matters, and few questions were asked on military subjects. Traffic continued sporadically on the subject of the money which was said to be on its way, but enemy messages were such as to lead us to suspect that traps were being set. It was for instance proposed that the enemy should send the money to Istanbul and we should send some-one to fetch it. This looked very like an attempt to kidnap a British agent on the Venlo pattern, or at least learn more of our organisation. We toyed with the suggestion over some messages, pleading lack of money for the journey and suggesting that we might find a 'neutral merchant' to act as an intermediary. A scheme was tentatively laid on for action at Istanbul, but the enemy appeared to lose interest, and it was not thought wise to persevere.

Perhaps because of this shadow cast over the channel, between 1 January and 25 June 1942, only three items of any significance were conveyed to the enemy. They were reports that an American aircraft factory was being planned to be constructed just outside Cairo; that American military personnel had been seen in Cairo's streets, together with a description of three different shoulder-flashes; and the correct location of the GHQ Middle East building in Cairo. Requests for spe-cific military information, such as the location of the 23rd Infantry Division and various Polish, Free French and colonial troops, and details of shipping in the Suez Canal, were simply ignored.

As an expedient on the issue of the factory, 'enemy enquiries about site, capacity, etc. were first evaded then answered with the excuse that the agent who supplied the original information had disappeared'. On the American military personnel, 'enemy enquiries for further details were met with a brief reply giving three shoulder-badges noticed'. As for the address of GHQ, it had actually been supplied several months earlier. SIME noted that this had been asked for, and correctly answered, nearly a year before. The address is such common knowledge throughout the Middle East that a trap was suspected. But it is possible that the enemy is even more ignorant of conditions in Egypt than we suspect. His second enquiry may imply that he had lost record of the first, or that he thought there had been a move.

Evan Simpson registered severe reservations about the questions posed by the Abwehr, as John de Salis pointed out to Dudley Clarke on 18 May that CHEESE's position was 'very precarious'.

Apparently Major Robertson had some information about him: 'the heavy hand of the British Secret Service is now apparent', do you know anything further about this? Up to now we have struck for money. '*Sans argent, nouvelles militaires impossible*'.

Remuneration has been promised but no sums have as yet materialised. The enemy are now asking for information about your aeroplane factory, location, details of equipment and whether manufacturing or merely assembly shops.

Simpson is now unwilling to carry on with this theme unless you insist on it. In my opinion there are several disadvantages. Sooner or later we shall have to locate this factory and tie it up with an existing building/installation, thereby exposing a building to bombing. We shall have to decide whether it is a factory or an assembly shop. The first is unlikely, owing to local conditions – total absence of primary materials, tools and skilled personnel. The second would have to be linked up with an area where considerable activity is already taking place where the associated features of a large factory, lodging capacity, rail/water communications, are to be found.

The enemy are also anxious to obtain the exact location of GHQ. This was given correctly by us as Sh.E1 Birgas (i) There is no record in the file that GHQ had been consulted. (ii) This might be an indication that our message had not been received, but would appear to be much more likely a check on our veracity.

The solution, produced by de Salis on 19 May, was to focus on three distinct themes and give the enemy the impression

- That LAMBERT is, and remains, loyal to the enemy;

- That owing to the lack of funds he has been forced to employ 'inferior' agents who had misled him and given him inaccurate and misleading information on – e.g. 18th Division;

- That he has now got rid of the lot and, should funds be available, he is now in a position to recruit better personnel who could and would produce the required information;

- With this new organisation we might allay the suspicion apparent ... and give us a possibility of having a new start.

SIME later recorded that

> it was not until the latter half of June that anything further was transmitted. Even then, the matter supplied was first of low grade, though in order to build up confidence it had to contain a high proportion of truth. 'A' Force was fortunately able to supply the enemy with information that he already possessed, new items that were unlikely to be of use to him, or truths that would probably confuse him more than a deliberate lie.

On 2 July the Abwehr suddenly expressed renewed interest and confidence in Nicossof and instructed him to begin transmitting daily, and TRIANGLE intercepts dated 4 and 12 July referred to him as 'credible' and 'trustworthy' although Athens noted that 'the reliability of this agent has not yet been proved'. SIME responded by having Nicossof welcome the chance to bring Rommel to Cairo and suggested that the arrival of the Germans would enable him to receive some medals and have his debts repaid. It was also SIME's chance to convey SENTINEL, a deception plan designed to encourage a German offensive in the period 10–20 August when the 8th Army supposedly would be in an especially advantageous position, with plenty of anti-tank artillery and minefields, to resist the attack. The objective, of course, was to delay the enemy's impending attack until after 20 August when Auchinleck would have the benefits of reinforcements. In the event Rommel, with only 200 panzers and conscious of his supply line back to Tripoli stretching a thousand miles, significantly over-estimated the British strength and postponed his attack until the night of 30 August, but it failed at Alam Halfa. His plan had been betrayed by ULTRA, thus allowing the 8th Army to reinforce the precise focus of attack, the Alam Halfa ridge with 400 tanks, 300 anti-tank guns, 350 field-guns and huge minefields. In terms of strategic deception, 'A' Force invented RAYON, a supposed plan to invade Crete which required Greek troops in Egypt to be mobilised. The intention, at the very least, was to prevent Rommel from drawing reinforcements from the German forces on the occupied island, and this certainly happened, as demonstrated by an Afrika Korps assessment of the Allied order-of-battle which included the fake 74th Armoured Brigade joining the genuine 7th Armoured Division.

The other 'A' Force strategic objective was to apply maximum pressure on Rommel's supply route from Italy, which in turn meant support for Malta, then besieged by the Luftwaffe and the Italian Regina Marina. The four submarines of the 10th Flotilla operating from HMS *Talbot* in Valetta's Grand Harbour, HMS *Unbroken*, *United*, *Unruffled* and *Unrivalled* took a heavy toll of Axis shipping, up to half of the cargo ships and two-thirds of the tankers, on which the Afrika Korps was wholly dependent for food, ammunition, fuel and replacements, so Malta's survival was a high priority for the Allies. The Royal Navy, with the benefit of well-protected submarine pens and high-grade intelligence derived from ULTRA, proved so successful in handicapping the enemy's supply line that the Germans developed a plan, codenamed HERKULES, to bomb the island into submission and execute a joint paratroop and amphibious assault, thereby eliminating the menace. However, the project was abandoned when it was realised that such an undertaking would siphon off too many resources from the increasingly hard-pressed Afrika Korps. By the end of the war the 10th Flotilla had fired 1,289 torpedoes, with an estimated hit-rate of 10 per cent.

Allied attempts to deliver vital supplies to Malta, from Gibraltar in one direction and Alexandria on the other, had failed. Both convoys, HARPOON from the west and VIGOROUS from the east, had been disasters. HARPOON was under attack for two full days, and four of the six cargo ships sunk, along with a cruiser and five destroyers. VIGOROUS was an even greater catastrophe, and returned to Alexandria after the loss of a cruiser, HMS *Hermione*, and five destroyers.

A third mission, codenamed PEDESTAL, was planned for August 1942, in the knowledge that another failure would leave the island, which had endured 3,000 air raids in two years, undefended from the air because of a lack of aviation fuel for the island's Spitfires operating from Luqa and its satellite fields. Surrender was contemplated, so PEDESTAL's fourteen merchantmen were protected by a huge escort on an unprecedented scale, which included two battleships, three aircraft carriers, seven cruisers and thirty-two destroyers. The Italians attacked in force, but suffered heavy losses, and HMS *Unbroken* severely damaged the German tanker *Regina*, the heavy cruiser *Bolzano* and the light cruiser *Muzio Attendolo* with torpedoes, putting all three permanently out of action.

The assembly and departure of such a vast concentration of naval force was next to impossible to disguise, especially as it transited the Straits of Gibraltar, so the deception planners tried to divert the enemy's attention to the eastern Mediterranean and promote the impression that the Allies intended to launch an invasion of Crete from Cyprus. This was reported by CHEESE which resulted in Luftwaffe and Regia Aeronautica Italiana reconnaissance flights being sent over Larnaca, Limassol and Famagusta to photograph landing craft and other preparations associated with amphibious operations. Evidently the combined evidence persuaded the Axis intelligence analysts who diverted Regina Marina surface vessels from engaging PEDESTAL, in preference to preparing for a major battle in Crete. In consequence, five of the PEDESTAL merchantmen reached their destination, including the SS *Ohio* carrying the vital aviation fuel, thus allowing Malta to survive. In David Mure's view,

> a large detachment of the Italian fleet which had been ruthlessly blockading Malta detached itself and shot off to Crete to intercept the invasion from Cyprus and the expected threat of the Italian heavy surface forces never materialised. The result was that a high proportion of the convoy got through to Malta and enabled it to remain a thorn in the side of Rommel's supply services. Fortunately the Italians chose to consider this scare, which may have tipped the balance in favour of the survival of Eighth Army in front of Alexandria, as a merciful deliverance enacted just in time.

The Axis failure to eliminate the threat from Malta would have many consequences. The ability of the RAF to deploy Bristol Beaufort torpedo bombers from 39 Squadron and Wellingtons from 69 Squadron, coordinated with the submarines, proved decisive when on 30 August a relief convoy destined for Tobruk was ambushed and three vessels were sunk. Then the *San Andrea*, a tanker laden with 3,198 tons of fuel for Rommel, was sunk. Increasingly desperate, the Germans assembled another convoy of nine ships, but it too was betrayed by ULTRA and five were sunk. In these circumstances, on 1 September, the Afrika Korps began its long retreat from El Alamein, in vehicles dependent on Luftwaffe fuel, thus making air protection from Albert Kesselring impossible. Further losses meant that during the first week of October, at an absolutely critical moment in the conflict, two tankers were destroyed, and the DAK received not a drop of gas.

During September 1942 the DAK took delivery of only 24 per cent of the 50,000 tons of supplies required each month to sustain the offensive. In that same month 33,939 tons of Axis shipping, mainly destined for Tripoli, was sunk.

In a prelude to the main offensive, Rommel attempted, at the end of August 1942, to break through the British defences at El Alamein to reach Alexandria, Cairo, and the Suez Canal, but his plans had been compromised by ULTRA. Instead of taking Montgomery by surprise and sweeping through relatively weak lines, many of Rommel's 203 tanks unexpectedly found themselves in a minefield sown with 18,000 mines and attacked from the air at night under the light of parachute flares. Worse, Rommel had gambled on the imminent arrival of six ships from Italy loaded with fuel and ammunition, but ULTRA had identified the vulnerability, and four of the merchantmen were found and sunk, and while the battle raged, the last two tankers, the *San Andrea* and the *Picci Fascio*, were destroyed as they approached Tobruk. After six days of intense fighting, in which the DAK lost thirty-eight tanks and 400 trucks, Rommel began to withdraw, blaming the failure on a leak from the Italians.

By the time the British offensive at El Alamein began on 23 October, ULTRA had revealed the extent of the DAK's plight, and on 25 October three tankers and one other merchantman were given a heavy escort and air cover, as learned from ULTRA, and another aerial ambush was prepared three days later, which resulted in the loss of three more tankers. Altogether the depleted DAK lost 44 per cent of its supplies in October, representing an increase of 24 per cent over September.

When Montgomery counter-attacked in October, Rommel was caught off guard and, short of fuel and ammunition, lost most of his tanks to new Allied weaponry. Overestimating his adversary's strength and down to his last thirty-two tanks, Rommel led his 70,000 men on a long retreat 800 miles across the Libyan desert, constantly harassed by the 8th Army and the Royal Air Force.

The options for the pivotal role in RAYON to be played by CHEESE (referred to as LAMBERT) were set out in a proposal dated 29 September 1942:

1. LAMBERT's friend (the BGM) meets a Polish officer in Cairo on a mission from Syria who says that the British seem anxious about the Russian threat and that there has been a large increase in the British troops in General Wilson's command.

2. LAMBERT meets a friend recently returned from Alexandria via the desert route who says that there is a marked decrease in military traffic on that road since his last visit in August. He reports many Greek soldiers in Alexandria and gathered from a Greek officer that they were destined for Crete.

3. LAMBERT's Greek merchant friend on his return from Aleppo reports seeing large troop movements by road in Syria and by road and rail in Palestine towards the North and the North East. He saw many tanks in the coastal plain in Palestine and US Airforce in Palestine and Syria.

4. The American officer back on leave does not speak of a British offensive but indicates that the British are consolidating their defensive lines. He has not heard of any new formations arriving with 8 Army and says that the British are keeping a wary eye on the Russian situation.

5. The Greek employee of the Egyptian State Railways mentions the specialist training at Qabrit and says that the Greek fleet is in the Port Said–Ismaelia area. He has seen landing craft near the canal on trains going east. Hears of Greeks going to Haifa after special training.

6. BGM's Polish officer friend returns suddenly to Syria leaving the impression of certain Polish forces moving towards the northern front and of impending action. He seemed very excited and pleased.

7. LAMBERT sees many British soldiers on leave from WD and gives idents of some units and Divisions of 6 Army.

8. Greek friends talking again of the liberation of Crete and the part to be played by the Greek forces. Greek officer hints at an invasion by Britain and Greeks in November.

9. LAMBERT hears of big conference at General Wilson's HQ and notices excitement among Greeks re. Crete.

When Rommel did attack his tanks encountered large minefields in their path, which made their progress slow. Making little headway because of mines, sustained air attacks, and short of fuel, Rommel ordered a withdrawal over three days from 3 September.

This was the crucial turning point in the war in the Middle East, and prepared the way for LIGHTFOOT, the Allied offensive scheduled for 23 October. The cover-plan for LIGHTFOOT was TREATMENT, which was intended to mislead Rommel as to the date and the location of the expected offensive that inevitably would be spearheaded, as usual, by the 7th Armoured Division. Clearly the ruse worked, for Rommel left Africa for medical attention in Germany on 23 October; his temporary replacement was General Georg Strumme who had arrived just four days earlier.

In the battle that followed the British deployed 1,200 tanks which faced a combined force of 525 Axis tanks, and the result was a shattering defeat for the Afrika Korps which lost 213, and for the Italians which had almost all their 278 destroyed, along with three complete divisions. By 11 November, 30,000 enemy PoWs had been captured. Rommel returned on 25 October, to find that Strumme had died of a heart attack two days earlier. Rommel himself would be recalled on 10 March.

Perhaps irrationally, based on this performance, the Abwehr concluded at the end of October 1942 that ROBERTO was once again 'reliable'.

Nicossof responded positively to the renewed interest and

> began to show a new energy and enterprise. Messages were even prepared to indicate that he was beginning to suffer from the monomania common among successful spies; it was not thought advisable to send these, and it was clearly becoming unnecessary to do so. CHEESE seemed to be completely re-established, and on the most favourable lines. The enemy had been given every excuse for forgetting the past: new contacts, which Nicossof represented himself as making, could be mentioned or dropped at will; mistakes and deceptions could be explained away on the plea of lack of funds, or of Nicossof's unfamiliarity with the business of collecting military information. Prospects were good either for a renewed course of misleading and fogging enemy intelligence or, with good luck, for a larger and more decisive stroke.

By the end of November 1942 the respective military fortunes in North Africa had been reversed, with the British taking the initiative, and able to operate with relative freedom from Malta which was resupplied in December by STONEAGE, a convoy from Alexandria which made the voyage without mishap. In the last naval battle of the year, at

Skerki Bank, off the coast of Tunisia, an entire Italian convoy of four ships, with an escort of three destroyers and a pair of torpedo boats, was wiped out. The merchantmen were carrying troops, ammunition, tanks and vehicles, and they were all sunk, killing some 2,000 Italians.

Between August 1942 and February 1943, at the height of the network's activities, CHEESE sent an average of six messages a month on the topic of money, and received four or five from the Abwehr.

After much pressure the Abwehr agreed to CHEESE's proposal, made on 25 September, to send a Greek merchant friend to Aleppo to collect his money, and the man travelled two days later on 27 September 1942. However, he returned empty-handed on 4 October, claiming to have been scared by the execution a few days earlier of five German spies in Aleppo. This left CHEESE very disappointed, as did another scheme which was for an intended delivery by a native labourer between 10 and 15 October. Finally, CHEESE was informed on 7 December that his money had already reached Cairo and he was asked for a delivery address. He nominated a flat supposedly occupied by a friend of his Greek girlfriend, and was told to expect Hamel to drop off a packet or a milk bottle containing the cash. However, at the last moment the address was raided by the Egyptian police over an unrelated matter, so the plan was scuppered. This unexpected incident 'electrified CHEESE' and gave him 'a severe attack of the jitters' which he reported to his controller on 17 December, explaining that he had instructed his '*amie*' to find a new and safer flat. Three days later he reported that the police raid had been 'a domestic affair' but that he had been 'badly frightened' by it. Nevertheless, on 15 January 1943 he was able to confirm that his '*amie*' had acquired a suitable flat and ask that the courier be diverted to the new address. However, on 6 February the Abwehr report that it has been impossible to change the arrangements, so CHEESE reluctantly agreed to use the old address.

Interception of the Abwehr's internal communications revealed the extent to which Athens shared CHEESE's frustration. On 7 January 1943 Captain Rolf von der Marwitz, the naval attaché in Istanbul, was reported to have paid a large sum to a German agent in Egypt identified only as ARMEN. Then, on 25 January, CHEESE was asked for his girlfriend's Christian name, which he supplied the next day. On 28 January Athens sent CHEESE more instructions about the delivery to the Rue Galal and suggested the password 'El Hakim'. This prompted an exchange with Zähringer on 2 February who was ordered to acquire the girlfriend's Christian name and to pass it on to headquarters so the delivery operation could proceed. In compliance, CHEESE identified Helene Cabri as an authorised recipient of his Abwehr consignment of cash, and described her as the tenant of a man named Kyriakides. Both, of course, were entirely imaginary.

In another TRIANGLE text, on 23 February, Zähringer was told that CHEESE was worried about his funds, and was directed to deal with the matter. On 18 March a message to Istanbul demanded to know whether Zähringer had solved the problem and, if not, why not? On 29 March Athens sent an urgent request to Rossetti in Istanbul, where he had arrived on 22 January, to provide an address in Syria where CHEESE's money could be made available. This development fascinated SIME, which speculated that the Abwehr might be contemplating the use of PESSIMISTS or even QUICKSILVER as an alternative to the Aleppo route proposed by CHEESE the previous September. Analysis of TRIANGLE later revealed that PESSIMISTS were also controlled by Rossetti.

The loss of *U-372*, a Type-VIIC of the 23rd U-boat Flotilla, off Haifa in August 1942, which was carrying his courier, Jawad Hamadi, codenamed HAMLET, also prevented further funds from reaching CHEESE. The entire crew of forty-eight, and the sole passenger, Hamadi, were captured by the Royal Navy, one of fourteen U-boats sunk in the

Mediterranean in 1942. Under interrogation Hamadi, a Druze student, admitted that he had been recruited by the Sensburg organisation in Athens to deliver money to CHEESE. When captured, Hamadi had been wearing a money-belt containing $3,500 and £500 in other currencies.

According to Walter Sensburg, who was questioned about HAM-LET after the war,

> HAMLET was recruited by Rossetti in Rome and transferred to Athens when Rossetti joined the Ast. An intelligent youth, probably an Arab, HAMLET had studied in Rome. He served the Germans out of idealism and would accept no compensation. HAMLET left Rome in 1942 aboard a submarine which was to take him to the Syrian coast. The submarine was sunk but, according to Rossetti, HAMLET survived and was interned by the British in Cairo. Nothing further was heard of him.

The voyage of the *U-372*, which sailed from the Greek island of Salamis on 27 July, commanded by Captain Heinz-Joachim Neumann, was compromised at the outset by TRIANGLE, and an ambush was prepared in which the submarine was attacked with depth-charges launched by the destroyers HMS *Sikh* and HMS *Zulu* and the escort destroyers HMS *Croome* and HMS *Tetcott*, and by depth-charges dropped from an RAF Wellington from 221 Squadron. The U-boat's entire complement was placed aboard the *Tetcott* and disembarked in Haifa where they were questioned by CSDIC personnel. On 17 August Hamadi, when cross-examined by SIME, admitted his role, disclosed his call-signs and radio schedules, and volunteered to work as a double agent. According to him, he had been instructed to make his way to Ranlkin, a village about 45 kilometres from Beirut where he was to set up his transmitter and contact Athens on behalf of a man he knew only as 'Paul'. SIME subsequently reported that the fates were unkind when, for a second time, a carefully-prepared plan had been made by CHEESE for his *'petite amie'* to receive the money at a suitably selected café on the Pyramids Road in October, the enemy were distracted and apparently compelled to abandon their side of the plan because of the shock of the British victory at El Alamein.

The next major Allied deception in which CHEESE was to participate was TREATMENT, a plan which suggested that Crete was about to be invaded. On 13 and 15 October 1942 CHEESE reported that troops would be landed on the island in early November, and on 17 October he described a commanders' conference called for 26 October, and on 18 October he said that Montgomery also planned a simultaneous offensive in the south of the desert, and declared that the attack on Crete was scheduled for 8 November. In response, on 21 October Hitler ordered the 22nd Infantry Division's occupation garrisons in Crete to be reinforced with valuable troops that might otherwise have gone to the Afrika Korps.

While working on TREATMENT, CHEESE was also setting the foundation for the cover story for TORCH, the huge Allied landings in Morocco and Algeria in which 1,500 ships would deliver first 90,000, then a further 200,000 troops to North Africa. The planners presumed that the preparations for what was to be the largest amphibious operation ever conducted would be impossible to conceal, so they concentrated on offering alternative objectives. Codenamed KENNE-COT, the campaign fell into two parts, with the first suggesting that Sicily and Italy were the targets, and TOWNSMAN, centred further east, implying that Crete was the likely objective of the massive invasion fleet which assembled in the Atlantic before venturing through the Straits of Gibraltar, which were under continuous scrutiny by the enemy. On 31 October CHEESE reported that the Allies intended to attack Italy, with Crete as a secondary target, and predicted large-scale

American air raids. In fact, of course, the TORCH beachheads were secured with ease on 8 November, the Axis having been taken completely by surprise.

Following the success of TORCH, and the liberation of Algiers, the local Deuxième Bureau agreed to cooperate with the British, and the result was the transfer from Cairo of Cuthbert Bowlby's ISLD headquarters, and the opening of an SIS station under Arthur G. Trevor Wilson and his energetic subordinate, John Bruce Lockhart. The French turned out to be running a stable of about a dozen double agents, among them RAM, a French NCO who was notionally employed at the French GHQ; a Spanish officer codenamed WHISKERS who was in contact with the Abwehr in Morocco and had created an entirely bogus network of sub-agents; and GILBERT, a French army officer and St Cyr graduate who had been infiltrated into Tunis in April 1943 to act as a stay-behind agent and was in radio contact with his Abwehr controller.

The Deuxième Bureau also controlled a SIM agent, LLAMA, operating from Tripoli and responsible for conveying a false order-of-battle to the Italians. SIM's efforts in the region had not achieved much success, their large stay-behind network in Tripolitania had been rounded up. They were also discouraged by an attempt to drop three agents by parachute near Damascus in December 1942 who were to establish radio contact with a station on Rhodes.

Levi was released from Tremiti on 15 May 1943 and, due to ill health, was put in hospital in Foggia but, due to heavy bombing, was transferred on 19 August to the military hospital at San Severo. In Cairo these events were monitored through TRIANGLE, and SIME reported that 'at the beginning of April 1943 we received information from a most secret source that Levi was to be released from imprisonment, and Rossetti was asked by Scirombo of the Italian Intelligence Service what should be done with him. There was an obscure reference to his being transferred to the Germans. Rossetti requested that Levi should be sent to Sofia to be at Rossetti's disposal. In mid-May 1943 Rossetti in Istanbul asked Athens if Levi could be brought to Sofia. Ten days later he again asked what had happened to Levi.

Two days later, on 17 May, owing to a shortage of beds, Levi was sent to San Severo prison, where he was liberated by British forces on 17 October and given a post as an interpreter by a Civil Affairs officer, Captain Cooley.

In October 1941 CHEESE was used as the principal channel for deception in conveying false information to the enemy on 20 and 27 October, in anticipation of the Allied offensive in the Western Desert planned for November. His role was considered both essential and completely successful, as was reported to MI5 in January 1942, although ISOS indicated some recent loss of confidence in him by the enemy.

At the end of September 1942 ISOS indicated that Rossetti had been rebuked by his superiors in Berlin for his excessive travel, but his reputation had been restored after Walter Sensburg had seen Hans Piekenbrock in Berlin. According to his British file, Sensburg had been based in Brussels in 1940 and had distinguished himself by landing a group of wholly unprepared spies, Sjörd Pons, Carl Meier, Charles van de Kieboom and José Waldberg on the south coast of England where they had been quickly arrested.

Between January and July 1942 the Abwehr, transmitting from a radio station in Bari, expressed renewed confidence in CHEESE and asked him to transmit daily, instead of merely twice a week, a request that was interpreted as proof of his perceived value.

In April 1943 Dick White, while on a visit to Cairo, was briefed on CHEESE and brought back to London a summary of the case prepared on 1 September 1942 by Evan Simpson so that MI5's B Division experts, T. A. Robertson among them, could offer some comments.

Simpson's *Report on CHEESE* covered twenty-four pages and started with a short account of Levi's prewar history but concentrated on his activities during the two months he spent in Cairo between February and April 1941. Although, at the time that it was written, Levi himself had been sentenced to five years' imprisonment and was still confined on Tremiti, Simpson had no knowledge of his fate beyond a single TRIANGLE intercept that suggested Levi had been detained for two to four months and then had been released. In his narrative Simpson concentrated on some of the technical issues that had arisen in developing the radio link, and catalogued the enemy's perceived failures in their poor handling of what should have been considered an exemplary agent. Simpson opined that most likely Levi had been managed by the Italians, which explained some the shortcomings, but this was one of several issues that would be dealt with in greater detail by Tommy Robertson, a man with vastly more experience of the Abwehr. Simpson observed

all outside evidence goes to show that, since the Italian declaration of war, and the prompt internment of Italians suspected of espionage, the enemy has been starved of reliable up-to-date intelligence from Egypt. He is consequently doubly greedy for it, inclined to swallow bad (in the absence of good) information and careless in his correlation and checking up. Though Levi was recruited by a predominantly German organisation it seems that the arrangements for his journey, wireless set, etc. were in Italian hands and he himself complained to Zähringer of the inefficiency of the arrangements. The handling of the CHEESE messages was done at Bari and linguistic evidence (the very Italianate idioms embedded in the French of the messages) seemed to show that the translation, and possibly the writing of the message was in Italian hands. Perhaps the whole case was being handled by Italians, and handled with a laziness and carelessness that the Germans would not have tolerated.

Simpson was very dismissive of how the enemy had mismanaged CHEESE and speculated about his imprisonment and subsequent release, unaware that Levi had been incarcerated continuously since August 1941.

> It is possible that Levi's release from prison with a new stock of plausible ingenuities on his tongue, may have had a hand in reestablishing what he had originally foisted on his employers, and found them even more ready to be deceived. All this must naturally remain pure speculation. If true it leads to the pleasing conclusion that 'wishful thinking' is not a monopoly of the democratic peoples. While on the subject of enemy methods, it may be remarked that had the enemy been handling genuine, loyal agents (instead of a pertinacious British organisation) he would almost certainly have soured their loyalty and lost their cooperation at a much earlier stage. The constant carelessness in encodement and (still more) in wireless procedure, endangered the whole communication and, strangely enough, it rose to a climax of inefficiency early in July just when the directorate of enemy intelligence seemed most eager for the information which was being transmitted. Meanwhile the failure to send money, the hollowness and monotony of the promises to do so, and the apparent indifference to the dangers which inefficiency would have brought on real spies concealed in Cairo, indicate a really lamentable lack of imagination and common sense.

Simpson concluded his *History* on a final note of triumph; 'CHEESE is still in action, and it is hoped that he will remain so, to the better confusion of His Majesty's enemies.'

The *History* was read in London by Tommy Robertson who drafted a six-page document of nineteen paragraphs dated 30 March 1943, quite critical of SIME's handling of the entire case. He saw the matter as 'an entirely Abwehr enterprise' and one, more specifically, managed by Einz Heer II through the Athens Abstelle, as disclosed by

TRIANGLE. Einz Heer II was the Abwehr's military sabotage branch, and MI5 considered it significant that this was the section handling CHEESE, instead of Einz Heer I, the intelligence collection specialists. Robertson also took up the issue of the Abwehr's 'degree of incompetence in the CHEESE case'.

> In our experience the Abwehr is often recklessly careless both in the way in which it trains, or fails to train, its agents, and in the way in which it superintends, or fails to superintend, their later activities. These haphazard methods even extend into the sphere of communications … We also have suffered from an Abwehr officer who did not listen, could not operate, or called on the wrong frequency, and from cipher clerks who could neither encipher nor decipher correctly. The standard, of course, varies from station to station and, with the Abwehr wireless network as large as it now is, it would perhaps be unreasonable to expect the general average to be very high. Nevertheless is it surprising to find it as low as it is. We can confidently say that CHEESE's experience with his control-station is a fair example of what any Abwehr agent may have to put up with.

By way of further explanation, Robertson explained that Colonel Sensburg, the head of the Athens Abstelle, was a familiar character who had been known to MI5 since 1940 when he had gained an unenviable reputation at the Brussels Abstelle for sending poorly trained agents on badly planned missions. In particular, while at the Brussels Abstelle in September 1940 Sensburg had sent four ill-prepared and poorly equipped agents in a fishing-boat to land on a beach in Kent, and all had been arrested within hours or their arrival. Of the four, Carl Meier and José Waldberg had been hanged. Robertson had relied on TRIANGLE and information from an Abwehr defector to conclude that Sensburg was incompetent.

Robertson then turned to what he termed 'the greatest strength and the greatest weakness' of the CHEESE case.

That is the return of Levi himself to Italy and his continued presence there. It is unnecessary to emphasise how great a weakness this is or could have been. At any point after his return Levi, a man reputed to be not entirely trustworthy, could have revealed to his employers what the true position was. In theory at least he could still do so, though probably he now feels (particularly since his imprisonment) that he has committed himself so far as to make any withdrawal impossible. Nevertheless, any operational deception put over by CHEESE contains this element of risk. If Levi were, from whatever cause, to break down, any deception then being practised would not only fall but by its nature reveal to the enemy precisely what we were attempting to conceal from them. On the other side the advantages of Levi's position (so long as he does not break down) are almost equally great. In the first place, the Abwehr is entitled to argue that no counter-espionage organisation and still more no double agent would have been willing to take the risks inherent in Levi's return. Indeed, from Levi's own point of view, the risks were fantastic. By returning to Italy at such an early stage he committed himself in advance to answering perhaps with his life for the good faith and reliability of an organisation of the nature and scope of whose activities he was necessarily ignorant. In these circumstances no one can blame the Abwehr if they regarded Levi's willingness to return and remain in Italy as an absolute guarantee that CHEESE was not working under control. In my view it is this fact which explains the rather cautious tone displayed in secret services of November 1941. The Abwehr never said that V-mann ROBERTO himself was under control, but only that 'the intrusion of the enemy Intelligence Service into the ROBERTO network is becoming clearer and clearer'. The picture in their mind was of SIME gradually penetrating the fringes of an organisation which was itself still sound at heart. Had they taken a different view, it would not have been possible for CHEESE at a later date to have restored his credit by discarding his network.

Robertson, who had been the MI5 case officer running Arthur Owens, the Welsh double agent codenamed SNOW, was adept at the complexities of managing difficult individuals who demonstrated uncertain or shifting loyalties, made some relevant points about CHEESE;

The return of Levi to Italy had, I think, another valuable result. With his going (since Fulvio Melcher had already fallen by the way) the Germans lost the only member of the Cairo organisation with whom they had any personal acquaintance. This, as we know from our own experience in England, is an incomparable advantage. A double agent whom the Abwehr has recruited directly, whom they have trained, and with whose personality they are acquainted, is always a little circumscribed as to what he can and cannot do. He cannot step too far out of character without arousing suspicion; it is difficult for him suddenly to change the type or value of his reports; he must react to new situations in a manner in keeping with what the Germans know of his character. An agent whom the Abwehr have never seen, or better still a network of imaginary agents, offers a wide scope. The Abwehr know only as much or as little about them as it is expedient that they should be told. They have no means to assess the probability, physical or psychological, of their saying or doing one thing more than another. Moreover, when necessary, imaginary agents can be dispensed with, changed or even captured without imperiling the remainder of the network or giving rise to inconvenient administrative problems.

Our experience in England has shown that the Abwehr, provided that its confidence in the original agent is unshaken, is very ready to accept new sub-agents recruited in the course of operations, and surprisingly unexacting in the particulars which it demands of their past careers and personalities. In this way we have been able to provide one agent with seven non-existent sub-agents, some of whom we have since put into direct communication with the Abwehr and who now constitute a network which has spread even outside the UK. Our experiences in this and similar cases also bears out the statement on page nine of the SIME report that 'the enemy is curiously unwary and eager to accept stories of the disloyalty of disgruntled colonials, Irishmen, etc. and even of supposed ex-member of Fascist organisations in England'. It may be unnecessary to draw the attention of SIME to the equally wide field of opportunity offered by disgruntled allies, nationalist (and even Republican) Spaniards; Indian supporters of Congress; and German-born Americans. The Abwehr is also prepared to accept on the one hand agents or sub-agents who work without any other motive purely for money, and on the other such ideological prodigies as Poles inspired by a disinterested love for the Greater Germany. The explanation is probably to be found first in the degree (always noticeable) to which Abwehr officers are the victims of Dr Goebbels's propaganda; secondly, in the slackness and increasing corruption of the organisation as a whole; thirdly, in the natural anxiety of an intelligence officer to see his estimate of the original agent justified by the skill and initiative with which he develops his work.

Robertson went on to observe that Clemens Rossetti was an Abwehr officer of great interest, and one meriting study, perhaps fulfilling a role close to that of the notorious Nikolaus Ritter, the spymaster who had spent some years as a businessman in the United States before the war and had subsequently returned to the Hamburg Abstelle to supervise the infiltration of agents into Great Britain. One of his early stars had been Owens, the spy known to Robertson as SNOW. Frequently mentioned in TRIANGLE intercepts, Rossetti was to be considered

a man of great energy. He travels incessantly to Sofia, to Italy, to Berlin, to Istanbul, and to Ankara. His name is constantly mentioned in connection with agents in the Middle East. Einz Luft Paris offers him one agent; on another occasion he declines an offer from Oberstleutnant Heidsschuch in Rome. He is the moving spirit of the HAMLET undertaking in Syria; he interviews a Persian agent in Sofia, he is authorised by Einz Heer Ost to operate on a considerable scale in Turkey and requires T£20,000 for the purpose. He is instrumental in planting false information on the Americans; he requires (for some nameless purpose) a pistol with silencer and supplies of the drug Pervitin which Ast Brussels has previously used with success. It may be questioned how great or of what value to the enemy is the practical result of this activity. Nevertheless it is clear than whether the Abwehr's machinations in the Middle East are successful or not, Rossetti is in some sense the centre of them. He holds, we may say, a position analogous to that occupied until the spring of 1941 by Oberstleutnant Ritter of Ast Hamburg in relation to this country.

Robertson then drew a parallel with SNOW, the classic case that he had supervised personally from September 1939 when the duplicitous Welshnan had been arrested in London and thereupon had promptly surrendered his transmitter which then had been used to dupe the enemy. As MI5's first double agent of the war, SNOW laid the foundation for the whole double-cross scheme, and was directly responsible for the identification of many subsequent German spies, in a role not entirely dissimilar to CHEESE's in Cairo.

We were greatly the gainers in knowing as much as we did about Ritter, his methods and his organisation. By far the greater part of this knowledge was a product of the SNOW case which was conducted almost exclusively with counter-espionage objectives in view. In one respect this case differed radically from that of CHEESE. SNOW was throughout his career in constant personal contact with the Abwehr. Between the outbreak of war and the final winding up of his case he made, or his sub-agents made on his behalf, six visits to the continent for personal conferences with Ritter or his officers. Each of these visits added something to our knowledge. On fourteen separate occasions (or as nearly as we can judge) the Abwehr either attempted, although not always successfully, to reinforce SNOW's organisation in England or put him in touch obliquely with other agents, some of whom might otherwise have remained unknown to us.

While praising SIME for what had been accomplished by exploiting CHEESE as a channel for deception, Robertson was subtly critical of the way his original contacts in Cairo, Georges Khouri and Madame Vigoretti-Antoniada, had not been pursued more professionally.

It does not appear that such opportunities as did present themselves were exploited to the full. The contrary seems rather to be the case. Levi, for example, went unaccompanied to see Madame Vigoretti-Antoniada and Georges Khouri, the two persons in Cairo who had been recommended to him by Count Scirombo. Nothing came of these meetings and no record survives of what passed. It is no doubt true that the practical difficulty of covering or recording such meetings were great, perhaps insuperable; it is also true that at the end of the operations SIME were no nearer to discovering the true sympathies of these people than they would have been had Levi not existed. At the same time a welcome opportunity was missed of testing the good faith of Levi himself at the very opening of the case.

Finally, Robertson turned to what he perceived as the central weakness in the CHEESE affair, which was the lack of funding.

Nicossof started his career in April 1941 with only £150. Nearly two years later, in February 1943, he was still without additional funds, but still apparently able to operate although during the intervening period his outgoing expenses must have at times been heavy. This situation must, until it is remedied, represent a grave weakness in the case. At any moment some senior Abwehr officer may from curiosity examine the back records and, if he does so, must reach the conclusion that Nicossof's accountancy can only be explained on the assumption that he is working under British control. SIME is, of course, fully alive to this danger, their report describes four attempts to secure additional funds: in August 1942, in October and again in December and the following January. None of these attempts was successful or at least had not been at the time the SIME report was written. It is, I think, pertinent to enquire whether this was wholly the Abwehr's fault. We know at least from the message already quoted that in August 1942 Rossetti was making a genuine effort to pay ROBERTO, and this was not his first attempt. Similarly, we know that he was exerting himself in Turkey to secure the latest payment in January this year. He has not, therefore, been entirely neglectful of his agent. On the other hand I received the impression (perhaps wrongly) from the first or introductory report forwarded by SIME that Rossetti had not always enjoyed their full cooperation in his efforts to pay CHEESE. It is said, with regard to the August plan, that at the last moment CHEESE's merchant friend was frightened off by the execution of five spies which had occurred a few days previously. Similarly, in December the flat at which CHEESE was to receive the money was raided at a crucial moment by the Egyptian police with the result that a fresh scheme had to be arranged.

I do not know if it was in SIME's power to have prevented either of these incidents: the report even seems to imply that both were staged. If so, I think SIME was following a false policy. In either case, apart from the general desirability of CHEESE's receiving money, there was a distinct counter-espionage advantage to be gained from allowing, even compelling, the payment to proceed. In equivalent circumstances in this country we should, I think, have felt that a contact with the Abwehr in Aleppo and still more in Cairo was worth the slight lapse from reality involved in inducing a Greek merchant not to be frightened or persuading the Egyptian police to postpone a raid.

I make this point because our own experience has been that the Abwehr is not adept at paying its agents and not infrequently fails to do so unless rendered active assistance. This is, I think, because they lack not the means but the imagination. The problem of making a clandestine payment to England should never be insoluble to an organisation with branches in the Peninsula and even in Eire. However, we have known long periods during which agents, whom it was clear that the Abwehr trusted, remained in urgent need of money, although during the same period there were other agents in England with surplus funds and yet others who might have acted as couriers on their way here. We should certainly have been wrong had we deduced, from the fact that these agents were not paid, that the Abwehr lacked the means to pay them. It was rather that it lacked the imagination and good sense to make use of the opportunities that were available. For this reason most, if not all, of the really successful schemes for paying agents in England have been our invention, not the Abwehr's, and have been carried through with our active, not to say pressing, collaboration. I suggest that SIME should find a similar approach to yield the same results.

Robertson's analysis was sent to Maunsell on 15 April 1943 and SIME prepared a rather resentful, four-page rebuttal of thirteen specific points dated 20 May 1943.

1. Special Station have read with very great interest the comments on their history of the CHEESE case which accompanied Lieutenant-Colonel White's letter of 15 April addressed to Colonel Maunsell. They are very far from considering the points made as merely academic or the criticism unhelpful. The truth is the contrary, and all those who have read the London comments wish that it could be possible to have a full-length personal exchange of ideas with their opposite numbers in London. Since the opportunity for this does not at the moment exist, the following paragraphs represent an unsatisfactory substitute for those personal conversations which, it is hoped may one day become feasible.

2. Paragraph 1 of the commentary contains, of course, the key to the understanding of what may appear to London to be the somewhat unbalanced

handling of the CHEESE case. Operating from behind the lines – at one time one might almost say within the sound of enemy guns – it has been natural that the principal and almost the only object of CHEESE's existence should be the practice of operational deception.

3. Since his 'rehabilitation' CHEESE has been almost exclusively used for the transmission of high grade operational material, with occasional interludes which have been devoted to 'building him up' for his next coup, while keeping him continuously at the disposal of the operational chiefs as a potential, rapid and reliable means of communication with the enemy.

4. This devoting of CHEESE to operational uses – almost entirely excluding any possibility of using him for counter-espionage purposes – to some extent explains what may appear to London to have been the over-cautious policy adopted in coordinating plans with the enemy for his payment. Special Section are only too aware of the weakness of the CHEESE story in its financial aspect, as pointed out in Paragraph 17 of London's comments. At the time of writing in fact, CHEESE has reached an almost unprecedented pitch of exasperation, and the slender thread on which depends the credibility of his story must be regarded as very near breaking point. Arrangements – approaching, it is believed, as near as was conceivable to the fool-proof – had once more been made for the receipt of money in Cairo, when CHEESE was informed (in response to querulous enquiries) on 9 May that the money had been delivered at the agreed address before 5 April. It was in point of fact certain that there had been no such delivery. Further irritable enquiries were made of the Abwehr; these produced information that the money had been handed over at the address which had been raided by the Egyptian Police in late 1942. While plans had remained in force for the receipt of money at this address, its unsuitability had been made clear to the enemy, and an alternative and much more satisfactory address given to and apparently accepted by them. It would seem that the Abwehr have failed once

more, through incompetence and/or dishonesty to take their fair share in the task of maintaining the probability of the CHEESE saga.

5. At this juncture the London comment is pertinent – have all these successive frustrations of the enemy's attempts to pay CHEESE been entirely the fault of the Abwehr? And – a question which has been of even greater interest to Special Section – will the Abwehr ever be capable of delivering money to CHEESE without more active assistance from us than they have hitherto received? In this connection it is felt that due emphasis should be given to certain aspects of the problem in Egypt, described in the following paragraph:

6. The necessity for giving absolute priority to operational considerations has been explained in Paragraph 1 above. The practical result of this has been the acceptance as an axiom that, for the sake of avoiding any possible prejudice to current operational schemes CHEESE and his story must be kept to a maximum extent free from the possibly fatal touch of such physical reality as, for example, is involved in contact with the enemy in the shape of his agents or couriers. Passivity has therefore been the keynote of all plans hitherto framed for the reception of the money; action has been confined to the making of such local arrangements as were necessary, and then merely inviting the Abwehr to do their duty – which they have systematically failed to do. The possibility that (notwithstanding the operational considerations involved) this policy may have been mistaken, is now demonstrated in the mounting danger which faces CHEESE as his impecuniousness continues without relief.

7. A certain timidity, therefore, occasioned by operational considerations of high importance, has been the first factor tending to hamper Special Section's schemes for guiding Abwehr money into CHEESE's pocket. A second restricting influence has arisen from the difficulty – possibly not quite fully appreciated in London – of working in a neutral country with

67

whose police and security authorities it is impossible to cooperate in matters ever approaching the degree of secrecy which attaches to CHEESE. The raid in December 1942 on the flat at which CHEESE was at that time expecting to receive money, is a case in point. This raid was not staged: it was due mainly to the fact that the premises and personalities chosen for the reception of the money erred perhaps too much on the side of verisimilitude – with the result that the Egyptian authorities (whom security considerations make it most undesirable to warn) did their duty with an embarrassing violence which could only be counteracted – after the event – by most devious methods.

8. The execution of the five Aleppo spies in August 1942 was deliberately advanced by CHEESE as an excuse for withdrawal from a plan for reception of money in Aleppo which had been necessarily improvised at short notice, in response to a snap request from the enemy. In justice to itself, Special Section may be allowed here to point out that considerable difficulties are involved in making such arrangements at a distance of some 600 miles through the agency of the local Defence Security Officer, in territory under French administration. This was a time, moreover, when Special Section was still suffering from growing pains accentuated by the always present difficulty of the lack (then particularly acute) of suitable officers for the handling of this type of work. It may be mentioned also that operational considerations applied at this time with a force which made it impossible (according to the CHEESE policy hitherto accepted as standard) to run any risk whatsoever of his reliability being exposed to danger. It was at this period that he was being nursed for the important part he was to play in the preparations for the El Alamein offensive, followed somewhat later by the TORCH operation.

9. No mention has so far been made of the part played by ill-luck (if one may be allowed exceptionally thus to describe the sinking of a German

submarine) in frustrating two other Abwehr plans for paying CHEESE. The first of these was when Jawad Hamadi fell unexpectedly into our hands in the summer of 1942 when a passenger on a submarine sunk off the coast, Hamadi had been recruited by the Sensburg organisation, had a large sum of money in his possession and had been told that he might expect to be contacted by 'a man called Paul'. CHEESE received no instructions which could be linked in any way to the Hamadi operation. The fates were unkind for a second time when, after a carefully prepared plan had been made by CHEESE for his '*petite amie*' to receive the money at a suitably selected café on the Pyramids Road in October, the enemy were distracted and apparently compelled to abandon that side of the plan by the shock of the British victory at El Alamein.

10. There is no doubt that CHEESE's records could not stand up for five minutes to the scrutiny of a chartered accountant and he continues to be in danger of a pauper's fate unless he can find some means of making both ends meet. At the time of writing he is at least able to keep body and soul together, having for some months been in the employment as an interpreter in the Cairo office of OETA – a post which not only enables him to pay his daily way but also to benefit from the indiscretions of his employing officers, who have a way of leaving their diaries about and discussing secret matters at the tops of their voices. CHEESE's salary, however, obviously cannot be expected to cover the overhead expenses of high grade espionage. Plans are at the moment under consideration for insuring against a continuation of failure on the part of the Abwehr paymaster, by initiating CHEESE into the profitable game of illicit diamond trafficking. It is hoped to be able to give to the enemy, as notional contacts of CHEESE, the names of actual persons known to the Abwehr as being involved in this traffic.

11. London's comments on CHEESE's financial status have served the useful purpose of clarifying still further an aspect of the case which has been the

principal worry of Special Section since the story began. Special Section would like also to express their appreciation of the constructive comments contained elsewhere in the London notes, and as stated before, only wish that the opportunity existed for the personal discussions which would be so much more satisfactory than the present exchange of necessarily abbreviated observations.

12. Paragraph 2 is a useful corrective to our previously not wholly clear appreciation of CHEESE's directing organisation; Paragraph 14 has helped to round off the picture which we have of the bizarre Sonderfuhrer Rossetti; Paragraph 10 has given some most useful suggestions for the introduction of new characters into CHEESE's *comedie humaine*, the analysis of significance in – and danger to – the case, contained in Paragraphs 6 and 7, is of great interest, especially in the light of Levi's recent dramatic release from internment Italy and summons to Athens (an event which caused Special Section to alternate between, on the one hand, serious misgivings as to exactly what Rossetti would require of Levi and, on the other hand, hopes that our old friend of 1941 might return to Cairo with money for Paul, and to claim the fatted calf for himself).

13. From the point of view of GALVESTON, the comments – especially in Paragraph 5 – on the value to be attached to the word 'reliable', have helped considerably towards a more objective assessment of ensuring standard on which, in the past too much reliance has perhaps been placed.

14. A certain amount of Schadenfreude has been derived from the information in Paragraph 3 regarding Abwehr incompetence – an incompetence which at the time of writing has reached new depths in the carelessness with which Athens encodes its messages. In this connection it is worth mentioning (in regard to London's Paragraph 11), that there has been no change in the CHEESE operator since the present writer first became acquainted with

the case in June 1942. Special Section have been extremely fortunate in their operator whose advice has been invaluable and who it is confidently believed has prevented any possibility of a technical flaw such as might arise from a changing transmission note or a blunder on the key.

Simpson's reference to GALVESTON concerned an 'A' Force order-of-battle deception scheme, later modified to DOWAGER, which owed its success to CHEESE. Just as MI5 assessed its own performance, and that of its agents in counter-espionage terms, identifying and neutralising enemy spies, SIME had opted to play a rather different game by actively engaging with the Abwehr. As Simpson had noted, the environment in which the MI5 and SIME operated were entirely different. MI5 had the geographical advantage of an island, populated by willing co-optees, with the full support of an efficient police apparatus and a vigilant military infrastructure. In contrast, SIME's territory was vast, with porous borders, a corrupt, incompetent police presence and a largely untrustworthy, hostile Egyptian Army. There was no comparison in their relative circumstances, yet CHEESE proved that even in such adverse conditions it was possible to gain the upper hand.

CHAPTER TWO

SIME

S oon after the outbreak of war MI5 opened negotiations with GHQ Middle East to expand the role of the local Defence Security Officer, Raymund Maunsell, the very first DSO who had been appointed in 1937. Within a year there were two more DSOs, at Gibraltar and Palestine, and 1939 saw the establishment of a regional organisation, Security Intelligence Middle East (SIME), which posted representatives across the Middle East in Cyrenaica, Tripolitania, Nicosia, Aden, Jerusalem, Damascus, Beirut, Habbaniyah, Eritrea, Istanbul, Ismaelia in the Canal Zone, as well as Gibraltar and Malta. There were also SIME staff in Persia and Iraq, attached to the PAIC command. Maunsell would take command of SIME with a deputy, K. W. J. Jones, while a new DSO, George Jenkins, was given responsibility for liaising with the Egyptian police's special section and the Ministry of the Interior. By the end of the war the DSO Egypt had four officers running the administration and organisation and six maintaining the office in Cairo which dealt with Egyptian subversion, and a further nine conducting vetting enquiries. There were also four officers based in the Canal Zone and two in Alexandria. In parallel, the DSO in Jerusalem,

Henry Hunloke, headed a staff of twelve, with sub-offices in Haifa, Jaffa and Nablus.

SIME would continue in existence for nineteen years, until it was wound up in 1958. In addition, SIME administered small prisons in Syria, Palestine, Egypt and Cyprus. At its peak SIME enjoyed a staff of 105 officers, and was divided into 'A' Division, with four sections (Records, Balkan, Post Security and Executive Administration); 'B' Division, also with four sections (Interrogation, Intelligence coordination and collation, Investigation and Most Secret Material); and the Special Section, handing agents. Initially the Balkan Section consisted of three officers (Edwin Whittall, H. L. Bond and J. C. D. Lassalle) while there were four in the Special Section (James Robertson, C. H. Roberts, Desmond Doran and John Wills). Later a Records Section was added with a staff of three headed by Captain J. Marcham, together with a Research Section of five, headed by Major G. E. Kirk. The Port section was just two officers, while the Interrogation Section employed seven. While Syria had a large DSO staff of ten, headed by Douglas Roberts, there was also a British Security Mission led by a baronet, Colonel Sir Marmaduke Coghill, consisting of twenty-two seconded personnel.

Because, by historical convention, Iraq had been run by the Royal Air Force from Habbaniyah, a separate organisation, Combined Intelligence Centre Iraq (CICI), headed by Squadron-Leader H. E. Dawson-Shepherd, conducted all counter-intelligence and counter-espionage operations on their territory, supported by a staff of five RAF officers.

In Tehran the DSO was Major E. Spencer, with just one assistant, Captain Rogers. In Turkey the DSO, G. R. Thomson had a staff of three, with one further officer each at sub-offices in Adana and Izmir.

Whereas the Middle East hitherto had been regarded as a security officer's nightmare, it was conversely an attractive environment in which intelligence collection operations could be conducted with impugnity. With its porous frontiers and tradition of cross-border smuggling, endemic police corruption, tribal rivalries, anti-Zionism and anti-colonialism, the region offered vast opportunities to a well-disciplined intelligence apparatus. Building on its comprehensive collection of prewar records of SIS reports, channeled through Passport Control Officers, and exploiting SIS's experience in the Great War which included the Arab Bureau, the organisation attracted members of some of the great trading families of the area, such as the Whittalls and Lafontaines, who retained their links with the Service over decades.

In parallel, SIS adopted Inter-Services Liaison Department (ISLD) cover to open offices in Tehran, Transjordan, Tripolitania, Cyrenaica, Eritrea and Algiers. Each communicated directly to both London and Cairo, and so were connected to SIS's prewar stations at Belgrade and Istanbul.

ISLD was initially headed by Sir David Petrie, a veteran senior Indian police officer and, until recently, Director of the Delhi Intelligence Bureau. In the summer of 1940 Petrie would be appointed to head MI5, and was replaced by Commander Cuthbert Bowlby who supervised an operations branch, designated 'B' Section, which had the advantage of having access to ISOS, referred to locally as TRIANGLE, which was a signals intelligence source, available from March 1941, offering an insight into the Abwehr's most secret wireless communications encrypted on hand ciphers. This traffic had been broken by Radio Security Service (RSS) cryptographers based at Barnet, in north London, who had made a study of messages transmitted by MI5's first double agent of the war, codenamed SNOW. The RSS cryptanalysts not only had the benefit of the Abwehr's side of the exchanges, but also the clear-text versions of SNOW's own reports which he encrypted with a quite straightforward transposition cipher. Using SNOW as a foundation, RSS extended its reach to all the Abwehr's traffic, and this would eventually lead to a solution of the machine traffic too.

Some TRIANGLE, usually in the form of summaries, was supplied to Major Jack Hester from England over the Special Communication Unit (SCU 4) circuit to Whaddon Hall in the Buckinghamshire countryside. Known to insiders as 'the link', it was established in August 1941, and the only SIS personnel authorised to handle this highly sensitive material worked for Section V at an entirely separate facility based at three houses on Lord Verulam's estate at St Albans in Hertfordshire. There the Middle East traffic was separated by a sub-section, designated VE, from other Abwehr communications and processed, meaning translated, turned into summaries and cross-referenced to other relevant data, before being put into the distribution system for circulation to indoctrinated Section V officers posted abroad to individual stations where only they could receive and look at the signal. These officers characteristically were assigned numerical code numbers ending '500' or '700' which immediately identified them internally as the only staff allowed to handle, and personally decode Section V communications.

Bletchley Park's satellite, Combined Bureau Middle East (CBME), based in the King Farouk Museum in Heliopolis, provided original intercepts through a local Radio Security Service organisation headed by Kenneth MacFarlan, a veteran signals intelligence officer who had operated in France in 1940. While the Abwehr material was available almost from the outset, being initially the decrypted hand ciphers, followed by encrypted messages on ciphers generated on the Enigma machine, the Wehrmacht's Enigma traffic, circulated as ULTRA, did not become available until September 1941.

RSS monitoring revealed that the Sicherheitsdienst (SD) ran two stations in Istanbul, one linked to Hamburg and the other to Amt VI in Berlin, while the Abwehr operated a single circuit from Istanbul. Scrutiny of all this traffic showed that the Germans were heavily reliant on the Turks for information, but as the tide of war changed in 1942, the Turks became less cooperative with the Axis and rather more enthusiastic about the Anglo-Turkish Security Bureau (ATSB), a joint liaison created by NID's Vladimir Wolfson in November 1940.

The ATSB's relationship with SIME became very significant and contributed to the success achieved by the DSOs who, between September 1941 and the autumn of 1942, captured twenty-five enemy agents. Among them were two Armenians, recruited by SIM, who were dropped into Syria in September 1941 equipped with a transmitter and a cover address in Switzerland, and detained in Aleppo soon after their arrival. A month later, on 10 October, another parachutist, Paul Fackenheim, was flown from the Phateron military airfield by a Heinkel-111 to a drop-zone near Haifa, but almost as soon as he had landed and buried his Afu set, he surrendered, claiming that as a German Jew recently released from Dachau, his mission for the Abwehr simply had been a method of reaching Palestine. Fackenheim, who had been decorated while serving as an officer in the 63rd Artillery Regiment in the First World War and later had travelled to the Dutch East Indies, was the grandson of Muhlhausen's chief rabbi, and underwent interrogation at the CSDIC facility at Rehovot, near Sarafand, by Arthur Dowden, formerly the British consul-general in Frankfurt. Fackenheim gave him a detailed account of his recruitment and training, and the DSO, having released a false statement announcing the discovery of the body of a dead parachutist, a calculated attempt to mislead the enemy about Fackenheim's fate, flew him to Egypt to face further questions at Maadi. There he was interviewed personally by Major Cleary-Fox, then John Wills, formerly of the 17th Lancers and the prewar Federation of British Industry representative in Paris, and even the DMI John Shearer who had been instructed not to reveal that the spy's transmitter had been dug up from its hiding-place.

Fackenheim would remain in British custody at Latrun, outside

Jerusalem, until 1946. According to his account, given after he had been duped into making incriminating statements by a very plausible stool-pigeon pretending to be a German internee scheduled for imminent repatriation, Fackenheim had undergone an Abwehr radio course in Brussels, at 5 rue de la Loi, and then had been transferred to Athens, ready for his mission. When confronted with a cousin, who lived in Jerusalem, the man was so frightened and ashamed of Fackenheim's work for Hitler's regime that he denied knowing him, thereby causing SIME briefly to wonder about his true identity, especially as there was another, rather notorious senior Nazi with a very similar name.

Codenamed KOCH, Fackenheim's task was to make military observations in Egypt and report troop movements, using a miniaturised Afu suitcase transmitter and a book code based on Henri Bosco's 1937 novel *L'Ane Culotte*. Great emphasis had been placed on the accurate identification, through unit insignia, of specific regiments and divisions so as to verify the enemy's order-of-battle. His principal objective was to establish himself in Haifa, posing as an illegal immigrant, and watch the main road and railway south of the port, sending daily logs of all military activity on those two routes. He was prohibited from recruiting any sub-agents, and instructed to concentrate on recording the number and types of vehicles spotted.

The difficulties encountered by the Abwehr in its attempts to collect intelligence in Egypt were heightened in June 1941 when two young Arabic-speaking agents, Mullenbuch and a Jew named Klein, both Palestinian volunteers from the Brandenburg Regiment, were to be flown to an improvised desert landing-strip sixty miles from the Egyptian border and then complete the rest of their journey on motorcycles. Accompanied by the Abwehr's most notorious spymaster Nikolaus Ritter, who flew one of the Junkers-88, the planes took off from Derna in Libya, but the Luftwaffe pilot refused to land when they reached their destination. Worse, they lost their way on the return leg so Ritter's aircraft crash-landed in the sea, three kilometres off the coast, killing Mullenbruch, injuring Klein and leaving Ritter with a broken arm.

The largest German spy-ring in the region was headed by a student named Latifi and consisted of seven Palestinians, Syrians and Lebanese, who were betrayed at the end of 1941 and of whom five were subsequently executed by a firing-squad at Aleppo. In April 1942 SIM parachuted two agents into Egypt, and another into Cyprus, but they were all quickly rounded up, the arrival having been presaged by TRIANGLE. Finally, in July 1942 two more were dropped near Aleppo, but did not last long.

Meanwhile, in Dar-es-Salaam, the local authorities interdicted Sobhy Hannah, a successful Egyptian lawyer who had been recruited by the Abwehr in France and sent on his mission via Lisbon. However, TRIANGLE had revealed his route, and under interrogation he revealed that he had been given a wireless transmitter, secret writing equipment and a large sum of money by the Abwehr in the expectation that he would establish himself in Cairo and cultivate contacts in anti-British circles.

All these efforts, apparently uncoordinated, indicated that intelligence collection in Egypt was a priority for the Abwehr, which was under some pressure from the Afrika Korps to supply Rommel with accurate estimates of enemy strengths and intentions.

As well as exploiting TRIANGLE, SIS acquired another significant advantage over its adversary on 19 November 1943 when an Abwehr officer, Otto Mayer, was captured by partisans between Trogir and Knin in Yugoslavia and handed over by Special Operations Executive's Force 133 to the British authorities in Brindisi. After a bullet had been removed from his neck in Bari he was transported straight to CSDIC in Algiers and then in February, via Marrakesh and Prestwick to London where, because he was well-known to Herbert Hart's study of ISOS in the Balkans, he underwent a lengthy incarceration at Camp 020. Because of his previous experience in the Balkans, having been attached to the Abstelle in Belgrade and Istanbul, he proved exceptionally valuable and acted as a human encyclopedia concerning the Abwehr and its personalities. Mayer's interrogations were assisted by information from DOLEFUL who had met him in Istanbul in January 1943 and instructed him to find a suitable sub-agent to operate a wireless transmitter in Syria. His nominee was to undergo training in Istanbul but, although Mayer had become insistent, the matter was taken no further and instead he fulfilled the role of a courier, delivering letters to a pair of recipients, a retired army officer in Damascus and another suspect in Beirut.

Under interrogation Mayer, who was aged forty, explained that he had lived in Yugoslavia for some years before the war and, following the Axis invasion, had worked for the Abwehr until July 1942 when he had been transferred to Turkey where he had remained for the following year. However, MI5's comparison with Mayer's information and ISOS references dating back to 1941 revealed that he had somewhat underplayed his own significance and involvement in espionage across the Middle East, but he could not be taxed with his contradictions owing to the delicate nature of the ISOS source. Accordingly, the arrival of another Abwehr source proved providential and this windfall was credited with having given entirely contrary information so Mayor would never suspect a breach of the Abwehr's communications security.

Mayor's extensive knowledge made available to MI5 was then enhanced by a high-level Abwehr defector who would be used against him, although the two men never met. In December 1943 the SIS station in Istanbul successfully cultivated a young Abwehr officer, Erich Vermehren, and his wife Elisabeth, both of whom were devout

Roman Catholics and opponents of the Nazi regime. He had been unable to go up to Oxford on a Rhodes scholarship because of the outbreak of war, and in October 1941 had married the Grafin von Plettenberg-Lanhausen, eight years his senior, in Freiburg. An aristocrat and committed Anglophile, Vermehren had studied law at the universities of Hamburg, Berlin, Leipzig and Freiburg until April 1941 when he had been called up for military service, but found to be medically unfit because of a shooting accident in his youth. Instead, he was assigned to be a welfare officer at several PoW camps, but in December 1942 was posted to Turkey for the Abwehr, under cover as legal adviser to the military attaché. His wife, who was related by marriage to the ambassador, Franz von Papen, tried to engineer permission to join her husband, even though she was a known anti-Nazi who had been interviewed by the Gestapo some thirty times before she eventually had been granted permission to travel to Turkey, ostensibly on a mission to liaise locally about a Vatican visit to Istanbul, and arrived on 20 December 1943 for what was intended to be a visit of short duration.

Even before Vermehren made contact with SIS, Section V already knew a certain amount about him and his wife, being information gleaned from ISOS, and about his mother who had been categorised as a 'very dangerous' Abwehr agent who had been flagged in Athens and then Lisbon, operating under journalistic cover.

Once in Istanbul his wife had met Nicholas Elliott's wife Elizabeth in church, and he subsequently had demonstrated his bona-fides to the SIS station's 'B' Section representative, by removing Abwehr papers from his office, including a complete roster of the organisation in Turkey, and allowing them to be photographed. One of these items consisted of 150 pictures of the Abwehr dossier on an SD source codenamed PASCHA. Until that moment, understandably, SIS had regarded the young man with some scepticism and suspected he might be an agent provocateur on a mission to embarrass his adversaries.

However, when the Turkish security bureau confided to SIS that they knew of Vermehren's link with Elliott, the decision was taken to accelerate his defection and, to protect his family and colleagues, make it look like an abduction.

Following his defection on Friday 28 January 1944, orchestrated by Elliott who codenamed him PRECIOUS, Vermehren's interrogation in Cairo revealed the extent to which the Abwehr had come to rely on sources across the region that were almost entirely under Allied control, although he was given no hint of the true situation. As personal assistant to Paul Leverkühn, chief of the Istanbul Kreigsorganisation Nahe Orient (KONO), Vermehren was exceptionally well informed and could offer a comprehensive and detailed overview of the Abwehr's operations right across the Balkan, eastern Mediterranean and Middle East area, amounting to around a hundred individual sources who had been assigned codenames. The greatest proportion of these spies, numbering ten, were waiters, sleeping-car attendants and other employees of the Taurus Express who regularly crossed the border into Syria. In particular, he singled out ARTHUR, a Taurus attendant and former NCO attached to the German Army during the First World War considered 'very reliable' who was known to the military attaché, General Hans Rohde, and was handled for Einz Heer by Erich Lochner. He collected information about troop movements in Syria and was thought to be friendly with a British NCO in Tripoli who gave him military information. ARTHUR's reports

contained very precise details on regimental badges and divisional signs. He made excellent sketches of them and even identified the writing on the Maltese Cross of the Queen's Own Rifles as scripture. He was not used by the Abwehr to recruit agents for them either among other Taurus employees or in Syria but in December 1943 ARTHUR did discover a sub-source (cover-name HELMUT) about whose identity and whereabouts he has told the Germans nothing. HELMUT writes in secret ink from, Vermehren thinks, Haifa to a cover address in Tripoli where ARTHUR collects the letters and delivers them to the Abwehr in Istanbul, where they are developed.

Naturally, SIME was especially interested in the enemy's activities in Egypt, and Vermehren revealed that in October 1943 he had been given responsibility for the recruitment of all Egyptian agents. He had been helped in his task by Prince Shahab, a member of the old Khedive's family who had volunteered to travel to Germany and help with propaganda. The offer had been turned down by the Reich Foreign Ministry but passed to the SD which had sent him to Cairo in the summer of 1942 to activate a transmitter hidden in the church of an Orthodox cleric, Father Demetriou. This attempt failed, so instead Shahab had made contact with a pair of cousins, Aziz and Mohsen Fadl, who had been recruited in 1941 by the Graf Meran, then head of the Istanbul SD, but later lost touch with them because of difficulties encountered when trying to send them instructions and codes.

This news was well received by SIME, which had first encountered Father Demetriou during the Eppler investigation. Demetriou had been detained in July 1942 and questioned when he had been compromised by the German spy who had been captured in Cairo (see Chapter Three). As a human repository of knowledge about the enemy's espionage, Vermehren was unequalled, and much of his information either neatly dovetailed with TRIANGLE or accurately reflected SIME's own information, garnered from its double agents.

After Shabab's successful return to Turkey, the Abwehr had sent Prince Mansour Daoud's mother-in-law to Egypt on a mission to deliver instructions and secret ink to the Fadls. Vermehren also knew about a Coptic Christian named Metaxoros who was supposed to repay a large debt he owed to AEG by passing cash to the Fadls. Another channel of payment had been Hassan Sirry, whose address in Istanbul, 29 Abe Sokak, and that of his mistress Sofia Misirli, had been used as a cover by the Abwehr. However, Vermehren said that he thought that Sirry, who had undertaken a mission to Egypt in November 1942 to establish contact with the Fadls, had been compromised by Prince Mansour's mother-in-law when she had been detained and questioned by the British authorities. Apparently, having had her face slapped in public in Turkey by Mansour, she had never forgiven him for the humiliation, and had been delighted to denounce him.

Then, in February 1943, Mahmoud Nitzi Sirry was sent to Egypt to report on Allied shipping, with instructions to send his reports in secret writing to his sister in Istanbul, and to recruit two sub-sources, one of whom was supposed to work in a British army workshop where he could access numerous different transmitters. However, within a fortnight of his arrival Sirry, who had been entrusted E£500 to pay the Fadls, had opened a club in Cairo and, according to a report from Berlin, had been arrested, so 'it was presumed the mission was unaccomplished'.

When tackled on the subject of his Abwehr networks, Vermehren was forthright, and listed the cases he was familiar with. Firstly, there was Anwar Sadr, the radio operator off the Egyptian liner *Zamzam* who had been in a PoW camp near Hamburg and had agreed to participate in a bogus escape and travel to Egypt as a spy. As far as Vermehren knew, this individual was still active and *in situ*. The SS *Zamzam*, formerly the Bibby liner *Leicestershire*, had been sunk on a voyage to South Africa by the Kreigsmarine raider *Atlantis* in the south Atlantic in April 1941. The Egyptian radio operator was one of 202 survivors, many of whom were repatriated to the United States through Portugal.

Another spy was Mehmet Narud-Din Sagun, codenamed REALTER and fluent in Turkish, Arabic and French, who was an officer in the Turkish army reserve whom he had first met in June 1943 through

Prince Shahab, and then sent to Egypt in November 1943. Although his mission included making personal observations and acting as a recruiter, this former member of the Turkish army's intelligence branch was to communicate to a cover address in Istanbul by using secret writing on newspaper wrappers. He only lasted six weeks, and then returned home because 'he lacked physical courage'.

Sagun had been directed to collect 'divisional signs; regimental badges; other indications of units; names of senior officers; existence of military establishments and repair shops, stating what types of vehicle or equipment was under repair; scraps of conversation overheard in bars, etc.' and, according to Vermehren's interrogators,

> Sagun brought back a very complete report to Turkey in his head, particularly regarding regimental badges and divisional signs. But even with this information at their disposal Vermehren claims that it was difficult for the Germans to locate units definitely in Egypt as Sagun failed to report how frequently he had seen the different signs and badges. Sagun subsequently stated that he had picked up some of his information by observing camps situated along the Cairo-Helwan railway.

What Vermehren did not know was that Sagun had declared his espionage mission to the British when he applied for his visa, and had also stated that apart from the E£3,500 he had been paid by the Germans, his motive for accepting the assignment was his wish to be out of the country when he thought he might be recalled for military duty.

REALTER had adopted the same methodology used by DAKHLA, a Turkish journalist and Abteilung II agent who had been reporting on shipping from Alexandria, Suez and Port Said since May 1943. He had links to the Egyptian nationalist movement, but DAKHLA's disadvantage was that his reports, also written in newspaper wrappers mailed to Istanbul, had taken four weeks to reach their destination, so he had been withdrawn in November 1943, after just five months.

According to Vermehren, 'in Turkey there was a gentleman's agreement between Abwehr and SD to exchange information, and the SD never passed the KO any military reports. Vermehren thinks all SD agents practised political espionage only.' He also identified the local SD chief as a wealthy officer named Fast who came originally from Palestine and before the war had owned two hotels, one in Beirut. He worked alongside Bruno Wolf and acted as deputy to Ludwig Moyszich, a sophisticated operator who was based under diplomatic cover at the embassy in Ankara.

In relation to CHEESE, Vermehren denied ever having heard of the codenames of two mystery couriers associated with him, ARMAVIR and NAHICHEVAN, but did mention Clemens Rossetti whose post in southern Italy, he alleged, had been taken over by his wife when he was transferred to Athens. Rossetti had also boasted to him about two of his most reliable networks, one of which was in Cairo. Unwittingly, Vermehren commented to his interrogators on

the technique of framing deceptive reports. He insisted that to be convincing reports must be based on a solid background of eye-witness facts, divisional signs, badges, etc. He himself had seen many reports framed by the Germans for issue to their double agents, and had been much struck by their compelling nature. Continuing on the subject of badges and individual signs, source claimed that the Germans knew by now all the signs and badges which were present in the Middle East, and that deception would have to be especially subtly carried out.

As a matter of general interest, though unconnected with the Middle East, source then spoke of the Allied order-of-battle in England. From reports sent from Berlin to Istanbul he had observed that we had some sixty divisions in England. It was clear, he thought, that this did not represent a sufficient force for the projected invasion of the Continent. However, while it was no doubt possible for us to conceal a few extra divisions here and there, he could hardly suppose that any large additional force could be hidden from German agents in England, and he had been much puzzled as to the truth of the matter.

Thus Vermehren unwittingly confirmed one of the cornerstones of 'A' Force's deception doctrine, that having successfully established an entirely false Allied order-of-battle at a very early stage, the enemy had not only come to accept its veracity, but had taken the view that any subsequent deviation was likely to be an easily detectable attempt to mislead the Abwehr's analysts. Certainly his understanding of the Allied strength in England, preparing for D-Day, was greatly exaggerated, and actually the 21st Army Group consisted of six armoured divisions, two airborne divisions and eleven infantry divisions, together with a number of independent brigades. Encouragingly, Vermehren's estimate seemed to include the imaginary five armoured divisions and six infantry divisions of the 'ghost' First United States Army Group.

When questioned about penetrations of the Allied intelligence community, Vermehren recalled that Clemens Rossetti, who he said had worked for the Abwehr for the past decade, had recruited the housemaid, perhaps named Carniglia Orlando, of 'a high British intelligence officer' in Istanbul who had provided 'fascinating' reporting on his 'sinister doings' at the time of the attempt on the life of Ambassador Franz von Papen in February 1942. He also named Edgar Yolland, a 33-year-old member of the US Office of War Information (OWI) attached to the US consulate-general in Istanbul, and son of a distinguished academic, Professor A. B. Yolland of the Royal University in Budapest who had been interned in England during the First World War. A naturalised American who had been a teacher at the American College, Yolland was handled by the Abwehr's Helmuth Hohne. Yolland was described as 'a great friend' of the deputy chief of the local

OWI, the former Associated Press correspondent Harold Lehrman, but also of Georg Streiter of the *Berlin Bösenzeitung*, a known SD agent. SIME later established that Yolland had been removed from his post after Lehrman had returned to the United States and investigated by OSS's X-2 but, to avoid embarrassment, no further action was taken against him apart from arranging his expulsion from Turkey after he had renounced his American citizenship. Vermehren also claimed to his SIME interrogator, Desmond Doran, that Paula Koch, a known spy in Beirut, had a source, allegedly recruited in the autumn of 1943 who was a French clerk or secretary, inside the local French Deuxième Bureau office with access to Sureté files, although an investigation failed to identify him (or her).

Among the gems in Vermehren's interrogation report was his admission that he had been responsible for handling a spy code-named PASCHA until the source had terminated in April 1943. This enabled SIME to question him with the benefit of PASCHA's recon-structed, 150-page file which showed that PASCHA was an SD agent in wireless contact with a network across the region, His reports, typed in French by a man living in the Ayas Pasha district, contained

> information about British and Allied military, naval and air forces in the Middle East; they cover an area ranging from Persia to Gibraltar and from Sicily to Capetown; they sometimes forecast a strategic plan, but gener-ally descend to the most particular details for which personal observation is sometimes expressly claimed. They appear from the notes to have been mostly communicated by wireless; in some places the language plainly refers to their transmission by wireless. Of all the sources quoted, by far the com-monest is a '*source militaire anglaise*'.

Vermehren described in great detail how the Abwehr had come to acquire PASCHA from the SD, and explained how his reporting was distributed.

PRECIOUS sent the collected reports off to Berlin by courier every Friday in the 'original' French, which he was forbidden by Leverkühn to alter or annotate. If he thought any report urgent, he would draft a signal for Hinz to send to Berlin and Sofia by the wireless transmitter of the German Consulate-General in Istanbul, the latter headed '*Spruch an andreas, zugleich fur Fremde Heerc West – Cura. fur KING*'.

Attgerer sent copies of all PASCHA reports giving air intelligence to the Air Attache in Ankara (first Colonel Morell, later General Kettembeil) and also to LOUIS (Einz Luft Berlin), and Murwitz or Zähringer sent PASCHA's naval intelligence to Einz Marine Berlin. But on Leverkühn's instructions all the PASCHA reports received from the SD were sent to ANDREAS. PRECIOUS believed that there were some purely political PASCHA reports, which Bruno Wolf of the SD did not hand over to KONO.

It was announced by KONO that PASCHA was, or directed, an organisation of agents and that PASCHA, or one or more of his hard agents, sent their reports by wireless to the SD's contact in Istanbul. This contact was not himself PASCHA, but received the reports of the PASCHA organisation by wireless and could transmit questions by wireless to the organisation. PASCHA himself had been recruited by Admiral Canaris before the war and was always regarded as an Abwehr, Berlin source; hence it was for Berlin to assess the value of PASCHA's reports and for KONO to pass them to Berlin unaltered. It was also assumed that the SD received the reports merely because there was no branch of the Abwehr in Istanbul to receive them until the middle of 1941.

PRECIOUS inferred from the dates and places mentioned in the reports that they were sent by wireless; they were sometimes written in telegraphic style. Indeed the 'original' reports typed in block capitals looked like wireless messages, not telegrams; PRECIOUS often saw them when or before Fraulein Schott copied them, and noticed also that they were sometimes crumpled, as it they had been carried in a pocket, presumably by the SD's contact, since the SD would have passed them to Angerer properly enclosed in an envelope.

The time taken by PASCHA in answering PRECIOUS's questions was not short, but nonetheless indicated to PRECIOUS that both questions and answers had alike been transmitted by wireless.

On the location of PASCHA's wireless transmitter or transmitters PRECIOUS made the following comments:

1. Alexandretta seems to have been the site of one of them when PRECIOUS arrived, but to have ceased about the end of March.

2. Alexandria or Cairo was probably another, as reports on areas all over the Middle East were represented as having come from those places.

3. PASCHA apparently had no 'residential' agent as far west as Tunis until July.

Despite these apparently authentic credentials, Vermehren explained that he had come to develop some doubts about PASCHA.

On 4 and 30 December 1942, 23 February 1943 and 6 April 1943 PASCHA reported the presence of parts of the 3rd American Infantry Division and 4th American Armoured Division in the Julfa region on the Russo-Persian frontier. This disagreed with other reports from agents of DENNIS [von der Marwitz], Zedow [Zähringer] and THEOBALD [Thoran] and made PRECIOUS begin to doubt at the end of April whether PASCHA had eyewitnesses in all the areas on which he reported, and to wonder whether he might not be relying on, e.g. truck (train?) drivers for sources of his information, as Zedow's agents often did. PRECIOUS therefore asked Wolf of the SD for particulars of the organisation; Wolf replied he knew nothing except that his reports were brought to him by his contact in Istanbul. PRECIOUS then asked if he might interview the contact; Wolf refused, but suggested that PRECIOUS should send any questions he wanted asked to Wolf for him to pass to PASCHA through the contact in Istanbul; the questions should be in French, from which PRECIOUS concluded that the contact could only speak Turkish and French. PRECIOUS therefore put questions to PASCHA on 30 April 1943 ending with one about the Egyptian Army to discover whether he was or had a source in Egypt. To this last question there was no reply.

A month or two later a fresh seed of doubt about PASCHA was sown in KONO's mind by Berlin with a signal asking if coincidences between PASCHA reports and material supplied to KONO by the General Staff might not be caused by KONO's passing this material indirectly to PASCHA. Berlin suggested that KONO night have passed it to someone, who might be, unknown to KONO, a member of the PASCHA organisation or in touch with it, or might have put questions to PASCHA leading him to give answers agreeing with the material. This suggestion alarmed Hinz and made him wonder whether there might not have been a leakage back to PASCHA through Lieutenant Ancora, the Italian assistant military attaché in Istanbul, with whom Hinz used to exchange military information. However, KONO asked General Rohde and DENNIS if they had been responsible for any such leakage, passed their negative answers to Berlin, and suggested that perhaps the leakage was in Spain.

The third blow to KONO's confidence in PASCHA was his report of 9 July, amplified on 17 July, that the 5th English Division was in Syria and consisted of the 13th, 15th Brigades and the 3rd, 9th and the 91st artillery regiments. On 19 July PRECIOUS asked PASCHA for an explanation of this report, as according to KONO's information this division had taken part in the attack on Sicily. On 24 July PASCHA reported that '*la repetition de la transmission*' had established an error in the transmission and a confusion in the text, which should have read 5th Indian Division. On 31 July PRECIOUS pointed out that this reply was unsatisfactory, because PASCHA had given the numbers of the brigades of that division, which could only be the numbers of the 5th English, and not of the 5th Indian Division; and he asked for further particulars of the source and channel of PASCHA's original information – a question which was never answered. PRECIOUS interpreted these reports as indicating that either consciously or unconsciously PASCHA was passing to KONO British 'smoke' concealing the fact that the 5th English Division was taking part in the attack on Sicily. PRECIOUS thinks, however, that PRECIOUS correctly anticipated the Allied attack on Pantellaria within two days.

In June or July a *'nouvelle convention'* was negotiated at PASCHA's suggestion. PASCHA offered to supply reports (a) more than once a day, (b) from new sources covering Malta, and Gibraltar, (c) giving greater details of divisional numbers, (d) in return for a further T£12,000 a month. Canaris told Hinz at the Sofia conference to pay PASCHA this further salary, but it was never in fact paid. The file shows that on 31 May in answer to a question about commandos in Malta PASCHA promised direct communication with Malta from 10 June; he had already produced one *'communication directe Malte'* on 29 April. The first fruits of the *'nouvelle convention'* were the longest single report ever received from PASCHA covering 14–20 July which contains one report on 17 July about Malta from a *'source directe'*; but the reports following it fell off instead of maintaining the improvement, and justified the complaint made in the questionnaire for PASCHA, drafted by PRECIOUS and amended by Hinz about the end of July, which repudiated the *'nouvelle convention'*. PRECIOUS formed the opinion that PASCHA had somehow recruited a British or Allied wireless operator receiving messages from Malta and Gibraltar, but had then 'lost' him and so been unable to fulfil this part of the new bargain.

The flow of PASCHA reports ended suddenly with the month of August. To PRECIOUS's enquiries Wolf replied that PASCHA had been put in difficulties by the Italian armistice, but hoped to re-establish his organisation on a smaller scale. He never did. After waiting a fortnight at Wolf's request, PRECIOUS was told by Wolf that he had seen his contact in Istanbul; Wolf was very upset, but helpless. At PRECIOUS's suggestion Leverkühn then summoned Wolf; Wolf came but, according to Leverkühn, said he would not be sending any more PASCHA reports. This collapse of PASCHA, at the time of the Italian collapse, first made PRECIOUS think that PASCHA relied on Italian agents.

When invited to speculate about PASCHA, Vermehren offered some interesting opinions about what had really happened.

In September or October 1943 Willi Hamburger was in touch with George Earle, the American naval attaché, through having stolen his mistress, and was trying to get information which he could take out to the British without hurting the Abwehr. He told PRECIOUS that he had heard that someone connected with the SD, that at the back of the PASCHA organisation was an Italian Jew connected with Marconi's office or shop in Cairo, and asked PRECIOUS for his name and further particulars. These PRECIOUS told him he could not give, because he did not have them.

PRECIOUS had always considered that PASCHA or his organisation might be Jewish. It was not until July 1943 that KONO received an order forbidding the employment of Jews. Canaris would have had no objection to recruiting Jews, as the fact that this ban was not laid on until 1943 indicates; at the same time if PASCHA or his organisation were Jewish, Canaris would be reticent about him and so would the SD. There were of course other guesses to explain Canaris's reticence, e.g. some promise made by Canaris. Leverkühn told PRECIOUS he was going to ask Canaris who PASCHA was; but so far as PRECIOUS knows, he never did. KONO in fact employed no Jews, because both Hinz and Ulshoefer were against employing them. The ban was interpreted in the spirit: 'You keep your Jews, but you don't mention them!' In PRECIOUS's opinion, the SD knew more about PASCHA than KONO, and Canaris more than the SD.

No further information about PASCHA had been acquired by KONO by the time PRECIOUS left. Leverkühn turned down a suggestion from Ludwig that he should 'trail' the SD contact in Istanbul in the hope of identifying him. KONO thought he lived in Ayes Pasha, where the German Consulate was. A theory held 'jokingly' was that PASCHA was connected with the British military attaché in Ankara, perhaps through his Security Officer (name unknown), who was betraying information to the Germans.

This theory was based on the '*source militaire*' which PASCHA often quoted, and which KONO thought he might have in 9th Army Headquarters. It was also supported by the scale of PASCHA's remuneration, which indicated (PRECIOUS thought) more than oriental greed; PASCHA was paid T£30,000 a month, not by KONO, but (KONO assumed) by the SD.

PRECIOUS asked the Interrogating Officer (a) if he thought PRECIOUS should have suspected that there was something suspicious about PASCHA [and] (b) if he knew of the PASCHA organisation as such before PRECIOUS gave his information about it. Evasive answers were returned. PRECIOUS seemed to think (i) that British interest in a defunct organisation was curious; (ii) that on reflection his own suspicions should have been aroused sooner and more strongly; and (iii) that PASCHA was at least partly under British control. (i) could not be disguised, but (ii) was not consciously suggested; nor was (iii), although it was not discouraged. PRECIOUS professed a complacent faith in the omniscience of Berlin, Berlin would know whether PASCHA's reports were true or false and while Berlin accepted them without complaint, KONO were content to be a conduit pipe for these. KONO had good reason to be satisfied with a source that covered so much ground with such an appearance of speed and veracity and was neither recruited nor controlled nor paid by them, as long as it satisfied the Head of the Abwehr in Berlin, by whom it was reputed to have been established. In the last few months of its life it came under suspicion both from PRECIOUS and from Berlin, but according to him its reports were still eagerly awaited. When it dried up, KONO were left to ponder how far it had ever really covered the wide regions laid suddenly bare and how best they could now be covered with new, and less bountiful, sources of supply.

This fascinating perspective showed that, after PASCHA had departed the scene, the Abwehr had been left devoid of reliable sources, and in those circumstances it was hardly surprising that it had come to rely even more heavily on CHEESE. As his interrogators, Stephenson and Eadie, noted,

> Vermehren says that he was always anxious to keep out of the dirty business of running agents but late last year Leverkühn asked him to lend a hand because of the urgent need for more agents, presumably to replace PASCHA.

Allegedly PACSHA had been recruited before the war, perhaps by Admiral Canaris personally, and had been handled initially by the SD but from the middle of 1941 by Gottfried Schenker-Angerer, the assistant air attaché at the Istanbul consulate. PASCHA's sub-agents were located in Iraq, southern Palestine, Cyprus and Egypt, and one of them, who communicated by wireless, had access to General Wilson's headquarters. On one occasion PASCHA himself had demanded E£12,000 to extend his wireless network to Malta and Gibraltar, but the plan fell through within a week.

> The Germans were always slightly suspicious of PASCHA as on several occasions its information corresponded to a marked degree with that already at the disposal of the OKW in Berlin. At one time, in fact, OKW asked Abwehr Turkey whether their questionnaires contained leading questions, thus indicating the expected reply to PASCHA. Vermehren claims that this was not the case. The Germans thought it possible that PASCHA was in touch with the British military attaché.

According to Vermehren, the entire PASCHA organisation collapsed following the Italian surrender, and the last message was received in October 1943. He also revealed that Willi Hamburger had confided in him that 'a Jew belonging to a Marconi institution', was 'behind the scenes' in the network.

As the interviews with SIME's Captain H. R. M. Eadie continued, Vermehren was judged to be 'gradually giving away more details', especially about Germanophile Egyptians. He named El Said Abubakr Ratib as a close friend of the Egyptian royal family who had decided to remain in Turkey rather than risk internment in Cairo. Abubakr had been a fencing umpire at the 1936 Olympic Games where he had embraced the Nazis, and was associated with Taher Pacha, a suspect in British detention, along with other influential sympathisers, including Prince Mansour Daoud, Prince Shahab, Ahmet Saabet, Hassan el Fekhe and Hassan Sirry. Fekhe had been acting as a recruiter since 1942, enrolling agents to go to Syria, but was dismissed the following year for faking his expenses.

With some reluctance Vermehren identified the four spies he had personally recruited, and named Nuradin Sagun, Hassan Sirry, Semsettin Kandemir and an Iraqi manicurist, Rahmiya Vedat, code-named BERBER, whose husband had been interned by the British in Asmara, but recently released to live in Basra. Vedat's mission was to travel to Basra and communicate using secret writing with a twenty-year-old girl in Baghdad codenamed BARRER who had been living there with her sister since December 1943, and would hand her reports to Muhharem Oysu, a Taurus Express employee and part-time smuggler. BARRER was also to act as a link for Kandemir, codenamed MONTLER, who was to be based in Ahwaz. Such detailed information, of course, was gold-dust to SIME.

Vermehren also described in detail the entire KONO staff in Istanbul, which amounted to about two dozen officers organised like any other KO, with representatives from the various Abwehr branches, Abteilungs I, II and III, and the three services, Heer, Luft and Marine. In a series of lengthy interviews conducted in a friendly atmosphere in

Cairo, he identified their individual roles, describing Robert Ulshöfer as the Turkish-speaking deputy chief of the Einz Heer who, he said, had attended Ankara University and was the principal recruiter. Professor Walther Hinz led the Einz Marine branch, and was responsible for liaising with the Turkish authorities. Hinz's deputy was Gailani, codenamed TAN, whose wife was the daughter of Persia's chief of police. He also said that Gottfried Schenker-Angerer, who headed the Einz Luft, had a radio interception facility in his office, run by an operator, Carl H. Clauss, monitoring British and Allied wireless traffic which was relayed to Berlin. Schenker-Angerer, who was described, along with his wife and daughter, as anti-Nazi, also had an agent codenamed MIMI who communicated through a link in the Iraqi consulate in Istanbul. Schenker-Angerer's deputy was Hermann von Sperl, a cotton merchant in Adana.

The head of Abteilung III was Hauptman Thomas Ludwig, codenamed ALADDIN, who worked under diplomatic cover at the Istanbul consulate. He was assisted by Helmut Braun and an interpreter, Robert Bendetsch, and Vermehren revealed that one of ALADDIN's coups was his regular access to the office safe of a director of the Walton & Goeland Shipping Company in Istanbul. As a result, Mr Walton's secretary, a Madame Dumont, was arrested in Beirut in May 1944.

Subordinate to Kurt Zähringer of Einz Marine was an agent runner, Ronald Lochner, who was based in Mersin and operated against Cyprus. His son Erich was responsible for drafting agent assessments and managing the agents employed on the Taurus Express.

When asked about Otto Mayer, Vermehren identified his codename as MURAT and said that he had operated in Istanbul under commercial cover, managing a refrigerator business. Although he had access to the KO communications and courier facilities, he apparently had operated independently under Berlin's direct control. Vermehren also predicted, correctly, that his Austrian colleague, Willi Hamburger, would also defect.

One focus of SIME's attention was the process by which agent reporting was assessed by the Abwehr, and Vermehren explained that when he had first arrived in Turkey

> the KO relied for its estimations of the worth of its sources entirely upon the comments passed by Fremde Heere West, upon the veracity and importance of the reports submitted to it via Abwehr HQ. These appreciations were not very satisfactory since they depended upon Fremde Heere West possessing independent evidence by which to check the veracity of the reports of the KO's agents. Later on KO was put on the distribution list, with the Service Attachés for OKW situation reports and order-of-battle charts. The KO then delegated to Lochner the task of collating agents' reports with those data from OKW. In some cases Lochner was able to show that the information available to the OKW was inferior to that got from some of the KO's sources. Vermehren gave the impression that there was no centralised grading-office responsible for assessing the bona-fides or the acumen of agents. Though Vermehren was not interrogated on the point, he did not seem to be aware of the existence of any machinery for scrutinizing the long-term record of an agent for symptoms of control or of indirect chicken-feeding.

One of Vermehren's interrogators, Captain J. F. C. Stephenson, noted that he was 'convinced that Berlin must have more than one wireless agent in the Middle East because they are so well informed' and concluded:

> Vermehren grows on one. It should be noted that he is not in any way anti-German but is anti-Nazi. He said that he tried to come to the Allies in April, July and September 1943 but only succeeded in doing so in January 1944 after his wife had joined him. He and his wife seem perfectly sincere in their reasons for coming over to the Allies. They say that her family has been persecuted by the Gestapo and she herself has been interrogated by them over

thirty times. They both claim to be devout Catholics and opposed to the
Nazi persecution of the Church. Vermehren is rather unwilling to divulge
details concerning German agents operating against the Middle East, and
I believe further facts could be obtained from him on much of the informa-
tion which he has given, e.g. the name of the Roman Catholic priest in the
St Antonin Church, Istanbul.

Because Elisabeth Vermehren fell ill with pneumonia in Algiers, her
husband was flown alone, carrying a British passport in the name
of Henry George Thomson, to RAF Lyneham from Gibraltar on 13
March 1944, and he found employment, under the alias Erich Vollmer,
in a prep school, the Bluecoat School in Horsham, and then at Worth
Priory, also in Sussex.

Elliott's cultivation of the Vermehrens was considered a great coup
at the time, especially as they were smuggled by train to Syria on false
papers, and then reached Cairo by air where they were interviewed at
length by SIS before the Abwehr even noticed their disappearance. In
his discussions with Vermehren Elliott had agreed that their departure
would be made to look like a crime had been committed by leaving
their apartment in disorder, a ploy intended to keep the Germans in
the dark about their fate. Implied in these negotiations was an acceptance that no public statement would be made, thus keeping the rest
of Vermehren's family safe, and maybe limiting the counter-measures
that any intelligence agency suffering the loss of key personnel would
be expected to take. However, almost as soon as Vermehren reached
Gibraltar, on his way to England, the BBC reported their defection.
The consequences were on a hideous scale as the incident proved the
catalyst for the subsequent absorption of the entire Abwehr into the
Reichssicherheitshauptamt (RHSA). Also, Vermehren's mother, Petra
Schwabroch, the *Das Reich* correspondent in Lisbon since February 1941 and living in some style at the Palacio Hotel in Estoril, made

a voluntary return to Germany in the hope that the disapproval of Erich's defection would not be misinterpreted, but she was arrested by the SD and incarcerated at the Oranienburg concentration camp, and her husband Kurt, a well-known Hamburg lawyer, other son, working for United Press in Berlin, and daughter Isa, an artist, were subjected to harassment. According to Klop Ustinov, who reported on Petra, she was privately anti-Nazi, but her SIS dossier suggested that she had been working for the Abwehr in Athens in 1937, and that her husband was also connected to the Abwehr. Klop, also living in Estoril, but reporting on the local German colony for SIS, complained that the BBC publicity about Vermehren and his mother had 'discouraged a great number of people from coming over physically to the British' while applauding the discretion exercised over the recent defection of Wolfgang Krauel, the German consul-general in Geneva. Another victim of the contamination was the Abwehr's Hans Ruser, a German journalist referred to in ISOS intercepts as having been in contact with Paula, who would himself defect to SIS.

Vermehren's own head of the Istanbul KO, Paul Leverkühn, was recalled to Berlin in February and imprisoned on 16 July. A prewar lawyer who had graduated from Gottingen and studied at Edinburgh University, and an old friend and colleague of Kurt Vermehren's, Leverkühn had worked in Washington, DC and New York. As he was in the Gestapo's custody on 20 July he survived the purge that followed the attempt on Hitler's life. His replacement, as head of the Istanbul KO, was Admiral Marwitz.

One of ISLD's many challenges was the management of double agents who may have been known to Vermehren, and might therefore be expected to come under suspicion as having been compromised by him. Under normal circumstances the Abwehr would have appointed a senior officer to undertake a damage assessment and then review the performance of any source likely to have been contaminated by the defector. However, in the chaos of the RHSA's retribution, followed by the 20 July plot, no such damage control study appeared to have been made, leaving the double agents, CHEESE among them, at liberty to continue their duplicity. One unexpected bonus from the defection was the discovery that INFAMOUS had been selling fabricated information to the Abwehr, without SIS's consent, so he was promptly terminated.

The interviews with Vermehren proved that the Abwehr had absolutely no concept of large-scale strategic deception, and actually thought the idea impossible. Furthermore, it had no capability for even considering the integrity and performance of individual agents, and certainly did not realise that some of its supposedly most reliable sources, such as ARTHUR, were actually double agents under British control. Furthermore, the fact that ARTHUR's sub-source HELMUT was entirely notional had also gone undetected, even though Willi Hamburger at least had been alive to the possibility of notional sources. He himself had invented a generic imaginary agent for all his Turkish political information, but purely as a security measure to protect the identity of his genuine informants. Among Vermehren's more notable revelations was his account of the Abwehr's attitude towards intelligence collection in Egypt. While his KO had taken the lead, other Abstellen, such as Athens, Sofia and Belgrade, also tried to run agents against the same target, although Vermehren had few specifics apart from some very helpful 'corridor gossip'. However, from his personal knowledge, the Istanbul KO had only occasionally mounted individual, short-term missions to Egypt, and had experienced very limited success, chiefly because of poor communications and a lack of a local support from an existing resistance movement. SIME interpreted this scenario as being extremely favourable for CHEESE who, run from Bari and then Athens, had been outside of Vermehren's purview. Based on the totality of the defector's insight, it rather looked as though CHEESE had become the Abwehr's longest-serving and most reliable source of military intelligence.

Another potential unintended casualty of the Vermehrens' defection was ARTIST in Lisbon. He was Johnny Jebsen, an Abwehr officer who had been recruited by his own agent, Dusan Popov, codenamed TRICYCLE by MI5 and IVAN by the Abwehr. Unfortunately, Jebsen was known to have been a close friend of the Vermehrens, and this connection automatically placed him in jeopardy, and in turn served to contaminate Popov. Ultimately, Jebsen was arrested by the Gestapo on corruption charges, and somehow managed to protect Popov.

For this defection to have happened once was bad enough, but ISLD was so active in Turkey that during the latter part of the war there were no less than three similar episodes. On 12 February, soon after the Vermehrens departed and Leverkühn was thrown into prison, one of his subordinates, Dr Willi Hamburger, received a similar summons. However, reluctant to submit to such an ordeal, Hamburger was persuaded by his lover, a glamorous Hungarian, Adrienne Molnar, to defect to the local representative of the American Office of Strategic Services (OSS). According to MI5, another of Hamburger's lovers, Edith Karakacievic, later became successively the mistress of two senior UK Commercial Corporation officers, Crabbe and George Howard, the 11th Earl of Carlisle, from whom she was supposedly directed by Hamburger to extract sensitive information. In one of his interrogations Hamburger denied that Karakacievic, a Serbian Jewess, had been his mistress, claiming to have met her only once, and he also refuted the rumour that he had conducted an affair with Frau Stille, the wife of the German consul.

Aged twenty-seven, Hamburger, who worked in Istanbul as the manager of Suedostrope, an import-export business, had first been identified as an Abwehr officer by Walter Aberle and Waldemar Weber, and then by Gottfried Muller, Georg Konieczny and Friedrich

Hoffmann, a trio of German saboteurs, collectively codenamed THE LIBERATORS, who had been arrested twelve days after parachuting into Iraq, near Mosul, on 17 June 1943 while undertaking what became known as the Marmut Expedition, to establish a local espionage and sabotage network among the Kurds. However, the three German officers, equipped with a transmitter and accompanied by an Iraqi interpreter, Nafi Rashid Ramzi, had been dropped some 200 kilometres from their planned landing zone, and had decided to split up, but they had been spotted by the authorities and detained just east of Erbil.

Codenamed TIGER and HARDY, Muller and Hoffmann admitted that they had been directed to blow up the Trans-Iranian railway and interrupt the delivery of oil to the Allies. The planning for the mission had begun in October 1942 and Muller had been trained at the Abwehr's school at Quenz and at a laboratory at Tegel, which he described to his interrogators in considerable detail. He also revealed that once they had been established, a second team, codenamed MAMMUT II, would then be dropped to them by the Luftwaffe. Research by the DSO Baghdad, Squadron-Leader Dawson-Shepherd, later identified these spies as Robert Baheshy and Louis Bakos, a pair of Iraqi students attending college in Istanbul, At one moment, when Dawson-Shepherd was coming under local political pressure to have the captives released from detention, the DSO sought testimony from Vermehren to not only implicate those he already had in custody, but to incriminate several other suspects.

Codenamed HOSIERY by his SIME, Hamburger described to his interrogator, W. B. Savigny, how, after he had learned Turkish as a student at Vienna University, where he wrote his thesis on the political reconstruction of the Arabic world in Asia, he had started his military service with the Luftwaffe in October 1940 and had been transferred to the Abwehr in March 1941 and posted to Vienna. He had then been sent to Istanbul and in August 1942 was placed under Paul Leverkühn's command. However, becoming increasingly disenchanted, he had made contact with Commander George V. Earle III of the Office of Naval Intelligence, but when he heard nothing more from the Americans, and when he was ordered back to Berlin, ostensibly for a new assignment in Paris, he surrendered himself to the British, and was received by Nicholas Elliott. After his interviews with SIME in Cairo, by prior agreement with the Americans, he was transferred to the custody of OSS.

Hamburger's defection, coming so soon after the Vermehrens switched sides, would have a lasting impact on German morale, and another Austrian, Karl Alois von Kleczkowski and his wife Stella, a couple operating under *Voelkischer Beobachter* journalistic cover for the Abwehr in Istanbul since the autumn of 1941, defected a week later in February 1944. And if this was not enough, in April 1944 Cornelia Kapp, an SD secretary based in Ankara, fell in love with an OSS officer and was also persuaded to defect.

Manipulation of the enemy's intelligence networks was coordinated with great imagination by a staff officer, Dudley Clarke, whose military intelligence experience dated back to Richard Meinertzhagen's exploits in Gaza during the First World War. Having served with Archie Wavell in the previous conflict, Clarke began lobbying for deception schemes in December 1940, the first of which was tailor-made for COMPASS later the same month when Marshal Rodolfo Graziani's Italian 10th Army, which had penetrated 54 miles into Egyptian territory, was defeated at Sidi Barrani when General Richard O'Connor's infantry division and a single armoured division equipped with the Matilda tank trounced ten enemy divisions. Initially intended as a five-day raid, the battle continued until February, with Graziani convinced that he was opposed by a vastly superior force. In the end, 130,000 Italians, including seven generals, surrendered, at a cost of nearly a thousand Allied casualties. This encounter, long before the ULTRA source became available, was a very practical demonstration of how the enemy's poor tactical signal security could be exploited, and the potential value of an order-of-battle based on deception.

Wavell was an enthusiastic exponent of strategic deception, even though CAMILLA, the cover story for his offensive in the Western Desert, did go entirely to plan. On that occasion the Duke of Aosta, fully persuaded that the British intended to attack in Somaliland, simply withdrew when it had been anticipated that he would do precisely the reverse, and reinforce his garrisons. Undeterred, Clarke embraced the principles of strategic deception and became its enthusiastic and persuasive exponent, to the point that he acquired no less than two pseudonyms: 'Major Constable-Croft' as the recipient of operation information, and 'Major Galveston' for all intelligence-related correspondence.

Despite the CAMILLA debacle, Clarke was authorised on 28 March 1941 to create 'Advance Headquarters 'A' Force', a title intended to mislead by implying some airborne unit. In reality the organisation consisted of Clarke and two officers, supported by a staff of ten soldiers, and was originally accommodated at the 'Grey Pillars' GHQ building before moving into two flats at 6 Sharia Kasr-el-Nil, directly below a brothel. Their objective was to develop a master-plan to conceal the Allies' future plans in the region, and this required not only the usual methods of conveying deception, mainly wireless traffic, the circulation of rumours and the 'planting' of false information on suspect neutrals, such as the Japanese consul in Alexandria, but the exploitation of double agents. Fortuitously, Levi arrived in Cairo in February 1941 and created the foundations of the CHEESE project, the spy-ring that would be the longest and most successful deception of its kind. One classic ruse adopted by Clarke was codenamed ABEAM, a plan conveyed over six months in 1941 intended to promote the idea that there were airborne troops based in Egypt planning to launch an attack behind the Italian lines in Italy. The intention was to exploit Italian fears, known from intercepted enemy wireless traffic, of just such a surprise. In support of it Clarke invented a non-existent 'First Special Air Service Brigade' and used ingenious methods to persuade the enemy it was training in parachute and glider techniques in the Transjordan desert. Captured enemy documents later suggested ABEAM succeeded.

Clarke's mission, defined and directed by Wavell, was in the first instance to buy time. The British position in the Middle East was difficult, if not disastrous, with Wavell having to weaken his defences in the west because of the need to deploy the 1st Armoured Brigade, the New Zealand Division and the 6th Australian Division to Greece, amounting to 50,000 troops and 8,000 vehicles. This left Wavell with just the 2nd Armoured Division and the 9th Australian Division to hold all of Cyrenaica.

The Germans occupied Yugoslavia in April, swept through Greece, and in May captured Crete. The Axis threatened East Africa, Iraq and Syria, and General Erwin Rommel arrived in Libya in February and was due to receive the 15th Panzer Division in April. The British were outnumbered, outgunned and isolated, and the 7th Armoured Division was in a parlous state. Worse, the Allies believed (wrongly) that Cyprus would be the next German objective, so Clarke was given the task of boosting the number of defenders, amounting to 4,000 troops of doubtful quality, by an entire division of 20,000 men. Of course, the 7th Infantry Division was fictitious, as was its armoured component, the 39th Battalion, Royal Tank Regiment, which was only equipped with dummy tanks. When, at the end of July, the British 50th Division reached the island, the defences amounted to a single genuine division, and a bogus one. Significantly, a captured German intelligence assessment was found to include the 7th Infantry Division and 10th Armoured

Division and estimate the British troop strength at more than 20,000. Having established the 50th Division, it would remain in enemy assessments of the Middle East until 1944. Indeed, in December 1941 a map retrieved from General Guglielmo Nasi's Italian Corps headquarters at Gondar was found to contain details of entirely imaginary defences on Cyprus, and an exaggerated estimate of 30,000 troops.

Under intense pressure from Churchill, and having received reinforcements in the TIGER convoy of 238 tanks and forty-three tanks, Wavell reluctantly launched a much-delayed offensive, BATTLEAXE, in mid-May. The attack faltered, leading Churchill to replace Wavell with General Claude Auchinleck, who proved equally cautious. Although BATTLEAXE failed, Wavell had succeeded in removing the Italians from East Africa, stabilising the situation in Syria and Iraq, and evacuating Allied troops from Crete. He has also become the first military commander of the war to embrace strategic deception, and had endorsed Clarke's tactics of inventing fictitious units such as the 10th Armoured Division, the 7th Infantry Division and the 39th Battalion, Royal Tank Regiment, to construct a thoroughly misleading order-of-battle. This was accomplished by sheer invention, but also by misrepresenting the true status of reserve, or headquarter units. Thus the 9th Amy, which was no more than at Corps strength, deployed against the Vichy French, became a full army, as did the 10th Army which supposedly was sent to the Caucasus to support the southern Soviet flank in August 1942. Also invented was the 12th Army, components of which were drawn from GHQ's substantial presence in Cairo and the Delta. The illusion was completed by Noel Wild's creation of a unit insignia, a seal balancing a globe on its nose, which was duly reported by CHEESE. Another of his inspired ideas was the unicorn as the sign of an equally fictitious 12th Army division. On this occasion, however, Wild over-reached himself as he learned too late that there was no French word for unicorn.

In addition to greatly exaggerating the size of the Allied forces across the Middle East, Clarke invented units, among them the 1st Special Air Service Brigade, to pose non-existent threats and exploit the enemy's perceived fears. Other imaginary units included the 37th, 38th and 101st Royal Tank Regiments, and in July 1942 Clarke won approval for CASCADE, an Allied order-of-battle that was composed of fourteen completely notional divisions.

The key to constructing a false order-of-battle was personal observation and this could be accomplished by the 'lowest grade of agent, whether he could speak English or not' who reported sightings of the divisional signs which adorned Allied vehicles. Such reports would become the staple of messages transmitted by CHEESE, but there was a fear that, after the mischief of October 1941, the enemy had turned rather cool on ROBERTO. Simpson, however, disputed this pessimistic interpretation, and on 3 June 1942 advised Dudley Clarke that

we believe that the enemy, thoroughly tricked in October 1941, has never quite recovered faith in this source. An attempt is being made to build it up again. Communications are sent in the name and character of Paul Nicossof, the only remaining member of the imaginary gang that Renato Levi was supposed to have built up in Egypt. Nicossof reports inability to secure any but the most trivial information; all the others, and all the sources of intelligence, have lost faith in the enemies' promises to send money and have left him hanging on alone in the faint hope that such money may yet arrive. This is the burden of every message, and it is only varied by occasional and unimportant tit-bits of information such as anyone could pick up in Cairo.

The enemy has gone to considerable trouble to convince Nicossof that the money is on its way, and is constantly asking for methods of getting it to him, etc. If they consider that the source is completely poisoned, this may be mere playing about. It is hoped that they are still in doubt, that they may actually send money, accept the information supposedly based on the enquiries this money pays for, and be gradually persuaded that Paul is real, loyal to them and more reliable than the agents who misled them in October. The whole case requires the most cautious handling, but it should not yet be regarded as beyond possible repair.

As British survival seemed to depend in some small measure on the concept of deception, Clarke needed a method of conveying the false information to the enemy, and this was the role to be fulfilled by CHEESE. In 1942 'A' Force's scheme, codenamed CASCADE, which was approved in July, invented no less than eight divisions and two armoured brigades, and in the beginning of 1943 he warmed to his task and created a further six British divisions, a US armoured brigade, the entire 12th Army and, finally in December, 14th Corps. In 1944 this ambitious campaign was enhanced by an even greater deception, WANTAGE.

By May 1942 more captured documents proved that the enemy had accepted the existence of the 8th Division, the 12th Division, the 2nd Indian Division, 1st SAS Brigade and the 101st Royal Tank Regiment, which was an over-estimate by 30 per cent of British strengths. Clarke's second task was to delay Rommel's imminent offensive, and this was achieved by pretending that the British were themselves about to attack, thereby forcing the Afrika Korps onto the defensive. Having built up a phoney strength, 'A' Force invented three successive dates for the launch, being 9 August, 30 August and 15 September, and perpetuated delays lasting four months by reporting that each operation had been postponed at the last moment. Finally, 'A' Force with 'full orchestral accompaniment', announced instead that the whole plan had been abandoned until after Christmas, so that when the attack really began on 17 November, the enemy was completely unprepared. During the really critical period, between

2 and 9 November, several ISOS decrypts directly cited CHEESE, characterising him as 'highly reliable'.

An Afrika Korps intelligence document captured after the victory at El Alamein suggested that seven of the eight CASCADE divisions had been believed by German analysts who also accepted a US tank regiment and a British armoured brigade. All told, the enemy had exaggerated the Allied infantry by 45 per cent, and tank strengths by 40 per cent. Gradually, as the conflict swung in favour of the Allies, the deception schemes changed. Having originally invented imaginary units to strengthen actual weakness, 'A' Force enhanced the true military position by using the false order-of-battle offensively to mislead the enemy about future plans. Thus in April 1942 FABRIC was devised to persuade Rommel that the next Allied attack would take place in the north of the Libyan desert, whereas the true objective was to be in the south. Furthermore, FABRIC's other purpose was timing, and to convey the impression that the British could not mount an attack before August, and would not contemplate action during the ferociously hot months of May, June and July. Additionally, Rommel also came to believe false intelligence reports that the newly-arrived American Grant M3 medium tanks could not be deployed until sufficient ammunition had been delivered. Accordingly, the Afrika Korps was taken by surprise when, in May 1942, it encountered fully operational Grant tanks on its southern flank. However, Rommel's attack on Tobruk on 26 May, which had been predicted by ULTRA, rendered much of FABRIC redundant even though he encountered unexpectedly heavy Allied forces and took a month to accomplish the capture of the port, a goal that he had estimated would take only a matter of a few days. Furthermore, by inadvertently launching his attack against strong Allied concentrations, his troops and armour paid a heavy price for what was achieved, which was the occupation of Tobruk on 21 June, taking 33,000 prisoners. Buoyed by victory and his promotion to the rank of field-marshal, Rommel continued in pursuit of the retreating 8th Army to the defensive positions at El Alamein, the last-ditch fortifications just forty miles from Alexandria. Fortunately, ULTRA revealed the enemy's plan, to attack El Alamein on 1 July, and the confrontation lasted a month, but stymied the German advance. Later Rommel would acknowledge that at this first battle of El Alamein 'the chance of overrunning the remainder of the 8th Army and occupying eastern Egypt in one stroke was irretrievably gone.'

'A' Force was now burdened with the responsibility of exaggerating the defences at El Alamein, most of the dummy tanks prepared for FABRIC having perished during the retreat. The plan called for the entirely notional 6th New Zealand Division and the 3rd South African Division, which had been part of the CASCADE deception, to be deployed as reinforcements, and the principal channel for conveying the false information, codenamed SENTINEL, was CHEESE. SENTINEL suggested that the British forces were due to be reinforced towards the end of August, and a grossly exaggerated assessment of Allied strengths persuaded Rommel to abandon his planned attack, thus leaving it to the 9th Army to seize the initiative, a plan concealed by yet another cover story devised by 'A' Force.

One news item that was considered impossible to keep secret was Churchill's impending visit to Cairo, scheduled for 4 August. He wanted to visit the 8th Army and confer with Wavell, who was summoned from India, and General Jan Smuts, who arrived from South Africa, and the cover plan, codenamed GRANDIOSE, was for CHEESE to report Churchill's movements accurately, but only after a delay of two days.

During Churchill's momentous visit, made while en route to Moscow, he replaced Auchinleck as commander of the 8th Army with General Gott, who was promptly killed when his aircraft was shot down, so the post went instead to Montgomery. Churchill also split the Middle East command into a Near East Command, taking in Palestine, Africa and Syria, with its headquarters in Cairo, headed by Harold Alexander, and a Persia and Iraq Command headed by General Maitland Wilson, who had been leading the 9th Army in Syria. Auchinleck would become Commander-in-Chief India, and Wavell would be appointed the Viceroy.

ISLD's principal task was penetration of the enemy's intelligence apparatus, and developed PESSIMISTS and QUICKSILVER for this objective. The PESSIMISTS were a group of three double agents run in Syria who had landed in Tripoli in October 1942 on a mission to Damascus, and had been quickly captured through TRIANGLE and turned against their Abwehr controllers in Athens. They consisted of PESSIMIST X, a Swiss-Italian named Costa who notionally acted as a courier for PESSIMIST Y, the group's wireless operator and a professional singer. Known to the Germans as MIMI and to SIME as JACK, he was a Greek named Demetrios, originally from Alexandria, and was described as 'a greedy devious shit and a stirrer'. He collected information from PESSIMIST Z, a thug with a criminal past involving drug smuggling. Of the three, only PESSIMIST Y retained his liberty, living in the same house as QUICKSILVER, a Greek air force officer, George Liossis, and nephew of General Liossis who had dispatched on a mission for the Abwehr in August 1942 with a prostitute, Anna Agiraki, codenamed GALA, and a Greek sailor, regarded as a Gestapo thug, named Bonzos and codenamed RIO. When questioned, Erich Vermehren confirmed that Costa had supplied details of Allied divisional signs and was 'well looked upon' by the Istanbul KO which had assessed his reporting as 'very good indeed'.

Their mission already compromised by TRANGLE, all three were picked up in a small boat off Latakia and, upon his arrival in Beirut,

Liossis, who had been in contact with SIS in Athens before the war, cooperated with the local DSO Douglas Roberts, who assigned John Wills of SIME to supervise the contact made with his German controllers by radio in October 1942, after GALA and RIO had been imprisoned. QUICKSILVER's notional network also included KHALIL, a laundryman working for the British 9th Army, and KYRIAKIDES, supposedly a Greek businessman with royalist connections in Cairo, where he was a frequent visitor.

In 1944 QUICKSILVER's diminishing funds were replenished with 200 gold sovereigns supplied by INFAMOUS, an Armenian double agent under SIS control since May 1943 who had been friendly with the Belgian consul in Beirut, and therefore was considered suspect. Famously his ISLD case officer in Beirut, Charles Dundas, complained to Cairo that 'plans which appear well-prepared at your end seem half-baked at ours'. Despite the protest, INFAMOUS was allowed to make his delivery, but took the opportunity to smuggle some watches into Lebanon, where he was caught and briefly imprisoned. This incident appeared to have no impact on QUICKSILVER's standing with the Abwehr, and in August 1944 he was appointed provost-marshal of the Royal Hellenic Air Force in Egypt.

Another important SIME double agent was STEPHAN, who was actually an Austrian named Klein who was arrested in Cairo in March 1941. Then there was INFAMOUS who became relevant to CHEESE when, in May 1943, evidence emerged that the Abwehr had decided to use an unidentified courier to smuggle money to CHEESE in Egypt. Naturally, all the parties involved were anxious to spot the man and place him under surveillance, and elaborate arrangements were made to watch the passengers on the Taurus Express which departed Istanbul on 17 May. According to INFAMOUS, the courier had been instructed to deliver the money and a document described as a directive to a contact at the Hotel Baron in Aleppo.

At one point, in late May 1943, information from INFAMOUS suggested the existence of an Abwehr network in Egypt, perhaps centred on Alexandria. On 26 May the Istanbul station sent the following message to SIME in Cairo:

> INFAMOUS has been instructed by Swiss to stand by for return of courier from Aleppo June 4 or June 5. He may however return before then. Courier expected to bring with him from ARNAVIR most important information concerning British submarines which transport arms for assistance of [group omitted] there. Numbers of notes will be available shortly.

SIS's man in Istanbul, Nicholas Elliott, designated 18700, announced that

> INFAMOUS reports that courier returned Istanbul 6 June and contacted him morning 7 June. Courier is Turk, aged about thirty-eight. INFAMOUS gained impression he travelled via Gaziantep and crossed Syrian frontier illegally. Description follows shortly.

On the following day, Elliott sent a further report about INFAMOUS:

> On contacting INFAMOUS... courier slit open lining of his coat and produced piece of linen similar to that brought by the priest. Typewritten on linen (which was sealed with adhesive tape) was letter in moderate English dated Alexandria 2 June 1943 from ARNAVIR to NAHICHEVAN.
>
> Following is paraphrase of salient points: (a) Letters dated March 22 and April 16 received. (b) 415 pounds Egyptian not yet received; we have only received from T£15,000 dollars. (c) We confirm arrival of very important convoys from England to Gibraltar already made to intelligence by 'transmission B.2 on May 31'. (d) B.2 will transmit exact date of convoys to Derna. Section of 10th Army proceeded Derna.

114

On 16 June the ISLD station in Istanbul reported that

> INFAMOUS confirms ASLAN left June 10 intended change trains after Ankara
> and take local train to Diarkbekir and Hardin. Destination probably Aleppo.
> ASLAN told INFAMOUS he might not be able to bring MOUSSA back to Tur-
> key as he is on a mission to Iran. ASLAN also stated MOUSSA brings parcels
> to Turkey from Syria.

When the directive and its covering letter reached SIME in Cairo, they were studied with great interest. The letter was signed NAHICHEVAN and proved to be instructions on how the sum of E£415 was to be delivered 'with every precaution to 'Madame MARIE' at 'Cairo, Rue Gogol 20, in the neighbourhood of the Neiogan Tawgig'. The directive turned out to be a request for 'information about British espionage, sabotage and counter-espionage organisations, together with the countries in which these are particularly interested. According to INFAMOUS, the person behind the operation was von der Marwitz, the German naval attaché in Istanbul. The others implicated were CAPPELLARTA, ODIOUS and ARMAVIN.

Rolf von der Marwitz was a familiar figure to British Intelligence, having been the prewar German naval attaché in Paris. A member of the nobility, he had been appointed to the same post in Ankara in April 1939, and was known to have commanded a squadron of minesweepers at Kiel and Wilhelmshaven during the First World War. Although not an Abwehr professional, he was implicated as the paymaster in several espionage cases across the eastern Mediterranean.

ODIOUS was Max Brandl, a Swiss watch salesman recruited by SIS in Istanbul in December 1942 as a double agent after he had volunteered the fact that he had been approached by the Abwehr in Vienna to spy in Syria. With SIS's consent he had returned to Vienna to agree his mission, and had returned in March 1943. He had been allowed to travel to Syria the following month but SIME interrogated him, aware that he had undergone undisclosed training by the Abwehr in 1940. He was arrested by SIME on a second mission to Syria in October when he admitted that he had been spying for the Abwehr in Spain, Tangier and Vienna since 1941.

Neither SIME nor SIS had any trace of ARMAVIN but it was believed that he was probably ARMEN, a character who had appeared in a TRIANGLE decrypt the previous December as having been the recipient of a large sum of money from von der Marwitz. In that same month ARMEN reported on the French fleet in Alexandria and later, most inaccurately, provided information about Gibraltar.

The issue for SIME was whether INFAMOUS was telling the truth about the existence of a hitherto undiscovered Abwehr spy-ring in Egypt, or if he was part of some elaborate test to check on CHEESE. The matter would never be completely resolved but SIS found a TRIANGLE reference dated December 1942 from von der Marwitz in Istanbul concerning a payment made to ARMEN in Egypt for information which included a map of Gibraltar and details of various warships. However, in Berlin's estimation, the information was 'highly inaccurate'. SIS noted similarities between ARMEN and ARMAVIN and speculated that they were the same person, remarking that both were believed to be Armenian; both had received large sums of money from the Abwehr in Istanbul and both are interested in naval information and pass material of dubious quality. Accordingly, SIS was inclined to conclude that INFAMOUS was telling the truth and that ARMEN was identical with ARMAVIN, in which case CHEESE did not seem to be under suspicion.

In October 1943 there was a further threat to CHEESE when an SIS agent in Athens, codenamed GROWNUP, reported that 'In Heliopolis, Cairo, there is a German transmitter worked by an Italian ROBERTO'.

After some discussion, it was agreed that SIS would declare the news 'very interesting'

> How did you get this information? Give full details of this source. Try and
> get further exact information to help us in running the spy to earth.

Fortunately, GROWNUP was not able to pursue the matter any further, and the subject was quietly dropped,

The single recurring problem was, of course, the transfer of funds to CHEESE which posed some challenges for SIME as well as for the Abwehr. Clearly the Axis showed little initiative in sending money to him, but in Cairo the debate was more about how to handle the expected courier. In October 1942, when it really looked as if an unknown individual was about to turn up in Cairo and hand over a packet of money to MISANTHROPE, there was a lengthy discussion about what she should say to the courier if she was questioned, and about the fate of the mystery intermediary. On 11 October James Robertson decided on a plan that would accomplish most, if not all of its goals while still maintaining the pretence that CHEESE was at liberty and working entirely independently.

1. MISANTHROPE will be given, verbally, a summarised version of the CHEESE case.

2. It will be most strongly impressed upon MISANTHROPE that her role is a DEFENSIVE one and that what she is defending is the false picture of Paul Nicossof which has so far existed in the enemy mind. Her task is primarily to prevent the enemy realising that Nicossof is not an Axis agent acting in liberty. Her task is NOT:

   (a) To get the enemy's money, or

(b) To arrest the enemy courier

although both (a) and (b) may be considered if we can at the same time be absolutely certain of security our primary objective.

It will be made clear to MISANTHROPE that to arrest the courier, while leaving possible accomplices at large, would give warning to the latter and at the same time cause them to suspect the integrity – perhaps even the existence of – Paul Nicossof.

She will therefore be told that, although she will have to prepare herself by learning the following 'part', it will be her role not willingly to reveal information about herself or Paul, but rather to remain constantly on the defensive. This will be naturally explained by the extreme nervousness of both herself and Paul. She will refer more than once to the recent execution of five spies at Aleppo; she may also mention the arrest of the two German spies on a houseboat, and the spate of arrests they brought in their train.

If pressed to introduce the courier to Paul, she will quote explicit instructions from him against this, and will plead his great nervousness. She will also advance the argument that a meeting between Paul and the courier would double the danger for both, as in fact it would.

Any further instructions which may be necessary will be communicated to MISANTHROPE verbally.

3. Name (Fictitious)

To be decided in consultation with MISANTHROPE herself.

4. Address

That of a flat in Cairo to be obtained by DSO.

5. [XXXXXXXXXXXXXXXX]

6. MISANTHROPE has already been briefly prepared for the part which she

may have to play. She has not been told that we have been in wireless communication with the enemy; it may be necessary to put her in the picture without any reservations – but this will be avoided if possible. Her 'part' is being prepared in detail and she will be instructed to learn it by heart.

7. If the enemy reply to the measure given in Paragraph 2 by informing us of the approximate date of arrival of the courier we shall send:

'Faur que messager aille a .... le ...... [date and time] ... Mons amie sera assise a ----- [exact positon of table in café or restaurant] ----[.] Elle s'appelle ----------[.] Taille 1 metre 62[.] Yeux bruns[.] Sourcils noirs[.] Cheveux bruns clairs[.] Sera habille en blanc sans chapeau[.] Portera sac rouge[.] Faut que messager lui dise[.] J'aiete chez Emile[.] Elle repondera[.] Comment va-t-il et Marie[.]

8. Description of MISANTHROPE to be in accordance with her altered appearance
Considerable discretion will be left to MISANTHROPE as to the policy she adopts but she will be told that our essential objectives are:

(a) To discover whether the courier is working alone or with associates, (b) If and when he proposes to return (c) If he had any other mission besides the delivery of the money (d) At all costs to allay or to parry any inquisitiveness on the part of the courier on the subject of Paul, She will plead ignorance of Paul's espionage activities – 'He is so mysterious about what he does' – and will lay emphasis on his extreme nervousness. If the courier expresses a wish to meet Paul, she may say that she will 'try to persuade him,' but will subsequently inform the inquirer that Paul feels that a meeting would be too dangerous for both parties. Paul's danger would in fact be doubled if the courier became too well informed about him; a policy of cautious mysteriousness would therefore be a natural one to adopt, but of secondary importance to the concealment of the real facts about Paul – to arrest the courier. It will be explained to her that this will be dangerous for our plans if associates of the courier remain at large, or if the arrest of the whole 'gang' does not take place simultaneously and secretly.

9. In case of emergency agents of the DSO will be present at a suitable distance at each rendezvous between MISANTHROPE and the courier. If the interview goes in such a way as to suggest to her that the courier has become suspicious, or is likely to slip out of our hands, she will communicate with the DSO agents by a previously agreed signal. In accordance with arrangements which will be left to DSO, the courier will then be arrested as unobtrusively as possible and immediately subjected to intensive interrogation on the points set out in Paragraph 3. It will be emphasised most strongly to MISANTHROPE that this plan will only be adopted in case of extreme emergency; and that unless compelled to it we are most anxious not to arrest the courier unless the conditions specified are satisfied. This emergency plan will require very careful planning in full consultation with DSO.

    1. MISANTHROPE has been instructed to look for a suitable place for the rendezvous, where the chances of her being seen by acquaintances are at a minimum.

    2. DSO will be asked to arrange a suitable flat in Cairo where Special Section or Advance HQ 'A' Force representatives will meet and instruct MISANTHROPE.

SIME, of course, was handicapped by the lack of a 'flesh and blood' Nicossof to appear for the courier, and there were other loose ends, such as the language to be spoken at the rendezvous, and even a physical description of MISANTHROPE and Nicossof. When Maunsell read Robertson's proposal he speculated about what might happen if *two* couriers turned up, Nevertheless, he gave his approval, and the DSO then began to assemble a suitable reception for the courier and his confederates at SIME's villa where two SIME officers, Majors Kennedy and Dunstan, gathered a team of Field Security NCOs to act as guards. The plan dictated that

> On arrival in the villa the prisoner will immediately be placed under guard in a room prepared for 'straightforward interrogation'.
>
> The BGM will have been brought with the prisoner to the villa. Out of hearing of the prisoner she will inform the interrogators of the substance of any conversation she may have had with him.
>
> The interrogation will then proceed in the light of such information as may have been obtained from the BGM. The interrogation will cover the following important points:

> I.   Name of the prisoner.

> II. How long has he been in Egypt (the Middle East?)

> III. Who gave him his instructions for the rendezvous at the café and the password?

> IV. The prisoner will be briefly questioned in order to discover how much he knows about CHEESE.

> V.   If as a result of the previous questions it is discovered that the courier is a 'principal' recruited in enemy territory for his task he will be asked how he was to report to his employers that his task had been completed, or by wireless it must be ascertained exactly where the wireless apparatus is and who besides the courier is aware, in Egypt, of its existence.

Frustratingly, with all these arrangements having been made, the Abwehr failed to send the promised courier. The dilemma for SIME was how to interpret the enemy's apparent reluctance to place their own personnel in jeopardy by undertaking the hazardous mission to Cairo. Was the adversary suspicious of CHEESE? Was the entire network compromised to the point that the Abwehr was now playing with SIME? If so, the implications for strategic deception were immense as the channel had developed into the Allies' main method of deceiving Berlin.

CHAPTER THREE

ROMMEL'S INTELLIGENCE

Rommel's arrival in Cyrenaica in February 1941 went unnoticed by the British because, at that stage in the war, CBME had access to some Luftwaffe Enigma traffic, but no Middle East Wehrmacht keys had been solved yet, and would remain opaque for another seven months. Nevertheless, the individual circuits dedicated to Afrika Korps administrative communications were identified as early as March 1941 and designated BULLFINCH, a channel accompanied by CHAFFINCH, for operational traffic, and PHOENIX, which was used exclusively by the Panzerarmee Afrika. These signals provided the very first indication of the deployment of German forces to Tripolitania, and they terminated at 0800 on 12 May 1943 after a series of poignant farewell signals, marking the surrender, and referred to within the network as KLARTEXT.

Initially designated 'AF5' and then LINNET in March and April 1941, CHAFFINCH included circuits connecting Rome and Berlin to Libya and Sicily. Whereas the latter were high-power static stations, the other sites tended to be low powered and mobile. Later in August 1941, a further network, linking Rome to Benghazi and Tripoli, were detected and monitored.

123

US military attachés based at embassies and legations in foreign countries were equipped with a cipher system known as the Black Code, a copy of which fell into the hands of the Italian Servizio Informazioni Militare (SIM) in August when the office of the military attaché in Rome, Colonel Norman Fiske, was burgled. The incident only became known when the diaries of Mussolini's foreign minister, Count Ciano, were published, causing acute embarrassment and prompting an investigation. The evidence suggested that SIM had revealed its coup to German codebreakers at the Chiffrierabteilung, who had ensured that all subsequent messages encrypted with the Black Code were intercepted and read.

It was in these circumstances that traffic for the period from October 1940 to August 1942 transmitted by Colonel Bonner F. Fellers, the US military attaché in Cairo, was read instantly by the Afrika Korps. Although not yet in the war, the Americans had been granted privileged access to British planning, and Fellers was a regular attendee at the staff conferences addressed by General Claude Auchinleck. His reports of these meetings formed the basis of a daily dispatch to Washington which Rommel found invaluable and came to rely on:

2 June, 1642HRS. Hachiem is still held by the Free French who claim to have destroyed two workshops of the 21st and 15th Armd. Divs. Axis lines of communications are believed by the British to be to be very unstable and General Ritchie is planning to push pursuits. Picture may be changed however by using units of the 1st Armd. Brigade as replacements.

Dispositions of 1 June

Axis Forces: Well covered by artillery and anti-tank guns in the general areas 36–40 and 36–39. Future moves are not apparent. 300 German tanks have been lost according to the British.

British Forces: It is believed that the Southern brigade of the 50th Div. has been completely destroyed. 1st and 7th Armd. Divs. In square 37–42 is the 4th Armd. Brigade with one regiment of the 1st Armd. Brigade. Balance of the 2nd and 22nd Brigades totaling approx. one brigade are in square 37/40. In square 38/40 is the 200th Guards Motor Brigade Exact position of the 7th Motor Brigade is not known but they moved south and west of Bir Hachiem and its car regiment of KGGs was in square U6-5 yesterday. [AQ6] June 4, 0749 HRS. On the night of June 2–3 Germans evacuated Eleut Ettamar, which position was then occupied by British Infantry Battalion, supported by remnant of 4 Armd. Brigade from the east. The position has again been attacked from the north by the German 7th Armd. tanks with unknown results. The main German position in minefields is unchanged.

At Bir Hachiem Free French withstood Italian attack of 2 June. RAF assisted with adequate air support. The 7th Motor Brigade is in a position west and slightly north of Free French. Right flank is being covered by 29th Indian Brigade of the 5th Indian Division. Axis lines of communication are being raided from south by 4th Armd. and from the north by 50th Div. and 3 South African Brigade. The 11th Indian Brigade from the 4th Indian Div. is now at Tobruk and the 10 Indian Div. is moving up in the rear of South African Div.

The detail supplied unwittingly by Fellers gave Rommel a massive advantage and he was quick to grasp the opportunity. Indeed, he became so dependent on what was termed 'the good source' that he would delay his own decisions until he had received the daily Cairo decrypts from his liaison officer, Leutnant Wischmann, and expressed his frustration if Fellers's transmission was unpunctual.

The 'good source' was terminated when, at the end of June 1942, a Luftwaffe signal encrypted on a vulnerable Enigma link was itself read and found to contain a reference to a recent British success in locating a particular Luftwaffe headquarters. This suggested a major security leak within the British command, but the ensuing investigation failed to make any progress. However, on 9 July 1942, Australian 9th Division tanks overran an Afrika Korps intercept site on the Tel-el-Eisa plateau manned by Wireless Reconnaissance Unit 621, some 600 metres from the front. All the sixty-nine PoWs, including the commanding officer, Harald Seebohm, and his adjutant, Leutnant Herz, underwent CSDIC's attention while analysts studied the captured cipher records which proved that the enemy had gained access to the Black Code. Consequently, Fellers was decorated and replaced by a suitably indoctrinated officer, Colonel Sivley. To prevent a repetition, Sivley's assistant, Captain John Brinton, was instructed to change the new attaché systems and procedures periodically.

This episode would severely handicap Rommel, although the activities of his Y Service would remain a mystery until April 1943 when SCORPION, the codename for the organisation's Enigma key in the Mediterranean theatre, was finally broken by Allied cryptographers. British understanding of the enemy's Y Service would be greatly assisted by Herz who agreed to cooperate with his debriefers in Heliopolis, thereby allowing MI8's Major Tozer to compile a handbook, *The German Wireless Intercept Organisation*. Herz's senior officer, Major Seebohm, later died in an Alexandria hospital of his wounds. However, with Rommel 'denied a vital source of intelligence' Sir Michael Howard observed 'from now on CHEESE had the field very much to himself'.

CBME made a critical contribution to the Allied victory in October 1942 at El Alamein, where an Oxford don, Brigadier Edgar ('Bill') Williams, acted as General Bernard Montgomery's chief intelligence adviser and kept him supplied with ULTRA summaries that provided a comprehensive view of General Erwin Rommel's order-of-battle, future plans, troop strengths, reserves, ammunition stockpiles, and fuel bunkers, together with daily updates of the Afrika Korps' tank inventory, vehicles under repair, and a tally of recent losses. He even received copies of his adversary's private medical reports (describing Rommel's low blood pressure), which were transmitted to Berlin by Rommel's personal physician, Professor Hans Hörster, then director of the Municipal Rudolf Virchow Hospital in Berlin-Wedding.

Rommel's attack at what he believed to be a weakness in the Allied lines at El Alamein proved to be one of the great turning points of the entire war. The DAK planned to overwhelm the supposedly thin British defences and sweep triumphantly into Cairo, but ULTRA had given Montgomery a very precise view of the enemy's intentions and, by now confident in its accuracy, he had taken the appropriate counter measures. This was a classic, textbook example of how to exploit reliable intelligence, and the scale of the defeat was immense. Its impact was all the greater because Rommel had gambled on capturing enough fuel to sustain his momentum but, in the event, the DAK encountered well-prepared positions and coordinated aerial bombing. Without any petrol reserves, the scheme designed to deliver a swift victory and closure of the canal was transformed into a wholesale rout of historic proportions.

In February 1944 Guy Liddell recoded a slightly different perspective on the battle, attributing an 'A' Force deception scheme codenamed FLESHPOTS as having contributed to the Allied success, claiming that Rommel had been influenced by the timely discovery of a misleading map, apparently abandoned in a burned-out armoured vehicle. On 18 February 1944 he dined in London with Montgomery's chief intelligence officer, Brigadier Bill Williams, who told him that

> Monty's first success at El Alamein was the turning point. The Germans did exactly what he had calculated that they would do. He had encouraged them to make their advance over the soft sand north of the Quatra depression by

planting false maps on them. These maps were left in a burned-out tank, and, according to General von Thoma, Erwin Rommel based his action upon them. Had the Germans, instead of turning north, gone straight on, there is no doubt that the 8th Army would have been in very grave difficulties.

The 8th Army's surprise counter-attack in October, supported by new equipment, proved to be the start of the Akrika Korps' disastrous withdrawal over 800 miles of poor terrain with no concealment from the Royal Air Force. Convinced he was facing a strong adversary, Rommel led what was left of the DAK men and tanks to an epic defeat.

This kind of comprehensive intelligence picture, a rare phenomenon, enabled Montgomery to exploit his opponent's weaknesses and mount credible deception campaigns, but the loss of Crete in May 1941 had demonstrated that, however impressive a commander's knowledge of the enemy's intentions, there was no substitute for the determined force of arms. Despite the defenders' overwhelming numerical superiority, with 27,500 British and Empire troops, supported by 14,000 Greeks, General Bernard Freyberg was forced to surrender to an airborne force of less than 16,000. Although 15,000 Allied soldiers were evacuated to Alexandria, some 1,742 were killed, 1,737 wounded, and 11,835 taken prisoner in a humiliating defeat. Yet before and during the German offensive, Freyberg had received ULTRA decrypts that had detailed the enemy's strategy and identified the precise date of the attack. He also had the benefit of the Australian 4 Special Wireless Section, an eighty-strong component of 101 Special Wireless Company, that provided Freyberg with high-quality tactical intercepts throughout the fighting until the unit was evacuated from Sphakia to Alexandria.

As SIME came to appreciate at an early stage, the Axis espionage network in Cairo essentially boiled down to CHEESE as the sweep of enemy aliens in June 1940 had effectively neutralised whatever preparations had been made by SIM. It would not be until May 1942 that the Abwehr attempted to infiltrate a new spy, Johannes Eppler, code-named KONDOR, into Cairo, taking an epic overland route across the desert from Libya.

Alias Husein Gafaar, Eppler had been born in Egypt and his plan, codenamed SALAAM, called for the noted Hungarian explorer, Count Laszlo Almasy, to drive Eppler on a hazardous 1,700-mile journey from Tripoli to Assyut and deliver him deep behind the Allied lines so he could make his own way to Cairo by train, accompanied by his twenty-five year-old wireless operator, Heinrich Sandstede, who held a forged British passport identifying him as 'Peter Muncaster'. Both men reached Cairo on 11 May 1942 but quickly discovered that although the E£600 they carried were fine, the Sterling notes worth £3,000 they had been given were banned in Egypt and difficult to exchange for usable currency. However, having changed some money, and spent most at nightclubs and bars such as the Kit-Kat and Rivoli, they were soon very short of funds and, suspecting their transmitter was faulty because they had failed to make radio contact with the Abwehr, they sought help from family, friends and contacts. Almost inevitably, this led them to betrayal.

On 11 June the DSO in Cairo, George Jenkins, was informed by Dr Radinger, one of his sources, who was a German Jewish abortionist, that Viktor Hauer of the Swedish consulate had been in touch because he had received a telephone call from someone seeking his help. Hauer had responsibility for looking after the interests of German internees in Egypt and subsequently he had agreed to meet two Germans who had asked for passports and a Hallicrafter wireless transmitter that had been stored in the consulate's basement, apparently since 1937. As Hauer had known since 1939 that the abortionist was an agent of the British, he asked him to act as an intermediary, and the result was that the DSO arranged for Hauer, whose precise diplomatic status was uncertain, to be abducted with his consent. This took place on the evening of 27 June, and as Hauer left the Metro cinema he was blindfolded and driven to the SIME villa at Maadi. Under interrogation, Hauer described his background. He was an Austrian diplomat who had served in Paris, and had married a woman from Alsace in Cairo in 1936. They had a five-year-old daughter who had returned with her mother to Europe.

Hauer confirmed that he had been visited at the consulate by Hassan Gafaar, and had agreed to see him again the same evening at Badia's Cabaret near English Bridge, where he had been introduced to Eppler. Together the trio took a taxi to Eppler's houseboat where he met Sandstede who had threatened him, and mentioned another transmitter buried five hundred kilometres away at Assyut. He had also said that in their messages they were known as MAX and MORITZ.

Having made this statement, Hauer's name was changed to Franz Miller and, at his request as he feared for his life, he was transferred to a PoW camp in Palestine where he remained for the rest of the war. SIME later concluded that Hauer had not told the whole truth, and had omitted to mention that he had also supplied Eppler with six maps of Egypt and a Mauser pistol, all of which were subsequently recovered. He had also acted as an intermediary for a group of Egyptian officers who had planned to block a British evacuation in the event that Rommel reached Cairo. They hoped to sabotage the bridges and maximise British casualties, but had no way of communicating with the Germans.

Eppler and Sandstede were arrested on the evening of 25 July 1942 at their rented houseboat at El Agouza, and interrogated separately by Harold Shergold and Giles Isham. Shergold, who spoke fluent German, having studied in Munich before the war, had joined the

Intelligence Corps upon the outbreak of hostilities, when he had been teaching at Cheltenham Grammar School.

The houseboat's interior was searched thoroughly, but no transmitter was found, and Eppler later claimed he had thrown it into the Nile four days earlier. From SIME's viewpoint, it was absolutely essential to ascertain whether this pair of enemy agents were on a short-term, tactical mission to collect military information directly relevant to the Afrika Korps' objectives in Egypt, or if Eppler had some other role, perhaps to check on CHEESE, supply him with money or complete some other mission.

From the outset, both men proved extremely compliant and not only implicated a large number of Egyptian co-conspirators but then appeared as prosecution witnesses at their trials. In return, both men were treated throughout as prisoners of war rather than enemy spies destined for the gallows. As a result of their testimony two Egyptian army officers, Flight-Lieutenant Hassan Ezzat and Captain Anwar el Sadati were court-martialled by a military tribunal headed by the Egyptian army's DMI, Kaimakam Moussa bey Loufta, and interned for the rest of the war, as was a pro-Nazi civilian, Aziz el Masri Pasha, the former chief of staff of the Egyptian army.

A pilot, Ezzat had been asked to fly Eppler back to the German lines, should the need arise. Anwar el Sadati was in the Egyptian Signals Corps and his function was to repair Eppler's radio and to transmit an emergency message if required. The signals officer, Sadati, was suspected of being a Nazi sympathiser, based on the a copy of *Mein Kampf* annotated in red ink, found at his home, and his admitted association with Eppler and Sandstede whom he had met at their houseboat.

Also implicated was an employee of the Ministry of Social Affairs, Frau Doktor Fatma Amer, the German wife of a local doctor, Ali

Amer, who had previously assisted escapees who had absconded from their internment camps. The most recent fugitive, Kurt Siegel, who had benefited from her help, was also detained. Eppler would later claim that Madame Amer would be his link to a pro-Nazi 'Egyptian Liberty Movement' and had introduced him to one of its leaders, el Masri Pasha.

Eppler willingly explained his own background. He said he was twenty-five years old, having been born in 1914 in Alexandria, the illegitimate son of Johanna Gafaar, and his father had been a British officer. He had been brought up in Germany between 1915 and 1931, and then had returned to Egypt where he had attended the Lycée Francais. He had travelled back to Germany in August 1937 and joined the Luftwaffe, holding the rank, and paybook, of a lieutenant.

Eppler would later say that while in Berlin in 1937 he had visited the Abwehr's headquarters in the Tirpitzufer, where he had been greeted by Admiral Canaris, and had been trained as a saboteur until October when he had been sent to Athens for a briefing on his first mission, in Istanbul. Following that he had operated in the Balkans, liaising with Colonel Morozow of the Siguranza in Bucharest, to investigate reports, leaked from the British embassy, of British plans to sabotage the Ploesti oilfields. His next assignment was to be Cairo, and Eppler described his journey through Palestine, staying in Jerusalem, before returning to Alexandria. By May 1941 he was in Baghdad but he gave several very different versions of his movements prior to his arrival in Tripoli in 1942 in preparation for SALAAM.

Fluent in English, Arabic, French and some Scandinavian languages, he was married to a Danish wife, Sonia Eppler-Wallin, and had lived with her at Godthaabsveg 90 in Copenhagen until September 1940 when he had been conscripted into a Wehrmacht motor transport depot, and was then then transferred to a signals unit. On another occasion he said that before the war he had run a cotton business in

Alexandria, but at the last moment before hostilities were declared he had fled by car to Germany, via Transjordan, Iraq and Turkey.

Eppler ended up in the same OKW topographical section as Sandstede, where he had been employed as a cartographer, but in the summer of 1941 both men had been moved to the 15th Company of the Brandenburg Regiment.

According to his version of events, Eppler initially had stayed at a flat at Sharia Bourse el Guedida belonging to a Frenchwoman, Mrs Therese Guillement, who was married to an Egyptian, but the location had proved unsatisfactory, partly because her premises were 'used for immoral purposes' and drew sporadic police attention, but mainly because the block was screened by other buildings which interfered with radio reception. He had then visited his mother at her home, Sharia Masr al Khadina 10, in Cairo's old town, and discovered that his step-father Saleh Gafaar, a retired Egyptian judge, had died seven months earlier, and that his half-brother Hassan Gafaar, was away.

Eppler described how he had befriended Hekmet Fahmy, a belly-dancer at the Continental Hotel, who had allowed him to stay at her houseboat which she shared with her lover, a British officer who had been posted with his unit to the desert, and had left behind a case containing personal papers, among which was a map of Tripoli showing the disposition of Italian troops prior to the British occupation in 1941. Eppler then asked Fahmy to find him a houseboat to rent, which she did, and he moved into Dahabia (houseboat) number 10. He also wrote a letter to Hassan Gafaar asking him to attend a rendezvous at the Bar Americaine in the Fouad el Awal. They met, and Hassan suggested they seek help from Hauer who, he claimed, had arranged an introduction to Hassan Ezzat at a bungalow in Heliopolis.

The SIME interrogators were particularly interested by Eppler's assertion that he had been informed that there was another active German transmitter in Cairo, allegedly run by the Gestapo and concentrating on political intelligence. At one point this radio, supposedly deposited at Zagazig before the war, could be accessed by a contact, Aziz el Masri, who might be able to send an emergency message to Rommel's headquarters for him.

Another espionage suspect was Prince Abbas Halim, an individual already known to be pro-Axis who had been the subject of correspondence between Alex Kellar of MI5's E2(b) and his colleague Helenus Milmo. According to Eppler, he had been instructed to contact the prince through his former servant, now employed at the Royal Automobile Club in Cairo.

Eppler also described how he had been given the details of a Hungarian priest at the church of the St Therese Carmelite convent in Cairo who would respond to a special password 'alma mater', and was supposed to have a 100-watt transmitter hidden on the premises. This statement led to the interrogation of Father Demetriou, a Carmelite lay brother who had been in Egypt since his arrival from Palestine in October 1939. Significantly, Demetriou, who was described by Hauer as 'thoroughly pro-German' had been nominated by the Swedish legation, which had taken over responsibility for Hungarian affairs when that country's legation had closed, as an interpreter and someone to liaise with Hungarian internees. Born in January 1912 in Maco, Pierre Demetriou had studied at the Keszthely convent in Hungary before moving to Mount Carmel in August 1934. Under intensive interrogation Demetriou admitted having known Viktor Hauer and a German woman whom he reluctantly identified as Fatima Amer, but denied that he had ever been entrusted with a transmitter by Laszlo Almasy or one of his representatives. He also denied ever having met Eppler, which was probably true as Eppler's diary noted a visit to the St Therese chapel on 30 May, when he had been informed that 'Father D' was away that day. As he had not repeated the trip, there was nothing else to link Demetriou to German espionage, apart from

Levi's instruction that he would receive a radio through the Hungarian legation, and various references to a priest working as an Abwehr courier. It would not be until Erich Vermehren's interrogation that more details of Demetriou would emerge.

Meanwhile Sandstede was also being cooperative. Born in Oldenberg in 1913, the son of a chemistry professor, he had emigrated to West Africa in 1930, then lived in South Africa, moving to Uganda, Kenya, Dar-es-Salaam and Tanganika, and in 1938 was working as the office manager for Texas Oil successively in Kampala, Nairobi, Mombasa and Dar-es-Salaam. He spoke English, French, Swahili and some Italian. He had been interned in Dar-es-Salaam at the outbreak of war, but had been repatriated in January 1940 with other civilian detainees in an exchange. Once back in Germany, he had been assigned to a topographical department where he had worked on maps of the parts of Africa he knew, correcting and translating them. He claimed that he had chosen the alias 'Peter Muncaster' as he had known someone of that name in East Africa, and the Abwehr had forged the passport accordingly.

Sandstede confirmed Eppler's story that the pair had first met while attending an interpreters' course at Meissen in the summer of 1941, and had been transferred to the 15th Company of the Brandenburg Regiment because of their knowledge of foreign languages. There they had both been recruited by Rittmeister von Hoesch for a mission in Africa, and had been taken in civilian clothes to the Grand Hotel in Vienna to meet Count Almasy. On this occasion Eppler had also met Otto Eisentrager, one of the Abwehr officers associated with CHEESE who had been an adviser to Emperor Haile Selasse in Abyssinia until the Italian invasion, when allegedly he had moved to Cairo.

When Hoesch was killed at Gazala on 8 October 1941 the operation was entrusted to a Captain Pretzl, a Muslim who had worked before the war at the Azhar University. Under his supervision, Eppler and Sandstede had attended a wireless operators' course in Munich, and then undergone further training at the Abwehr radio station at Berlin-Stahnsdorf. However, Pretzl would be killed in a plane crash in November 1941 while on a flight to Vienna, and in his absence Almasy took over command.

Almasy, who would travel to Tripoli at the end of December 1941, assured both men that their mission, to collect military information in Egypt, was entirely safe, and that if they were caught the Germans would take immediate steps to exchange them for Major Patrick Clayton, a founder of the LRDG who had been captured on the last day of January 1941 during a raid by his 'T' Patrol, deep behind enemy lines at Kufra. Clayton, who was wounded in the engagement, was an explorer who had been on several prewar expeditions when he had worked for the Survey of Egypt. Evidently the Germans regarded his capture as a considerable coup, and served to provide them with a potentially valuable bargaining chip, should the need arise.

By February 1942 the Abwehr had assembled a large group to finalise the details of Operation KONDOR, and among them were Steffens, von der Marwitz, Waldemar Weber, Wöhrmann, Munz Korper, Stringmann, and Beilharz.

The mission began on 12 May when Almasy led two columns of six captured British Ford V8 trucks into the desert at El Dibo on the journey across Libya, leaving fuel and water dumps along the route for use on the return journey. Conveniently, Almasy maintained daily radio contact with his base in Tripoli, thus enabling the British Y Service to monitor the traffic. The last part of the expedition was completed with two trucks, and some seven kilometres from Assyut Eppler and Snadstede, having buried their German uniforms, replaced them with civilian clothes, and concealed one of their two transmitters under some stones. This set, identical to one recovered from the houseboat, would later be retrieved by SIME. Finally, on the afternoon of

Sunday 24 May 1942, they caught a train to Cairo where they found rooms, for two nights, at the Pension Nadia, before finding accommodation at Therese Guillermet's brothel.

Sandstede described how he had attempted to raise the Germans with his radio, using the callsign HGS (his initials) and hoping to hear HWB in reply from Weber. After two weeks of failure, they decided their equipment was faulty and took steps, which proved disastrous, to obtain a new set. Sandstede also confirmed that the book code he had been assigned was based on *The Unwarranted Death*.

Both Eppler and Sandstede agreed that Almasy had briefed them on a Hungarian priest, Father Pierre Demetriou, of the St Therese Convent in Shoubra, who was alleged to possess a wireless and be in radio contact with Budapest. When SIME followed this lead and questioned the priest, the allegation was denied and no further action was taken. In any event, Eppler failed to find Demetriou.

SIME was able to verify the statements made by Eppler and Sandstede by comparing their versions with TRIANGLE intercepts, which became available from January 1942, and CSDIC interrogation reports of interviews with two NCO drivers, Waldemar Weber and Walter Aberle, two Palestinian Germans who had been captured at Bir Hachim on 27 May and questioned before Almasy ever reached Egypt.

According to a report drawn up by Blanshard Stamp of MI5's B1(b) section in January 1943, Weber had been born in 1912 and spent most of his life in Palestine. He had joined the Nazi Party in 1934 and undergone military training in Germany in 1936. Shortly before the outbreak of war he had returned to Germany and in October 1939 had been assigned to the 25th Infantry Signals Depot to undergo wireless training, but in the spring of 1940 had been transferred to the elite Brandenburg Regiment. He had completed a mission in civilian clothes to Bulgaria, returning to Germany in November 1940, and in July 1941 had been posted to Istanbul as a wireless operator.

In September 1941 he was ordered back to Germany, in preparation for a mission to Syria, but only reached Athens when it was decided that his grasp of Arabic was not good enough. Instead, he had been transferred in January 1942 to the Abstelle in Paris to study the British order-of-battle, and then in February sent back to Berlin in anticipation of his posting to Tripoli and participation in SALAAM. He recalled having met Eppler and Sandstede for the first time in Berlin in September 1941, when the pair had attended a course on the composition of the British Army.

Aberle, aged thirty-seven, also had been born in Palestine and from 1936 had run a garage in Haifa with Weber. He had returned to Germany upon the outbreak of war and had been assigned in the autumn of 1939 to an anti-tank depot company before being transferred to the Brandenburg Regiment in the spring of 1940. After a period on the Belgian coast preparing for the invasion of England, he was posted to Tripoli in October 1941.

More corroboration came from the diaries which Sandstede had maintained. Although some entries proved to be false, such as the claim that they had visited Suez and Port Said to recruit local informants, they had kept these incriminating documents to prove, when Rommel entered Cairo, what they had accomplished for the Reich. At the moment of their arrest Sandstede had thrown Eppler's diary into the Nile, but had failed to destroy his own.

Eppler's half-brother, Hassan Gafaar, was also arrested, and when questioned he explained that he had been born in Germany, where he had spent the first seventeen years of his life, and had been educated in Stuttgart. He then had been apprenticed to a firm of ironmongers for eighteen months in Backnang, where he had lived with his grandmother.

He said he had had not heard from his half-brother until a fortnight earlier, on Saturday 11 July, when he had received a handwritten letter instructing him to meet Hans at the Americaine that same evening. He had gone to the rendezvous and later had visited his houseboat, and thereafter had seen him every day. He also admitted introducing Eppler to Hauer in the hope of replacing the transmitter's faulty quartz crystal.

Thus SALAAM, one of the great adventures of the Second World War, later to be recounted in films such as *The English Patient*, ended as a series of interrogation reports, studied by MI5 analysts in London eager to learn if the Abwehr was planning to establish a spy-ring in Cairo to rival CHEESE.

CHAPTER FOUR

THE CHEESE NETWORK

Between July 1941 and April 1945 CHEESE transmitted a total of 432 messages from Cairo, and provided the enemy with a vast quantity of information, much of it misleading, which had been carefully processed by 'A' Force for the purpose of giving the enemy an entirely false impression of the Allied order-of-battle, the strategy adopted to prosecute the war in North Africa and protect Egypt from the Afrika Korps, and to convey a wholly bogus picture of British priorities. Such an undertaking required great force of character on the part of the principal coordinator, Dudley Clarke, who had to persuade much more senior officers of the value of deception and unorthodox warfare, and SIME which otherwise might have been expected to adopt a very insular, defensive role if it had not been for the imagination of a handful of officers who would later take up the intelligence business on a professional basis. Charles de Salis, Geoffrey Hinton, Douglas Roberts, Terence Robertson, Nicholas Elliott, James Robertson, Rex Hamer, Michael Crichton and Desmond Doran found their natural *milieu* in the postwar secret world, but it was the CHEESE case that enabled them to realise their vocation. No such double agent had ever been managed with such ambition, and the proposition that an entirely notional spy could dupe a relatively sophisticated enemy over a period of four years remains a veritable milestone in intelligence history.

Until he found a job with OETA, CHEESE himself relied on personal observation, open sources (such as the Cairo newspapers) and his sub-agents, principally MISANTHROPE, for his information, but as the channel developed, probably beyond the wildest expectations of SIME and ISLD, he became something of a cottage industry. From the Allied perspective, the priority was to put over dangerously false material, mixed in with sufficient truth to make it palatable, to an enemy that might have other comparable sources. This was an extraordinarily hazardous undertaking, and demanded great concentration and an appreciation of the subtleties required. These talents are not always associated with the military mind, but the remarkable personalities associated with CHEESE proved themselves to be entirely up to the task, ready to engage the Abwehr at their own game at a time when such large-scale schemes were entirely unknown. CHEESE himself had the benefit of a committee which carefully rehearsed each scenario and enjoyed sufficient prestige to perpetuate the fraud over a long period with support from London, Istanbul, Athens and Damascus, not to mention the military authorities across the entire Middle East. The stakes could hardly have been higher, but how did the case officers and their senior management develop CHEESE's sources and choose his sub-agents?

The sheer variety of contacts fabricated by SIME's Special Section is testimony to their fertile imaginations and their skills at exploiting and manipulating their adversary. Every message, every casual observation, was carefully logged, recorded on a card index and scrutinised to ensure there were no internal contradictions in the traffic. The narrative may have been constructed from whole cloth, but it had undergone plenty of study by skilled analysts to ensure that it retained an essential verisimilitude and would be likely to be accepted as at least plausible by their Axis counterparts. SIME never made the mistake of underestimating their opponents, and paid them the compliment of fabricating themes that *might* have been authentic.

What distinguishes 'A' Force from any other Allied organisation was the very comprehensive nature of its mission, and the amount of attention paid to detail. For example, to develop a completely false Allied order-of-battle, which was part of the general strategy of exaggerating the strength in the Middle East, Dudley Clarke not only invented non-existent military units, but embroidered reports of individual sightings by including details of unit emblems and shoulder-flashes. For a professional analyst, such observations added verisimilitude to the reports, and 'A' Force mastered the technique by keeping track of every item passed to the enemy so there were no internal errors that would have tipped off the Abwehr.

In his early reporting, CHEESE appeared to concentrate on his own observations, but gradually, as his confidence grew, his messages grew wider in scope. An analysis of his first eighty transmissions illustrates the diverse range of the topics his information covered:

–   South African troops in Cairo and the Western Desert; the Polish Brigade leaving for unknown destination; the 18th Division HQ; possible deception, Australian, New Zealand and Greek HQs.

–   The 6th Australian Division in Palestine and Syria; No South African or New Zealand troops in Persia. Australian troops en route for Middle East; the 4th Armoured Brigade west of Alexandria. The 2nd Armoured Division in the Western Desert.

–   18th Division HQ; General Sir Alan Cunningham in Cairo; a bomb was dropped on Abbassya.

- The situation at GHQ.

- No Free French or British troops arrived from Syria; equipment from West Africa.

- General Sir Alan Cunningham is Commander-in-Chief; No New Zealand cavalry division in Egypt; An infantry division in the Western Desert. No American units in Cairo.

- Aircraft arriving in crates by sea.

- Ships damaged in Alexandria harbour.

- No cavalry in Egypt.

- The 2nd New Zealand Division, the 5th Infantry Division and new English division leaving for Caucasus in mid-November.

- British warships at Alexandria.

- The 70th Division formed. Voltage of Cairo and Alexandria.

- The 50th Division is in Palestine en route for Caucasus.

- An American aircraft factory is to be built here.

- An Australian brigade in Delta. The 43rd Australian Battalion in Cairo. The 11th Hussars officers are in Cairo and the rest of their regiment arriving.

- General Moore is in Cairo. No Australians are here but South African and New Zealand troops are.

- The New Zealand troops in Cairo are the 9th Brigade and the 6th Division.

- Egyptian cigarettes have been sent to the officers mess of the Royal Sussex regiment in Cyprus.

- United \States and South African troops are leaving, but not for the front: fortifications in west.

- The 44th Infantry Division and HQ of the 15th Armoured Division arrive.

- The 1st Indian Division is to go to Cyprus; The/British admiral is in charge of the Greek fleet.

- The 44th Division is building fortifications between Cairo and Alexandria.

- Leave for the Greek Navy has been stopped. Many troops are on the Canal and Sudanese border, and the 12th Division.

- The 44th and 50th Division is in the Cairo area. The American Tank Destroyer Command in the Delta/and the 6th Regiment of Engineers.

- British subjects registering for military service.

- Two German spies and many civilians have been arrested. News of a possible attack on Crete.

Study of CHEESE's second tranche of messages, transmitted mainly in 1942, reflects his self-dependence in the absence of funds to recruit and maintain a well-informed spy-ring. Thus he made transmissions on topics that were within his grasp, including

– Churchill passed Cairo eastwards. Landing exercises at Tabrit by Greeks and British. Remainder of Greek Division. Arriving at Alexandria, possibly for Crete.

– A Greek Brigade left Kabrit.

– The appointment of Generals Harold Alexander and Bernard Montgomery.

– New armoured division arrives at Suez from England.

– Possible that the 87th Armoured Brigade is part of the new division.

– Charles de Gaulle remained three days at Cairo.

– The 15th Armoured Division is still in the Cairo area. The Greek Brigade is moving from Alexandria to Kabrit for landing exercises.

– Reaction of population to desert battle. Jews returning. Spitfire flying.

– Troops crossing Canal possibly new armoured division of 20th Armoured Division.

– British warned about the Caucasus and transferring troops from Africa.

– Reshuffling of high officers in GHQ continues.

– The white unicorn is the totem of the 15th Armoured Division.

– Some Greek officers and NCOs remaining at Kabrit.

– Greek training at Kabrit under Field Security supervision. Gliders have left the Canal area.

– No troops left Alexandria for the Levant. Training at Kabrit will probably last a month.

– Last convoy at Suez only British troops. Much artillery.

– Senior officers arrive from England (linked with invasion of Italy).

– Montgomery at the British Embassy, Conferred with Admiral Sir Henry Harwood, Harold Alexander and Arthur Tedder.

– Supplies to 8th Army hampered by bad weather.

– Civil population of Zuaha supplied by truck./Civil traffic allowed on the Cairo to Alexandria road. Restricted on the Suez–Port Said road.

– The King of Greece in Cairo.

– General Bernard Montgomery in Cairo.

CHEESE also relied on the newspaper for some of his material, and his reports drawn directly from what had just been published included Indian troops in Persia; General George Brett in Cairo; air-raid damage; General de Gaulle in Cairo; the death of General William Gott; General de Gaulle and General Georges Catroux in Tripoli; Charles de Gaulle left the Levant; photo of General Alexander reviewing Polish artillery with heavy tanks; de Gaulle arrives at Brazzaville; five spies shot at Aleppo; General George W. Casey arrives from Iran; Greeks at the front; Air Marshal Arthur Tedder's appointment; troops in the 9th Army; desert disaster; the Greek Commander-in-Chief; General Sir Bernard Paget succeeds General Sir Henry Wilson; General Sir William Holmes appointed to the

9th Army; Air Marshal Keith Park replaces Sholto Douglas; General Lloyd killed in an air accident; The King of Yugoslavia in Cairo; German traitors in Turkey; 2 Polish Corps containing Carpathian and Cresows Divisions fighting in Italy; The King of Yugoslavia in London; General Paget visited Cyprus; Brigadier Fitzroy Maclean is head of a British Military Mission to Tito; General Wilson and Lord Macmillan in Cairo for a conference; The King of Greece in London; Greek Brigade to be reorganised so as to help in the liberation of Greece; Nineteen delegates of political parties in Greece and in exile meeting in the Near East; Air Marshal Park returned here from a tour of Syria and Palestine.

The wife of a Polish officer supplied the content of four messages; 'her husband embarking at Port Said'; 'Leave cancelled and rejoined his regiment in Cyrenaica; A Polish officer at Quassassih belongs to 2nd Armoured Brigade; Husband thinks Poles in Italy will soon launch an attack against the Albanian coast.'

A 27th Lancers officer 'arrived from England. His 'leave cancelled – to rejoin his regiment in Cyenaica'; His 'regiment is part of 8th Armoured Division which has left Cyrenaica and returned to Egypt'. He was 'leaving for Syria with his regiment. Thinks other units of his division soon embarking for Europe.'

Another source, a Hungarian interpreter, had been 'chosen by Civil Affairs branch for his knowledge of Bulgarian'; Bulgarians frightened that they will undergo the same fate as Hungary'; Assisted at discussions in November and training branch on port of Varna'; 'Going to 9th Army HQ at Aleppo'; 'The English will soon be fighting side by side with Russians.'

CHEESE also asserted, on his own account, that he had 'seen no sign of 4 Division. Thinks must have left Egypt; South African troops at Heitan of the 7th Division; The railway line to Palestine blocked by a sandstorm; Divisions in Egypt: the 7th

South African and 6th South African Armoured, 10th English Armoured, also division with the sign of a white unicorn; Many Greeks around Alexandria – perhaps a whole division. Also New Zealand and Polish and Indian troops at Congos. 8th Armoured and 4th Airborne Divisions to Libya and Cyrenaica; Troops with sign of green tree and black cat in Cairo; Greek Government crisis, Teomoninos resigned. Rumour that Venezilos or Romenos will be president. No Australian troops here, only airmen. Still many New Zealanders; Green tree sign belongs to 46 Division. It is London Division, were formerly in Italy. A summary of CHEESE's sub-sources and the information they supplied implies that one of SIME's tactics was to overwhelm the recipients with such volume and detail that it would appear inconceivable that anyone could devote the necessary resources to the creation of a dangerous fiction. And yet, that is precisely what was accomplished.

Initially CHEESE started off with a relatively limited group of conscious and unconscious informants who relayed interesting gossip or reported their own observations, but gradually the network grew to encompass more than a dozen sources who occupied positions which gave them access to military secrets. Clarke's methodology was to drip-feed the Abwehr with what might be termed pieces of a jigsaw, thereby allowing the enemy analysts to build their own picture, rather than hand the entire story to them, almost on a plate, an approach which would be more likely to cause them to question its authenticity, By allowing them to reach their own conclusions, apparently independently, using their own military doctrine, Clarke believed that the objective could be better accomplished.

Among the first was described as 'ESR friend' who reported military observations, such as gliders spotted near the Suez Canal, troops crossing the canal to Palestine despite the desert battle, possibly a new armoured division or the 20th Armoured Division; the bridge at

Firdan; Australian troops at Kabrit, troops crossing the Canal; Australians leaving Kabrit; American gliders in crates at Suez. Another source was a BOAC employee who claimed that General Martel passed through Cairo while on a visit to Benghazi; reported that Generals Richard Casey and Alexander, and Air Marshal Tedder were going to Baghdad; noted that a BOAC pilot had remarked that there would be an Anglo-American invasion of Italy in November 1942.

A South African sergeant, Piet, was employed as General John Whiteley's confidential secretary. He submitted reports about Canadian troops in Palestine and Syria; that there was no Canadian armoured regiment in Cairo; that the 19th Division was not in Tobruk, but Polish troops of the 50th Division were. That the British were dissatisfied with American tanks; that British and Australian troops were to leave Tobruk; that reinforcements were to be delivered from Alexandria to Tobruk; that British forces feared an imminent German offensive; that Australian troops from Tobruk were being transferred to Syria; that General Wavell had made a secret visit to Cairo; the 1st Armoured Division and three infantry divisions were to be sent to the Russian front on the Caucasus; that the British were expecting tank reinforcements; gave false dates for a British offensive in November to delay a German attack. That only Indian and South African troops, and the 1st Armoured Division, would be left in the Western Desert; that the 50th Division was being withdrawn.

Some of CHEESE's sources only appeared once in his traffic. AHAN reported on 23 January 1945 that there were twenty cargo ships and one destroyer at Suez. An unnamed British officer mentioned that General Carton de Wiart had passed through Cairo recently on his way from the Far East.

CHEESE's fifth sub-source was an American journalist who mentioned a naval attack on Tripoli; had been ordered by the navy to report to Alexandria on 1 January; that naval plans had been spoiled by bad weather; that Australian troops were in Alexandria, en route to Palestine.

MISANTHROPE, of course, turned into a key source, and she pumped a friend, allegedly a US Army Air Force sergeant, William Schultz, for details of American troops in the Middle East, and the deployment of American aircraft leaving for Syria and Cyprus. Schultz was first mentioned by CHEESE who reported on 11 September 1941 that 'my girlfriend has got to know a sergeant in the US Air Force'.

She also reported seeing tanks in central Cairo, and one of her acquaintances, a Polish officer, of the Carpathian cavalry, from Baghdad, told her that General Wilson had received reinforcements, including Polish troops; and rejoined his regiment in Iran. Her other messages included reports that the green tree unit insignia was no longer seen in Alexandria; two British destroyers had arrived in Alexandria, having escorted a battleship to Port Said; the London Division had left Alexandria 'some days ago by sea'. Six large merchant ships had arrived in the 'port on the 22nd; carrying English troops of which several thousands are already in the town. Heard they had come from Italy'. She also claimed to have seen 'three aircraft carriers at Alexandria on the 1st. Heard they had arrived on the 25th accompanied by American destroyers. About fifty merchant ships in Alexandria harbour'. Three transmissions later CHEESE noted that she had said there were still about fifty freighters in Alexandria and some small warships – destroyers – but no battleships or aircraft carriers. She also saw about forty big tanks on the quay bearing the words 'USA-Turkey Lease Lend' and mentioned that there were only a few troops in Alexandria.

MISANTHROPE continued her observations, reporting that 'four destroyers left port yesterday after a stay of a few days. An Italian submarine and the Greek cruiser *Georgios Averof* were in Alexandria where South African troops were based at the garrison at the Moustapha barracks. Soon afterwards she noted seven aircraft carriers, accompanied by several destroyers had arrived recently at Alexandria. These participated in the invasion of the South of France and are undergoing repairs while the crews rest. Three messages later she reported that 'English sailors very numerous in town last few days. Only two of aircraft carriers left; several destroyers and a cruiser in port. Other aircraft carriers on maneuvers along the coast several kilometres from Alexandria'. Her next transmissions were:

> About fifty merchant ships at Alexandria. Of aircraft carriers which arrived and left, there are still three or four. Not many troops in Alexandria. Mostly South African or Palestinian.

Seven messages later she reported:

> Much maritime activity last few days. Two big convoys of battleships and transports left port 15th and 19th for Greece carrying soldiers who mostly wore sign of chequerboard or little black bird.

Three messages later she elaborated, 'black bird resembles stork standing with a branch in its beak. The Jewish Brigade has left for Italy. Intense shipping movement to Greece'.

MISANTHROPE's reports from Alexandria continued, mentioning 'a big battleship at Alexandria on 13th. Do not know destination'. Soon afterwards, 'several trucks seen with sign of chequerboard in Alexandria last few days. Also seen sign of red goat on white shield. Two cruisers, several destroyers, about forty cars in port on 2nd. Still plenty of traffic with Greece'.

Another of MISANTHROPE's sources was an Australian artilleryman from the 9th Division. She also knew a US Army Air Force officer,

Sam, who confided that he thought an Anglo-American invasion of Italy was imminent; that American bombers were due to arrive in Egypt to participate in air raids on Italy. Sam also speculated about an attack on Sicily, but SIME went to elaborate lengths to promote him as a credible personality. He was aged thirty-three but looked younger, and had a

> cheerful personality but has occasional (of short duration) bouts of gloom. Moderate drinker except when out for a deliberate 'binge party'; good mixer, an infectious chuckle rather than hearty laughter. Definitely a way with him so far as women are concerned. Pleasant manners, dresses neatly, even when in flying kit.

Sam's SIME dossier described him as an 'experienced navigator and pilot' who had spent 'the early part of the war on the North Atlantic 'run'. For the last nine months however, has been on the South Atlantic and similar crossings. Sam also had a 'great friend who is now with American forces in the desert, and through this friend was introduced to the *amie*, some weeks back. Finds the *amie* definitely attractive, apart from her looks. Thinks that it must be her accent. *Amie* finds her a much better dance partner than the other American,

> One day, checks in with American Air Force headquarters enquires for his friend. Told that his friend is at Shepheard's Hotel, but due to report back to his unit within a few hours. Contacts friend, who is in a hell of a hurry, and pretty mad at having to miss date with *amie*. Sam learns 'what to do' and in his turn is fed up because he will miss the fun. Lunch is more liquid than solid. With the wisdom engendered of whisky, friend suggests that he should keep his date with the *amie;* after some bibulous argument, he agrees for friendship's sake although he would rather accompany his pal. They part, the friend to his unit, Sam to bed for the afternoon. When he

wakens, and has one or two to remove taste of his sleep, he rings up *amie*, tells her that the other fellow has had his leave cancelled, and can he keep date instead? *Amie* pricks up her ears about the cancelled leave.

MISANTHROPE also noted having seen American and South African troops in Cairo; Tanks with German totems had been spotted in Cairo; French and Greek troops; Sudanese troops bearing a giraffe totem; Indian and Cape Corps South African troops noted, along with American sentries; Rhodesia, Commandos and Rand Rifles spotted; Guns on the Mena road, New Zealand vehicles bearing a bird totem; South African instead of American sentries. Trenches and barbed wire seen beside a desert road; Tank Corps, Scottish and South African troops observed. Lorries from the New Zealand 6th Division seen; Cargo ships at Alexandria were said to be destined for Malta; Reports of the 51st Division, Greek and Australian troops; Armoured cars and Polish troops seen near Barrage; many Scottish troops, parachutists and vehicles with scorpion emblems seen in Cairo; large American aircraft in the Delta; about 100 planes seen over Cairo; Totems bearing a white unicorn and white bird on a black background; A black and white dagger on a red background seen; Free French soldiers seen; American aviators in Cairo, also New Zealand trucks bearing emblems with four white stars on blue; Australians on leave from the desert; no visible air-raid damage at Heliopolis; South African and New Zealand troops on leave; American aviators and troops seen in Cairo; new South African troops on guard at the embassy; wounded soldiers seen from British regiments, among them the Durham Light Infantry, the East Yorkshires and the East Kents; lorries on desert road with totem 'GO' and Tank Corps drivers; soldiers of the South African Division; infantry sentries at GHQ; increase of Americans; RAF convoy on Abbassia road; more English naval officers in Cairo.

Thirteen of CHEESE's messages directly concerned his office where he kept his ear to the ground and reported on such diverse topics as headings on the agenda, 'Leaving for Derna' and 'News planning staff HQ/GEORGE'. He also spotted a document entitled 'the civil evacuation of Tripoli' and in two signals referred to an unnamed officer who had 'returned from Cyrenaica with General Wilson via Benghazi and Tobruk', and had been heard to remark that the 'British had underestimated ammunition supplies at Mareth.' CHEESE also reported that one of his colleagues 'was with the 12th Division in Cyrenaica. Heavy traffic on the Tobruk line. The Tobruk-Benghazi line being extended'. The officer to whom CHEESE allegedly answered was responsible for several items, including

> Recruiting Arab labour for Cyrenaica landing grounds; The visit of Turkish officers to the Tunisian front, friend from Ninth Corps; Still recruiting Arab labour.

CHEESE's office underwent a reorganisation, an event which he said had been 'delayed until after the final attack of the 8th Army'. This allegedly would not take place 'before May' and on 15 May announced the formation of the ATB'. Another office contact was the interpreter employed by the Telegraph Officer, and he was credited with the news that a new railway line had been built between Tobruk and Derna.

Without any money to buy top-level information, CHEESE often resorted to peddling rumours that were in circulation, and the topics he passed on included:

> - Auchinleck offensive in Libya; Possible landings at Benghazi, Tripoli, Crete, Rhodes. Airborne troops leaving for Palestine.

> - British offensive in Libya if Russian resistance continues.

- Approaching British offensive.

- British offensive mid-October.

- British offensive shortly.

- South African troops leaving for the desert; Artillery and tanks on the desert road.

- 'German' tanks for an American Brigade.

- Activity in the cacan zone.

- Soldiers arrive from Shallerfa.

- Told that the new Infantry Division is the 30th.

- Approaching British attack in the desert.

- Invasion of Italy imminent.

- General Alexander arriving in Cairo.

- The invasion of Italy.

Occasionally CHEESE would insert into the text of his messages some indication of his source, such as 'I had heard information received that' or 'a good source…' Into this category were subjects such as '5,000 South African troops arrive. Allied equipment/troops arrive at Suva'. 'British troop movements postponed; Canadian troops'. '19th Division HQ in Cairo; Polish Brigade in Western Desert'. 'The 4th

Indian Division and an armoured division; Canadian tank brigade left for Palestine; American tank and aircraft experts'.

Another prolific source for CHEESE was AMAN, clearly located near the Suez Canal, whose first report mentioned 'many troops with sign 'GO' in camps near Gaza. Think they belong to 8th Armoured Division'. AMAN went on to mention 'many troops with chequerboard sign around canal'. Then he 'saw a battleship last Thursday passing southwards. Think it was the *How*' which was a deliberate reference to HMS *Howe*. In the same message he also mentioned 'several trains recently carrying soldiers towards Palestine, wearing letter 'Y'. A little later he saw 'several trains of English paratroops and Indians passed canal towards Palestine recently. Think it must be 4 Airborne Division'. In his next observation he reported:

> Still many troops about canal wearing signs of: black and white chequerboard – white unicorn – yellow hammer – yellow axe.

This was followed by:

> Recently seen many Arab troops wearing on their heads a red and white cloth – belong to Arab Legion.

AMAN's last five reports mentioned '33rd Division and troops wearing sign of chequerboard still about canal' and 'not seen sign of 8th Armoured Division for a long time'. Then '*Valiant* at Suez on the 11th 'coming from the south' and 'soldiers of the 33rd Division no longer to be seen about the canal. Big battleship was at Suez and left southwards'. His last message was

> about twenty cargo ships, one tug at Suez – 25 December. Plenty of traffic South-North through canal. Think battleship that left southwards was the *Valiant*.

CHEESE's seventh unconscious source, mentioned in just two messages, was an Airborne Division major who was reported 'still at Alexandria' and was visited by ARMIN who was told that he thought he would soon go to Palestine with his unit. He also let slip that an Indian battalion was part of his division.

'There was also an officer at 3 Corps Headquarters who was here yesterday. Many troops have left their camps at Alexandria. His old division to leave for Palestine.' His second and last use as a source read

> Leaving soon for Palestine. Says English counted on a German retreat from the Balkans following Allied landings in France but German forces in Balkans now still too strong for an attack.

After CHEESE found a job at OETA's Cairo office, he was able to pick up some useful information which formed the basis of five messages which were more political in nature.

> Officer in branch of opinion that rupture of German-Turkish relations will facilitate British strategy of invasion of the Balkans.

This was clearly intended to perpetuate the threat to the German southern flank, whereas his next signal merely recorded that 'all superior officers of Middle East met here last week for talks with Paget and his staff'. Then he reported that 'officer who accompanied head of OAB on tour of Libya says most of the troops there are indigenous Africans and are part of the 12th Division'. Finally, he observed that an 'officer says he thinks all islands in the Aegean will soon be occupied by English and Greek troops'.

One of CHEESE's contacts was a Lebanese merchant referred to in two messages, who noted that there were 'many French troops in Beirut, Lydda aerodrome had been enlarged. Heavy bombers stationed there' and later stated that there were 'many paratroops in Palestine. Rumour goes that they will attack Rhodes'.

In December 1942 SIME undertook a review of CHEESE's sources, noting that he was reliant on just four, being a BOAC pilot, a US Army officer, a US Army Air Force officer, and a naval petty officer. The recommendation was that this group should be expanded to embrace two wounded men, a Royal Army Service Corps officer and a Long Range Desert Group sergeant, and an OETA officer from Benghazi.

The BOAC employee worked on the Benghazi to Cairo route, and the proposition was that he was in an ideal position to overhear useful conversations. The OETA officer could be expected to have a knowledge of future plans from Cairo,

> This man could be fairly insecure and could see shipping and especially landing craft in Benghazi and could pick up 8th Army line of communication gossip.

The American could offer USAAF and RAF news, although SIME preferred to drop him as he should be somewhat discredited in CHEESE's eyes if not in the enemy's. The idea of developing a USAAF officer had originated when SIME had first contemplated widening CHEESE's contacts:

1. The American Air Force officer tells *Amie* that the rumoured attack on Crete is to be no more than a demonstration, if that. All the special training that the Greeks and other troops have done, is for a combined operation somewhere else. Where, he will not say.

2. CHEESE's Greek friends maintain that, although the date of the Crete attack has been postponed to coincide with operations elsewhere in the Levant,

these other operations are simply feints to draw attention away from Crete so the latter affair will come as a complete surprise to the Germans.

3. CHEESE has not yet been able to discover whether the other objectives are the Dodecanese Islands or the Greek mainland.

4. Some Greeks say that Italy is the objective.

5. CHEESE finds that it is difficult to sort out all these rumours because he has to rely, outside of Cairo, entirely upon the hearsay of his own and *Amie*'s friends.

6. In view of recent events, it is now essential that he shall be able to travel around himself so he can assess the value of all this talk of operations in the Levant.

7. His usefulness is at an end unless he has funds which must be fairly substantial.

CHEESE's naval source could give news of landing craft and supplies going by sea from Alexandria to Tobuk and Benghazi. The RASC officer 'could talk of the supply situation, difficulties, plans and give identifications (this source should be important because the supply problem is bound to be uppermost in the enemy's mind).'

The wounded LRDG NCO could give indications of a flank attack and news from Kufra district. SIME also concluded that ROPE should make a practice of visiting the wounded in the hospitals, and that CHEESE 'ought meet his old friends in bars while looking for work and not appear too keen and must not be brought up to such a boil as he was recently'.

CHEESE also had a wide number of casual contacts, such as an

Egyptian technician who remarked to him about an advertisement in a newspaper concerning a factory at Shoubra; a Greek sergeant pilot who was being taught to fly Mosquitos; a colonel visiting a Civil Affairs office who commented that there would not be an invasion of Greece this year; an officer in the Indian Division, destined for Italy, which he thought was about to embark; a Merchant Navy officer who mentioned ships assembling at Durban for a voyage to perhaps Crete; a Greek friend who claimed that Free French agents in Alexandria were contacting French sailors in Alexandria who were preparing for an attack on Italy; that many ships were docked in Alexandria, and the Hampshire Regiment had arrived from Malta; a Greek officer said a Parachute Brigade was moving from Kabrit to join the 8th Army; some supporters of General de Gaulle had predicted the invasion of Italy on 11 November; a drunk Australian was rejoining his regiment at Kabrit, and other Australian soldiers talked of an Australian division in Palestine; a Free French sergeant under the command of General Leclerc's 21st Battalion de Marche was moving to Tripoli; a Greek corporal from the 1st Brigade had arrived from Syria where he had undergone mountain training, and said his unit was part of the 3rd Corps in Syria.

Because CHEESE based himself in Cairo, few of his reports necessarily concerned the war at sea, and any reporting from Alexandria of the Suez Canal entailed considerable danger and required the closest liaison with the Naval Intelligence Division. The central and eastern Mediterranean was an area of absolutely vital strategic importance, with Malta in the frontline as the Royal Navy's base for submarine operations designed to disrupt Axis shipping destined for Libyan ports supporting the Afrika Korps. Similarly, the Suez Canal was a lifeline for the Empire, shortening the sea-routes to the Far East, so the Allies regarded any information being passed to enemy as being potentially very sensitive. Three messages in particular were considered critical, and the first, CHEESE's 423rd transmission, sent in January 1945 at a time when he was supposedly convalescing in the port, included sightings at Alexandria of two cruisers and five destroyers; that there were more freighters in port than usual; that there was still plenty of traffic between Greece and Alexandria; that nothing had been heard of transports from Gibraltar; and that a chequerboard had often been spotted. A second message, his 428th, reported plenty of activity in the port and the embarkation the previous week of an Indian battalion with an emblem of a goat. He also mentioned the sign of the local naval headquarters as a ship with a white sail on a black and blue background. Another sign noted was a camel on a chequerboard, and he observed a large number of black colonial troops. The third signal, the 432nd in the series, and his very last transmission, described five cruisers, six destroyers, fifty cargo ships and a large liner at their moorings, on 2 January 1945. He also speculated that most of the sea traffic was with Greece and India, and identified the black troops previously mentioned as having come from South Africa.

Five of CHEESE's messages simply repeated information that had been published in the newspaper, the cuttings including articles on a visit by General Alexander to Syria, Palestine, Jordan and Cyprus; that the Allied air forces had come under the command of General Carl Spaatz; references to General Doolittle as chief of Bomber Command; and the appointment of Alan Cunningham as chief of ground support. He also mentioned references to diesel engines being used on the Mersa-Capuzzo line, two reports about a visit made by General Wilson to Ankara, and an announcement that commercial shipping between Egypt and Turkey would resume shortly. On one occasion, in early 1945, CHEESE said he had encountered a British officer of the 5th Division who had been on leave. After a conversation with him, CHEESE concluded that the 5th Division was not in Egypt. In similar circumstances a New Zealand NCO remarked that most of New Zealand's troops had gone home, although some had been sent to Italy.

CHEESE's military reporting was wide-ranging but much of it related to his observations of unit insignia, a very useful method of developing an order-of-battle. For example, he identified particular badges seen at Abbassia with specific components, so he said the yellow camel was GHQ; a white unicorn was the 15th Armoured Division, the green fig-leaf as belonging to 3 Corps, and a seal on a globe, the 12th Army; that he thought the sign of the New Zealand 6th Division was a Kiwi bird with other troops simply bearing the words 'New Zealand'; the head of a blue bird in flames associated with the Royal Electrical and Mechanical Engineers. He also said there were still many Greek troops in Alexandria. In other individual messages he reported in April 1944 that Sofoklis Venizelos had formed a transition government, that there were still many Greek troops in Alexandria; and that following a visit of Soviet personnel the Bulgarian section of the Civil Affairs branch would close as the Russians were to take responsibility for Bulgaria.

In more general, low-level reporting, CHEESE picked up casual gossip and described how a Greek had recently arrived from Syria; that some American officers expected an imminent British attack on Derba; that a Greek naval officer had talked about the British fleet at Gibraltar which had been deployed in a feint to the west to cover an impending attack on Crete, and who claimed that most of the Greek navy was now based at Kabrit and Port Said. CHEESE was adept at picking up disparate items opportunistically, and examples included a 78th Division officer who was a member of the London Irish regiment which, he said, was a part of the Irish Brigade; a Jewish officer in the Polish Army who asserted that the 'English had arrested at Alexandria several Jews who were organising riots to take place during Pan-Arab congress. The Jews meet in a club, the president of which is a lieutenant in the British navy.'

This sort of material was intended to support CHEESE's bona-fides, bolster the enemy's confidence in him and even the most innocuous morsel of gossip might have a special significance for enemy analysts who, essentially, were being invited to draw some very faulty conclusions from the misleading information with which they had been provided. Some of these items were of no great strategic significance, but were part of the 'pocket litter' of espionage, the tiny background details that served to authenticate the larger picture. Thus, a Greek staff officer confided that 'news of the evacuation of Athens would be the signal for larger scale landings in Greece which would take place any minute'. Also, a staff officer at GHQ mentioned that 'General Laycock, Commander-in-Chief of the commandos, was here on his way to India'.

One of CHEESE's most prolific sources was ELIF who provided material for eleven messages. In his first he reported that two aircraft carriers in Alexandria had departed through the Suez Canal on exercises but their escort destroyers were still in the harbour. He had bought shares in the Bank of Athens which he thought would rise in value after the Allied invasion of the Balkans; he noticed that restaurants were full of English and Greek troops; that the 2nd Greek Brigade had been at Amriya during the rebellion; that the 1st Greek Brigade had been deployed to the desert so a purge could be conducted; that the same unit had left Amriya for the Lebanon where it would be joined by a newly-reorganised 1st Greek Brigade. In one quite long signal he was reported as having observed plenty of troops from the London Division in Alexandria, and had seen RAF trucks towing trailers carrying large wooden crates. He also claimed to have seen two cruisers in port, including HMS *Birmingham*, accompanied by three destroyers and five corvettes. On 7 June he said that the entire port had been obscured by a smoke-screen, and finally noticed that plenty of troops in Alexandria wore unit insignia bearing a black cat and a green tree.

A Merchant Navy officer contributes to just three messages. He was reported as having speculated that 'we are on the verge of important events'; that from mid-June there would be major troop movements from Egyptian ports; and that two aircraft carriers had left Alexandria on manoeuvers through the Suez Canal.

A South African corporal who had been exercising with the 8th Armoured Division provided the content of four messages and disclosed the authentic news that General Wilfred Lloyd had been killed in an air accident. He had also mentioned that the South African troops at Heinan were infantry, and not part of his Division. His last report indicated that he was in Italy with his unit.

The wife of a security officer was helpfully indiscreet and revealed that the Allies were about to impose travel restrictions across the Middle East, and especially on Syria's border with Turkey. Her husband had recently returned from Syria where there had been plenty of troops, including an English armoured regiment. She also said that her husband hoped for leave after an imminent attack had been executed. Later she reported that her husband had told her that the frontier restrictions had been relaxed, and that 'several groups of German PoWs will be repatriated through Turkey'.

A major serving in the 4th Airborne Division based in Palestine, a unit that had its insignia of a winged horse replaced with a parachute bearing black wings. He mentioned that his division was in Tobruk, then was reported as going to Alexandria to rejoin his unit which was to soon embark.

A source described only as 'an American from the desert' was responsible for four messages, the first mentioning General Andrews in Cairo. He also spoke indiscreetly about forty US transport aircraft delivered to the 8th Army, and in another signal described how the British had adopted a tactic of drawing German tanks onto Allied minefields, and suggested that many troops had left the Delta for deployment in the desert. He alleged that the Afrika Korps had been drawn into a trap previously warned of by CHEESE, and predicted a British attack in the desert in November.

CHEESE's circle of friends appeared to be mainly Greek and they discussed many military topics, such as tanks leaving the Canal Zone for Palestine; speculation about a new armoured division with Greek officers and NCOs that was to undergo special training in Syria; that the defeat at Tobruk had prevented the British from launching a planned assault on Crete; that Greek troops had recently left Kabrit; of an invasion of Crete set for October or November; of a Greek brigade in Alexandria; and news of a Greek brigade in the desert; and of special training at Kabrit.

A casual acquaintance in Alexandria told CHEESE that he had noticed less traffic on a desert road, and seen many Greek soldiers in the port. A Greek merchant friend was credited with the news that there were troops in Palestine wearing black berets. A French sailor claimed there were many small troop transports in the harbour at Alexandria, and he had encountered members of the Queen's Regiment on leave, some Greek aviators and soldiers from Australia. A Greek soldier had asserted that Greek troops were only sent to the front for training. And a group of Greek contacts opined that the departure of the Greek Brigade from Kabrit meant the planned attack on Crete would be postponed until September, and disclosed that no assault on Crete could take place until the training at Kabrit had been completed.

A journalist, codenamed SYRIAN, gave CHEESE two useful political items in early 1945. One was that relations between ministers had broken down to the extent that Marram had threatened to resign; the other was the news that there was to be a pan-Arab conference held in Egypt later in the year to which the leaders of all Arab countries would be invited.

Other items came from radio broadcasts, such as the news that

General Sir Bernard Paget had replaced General Wilson, and sheer rumour, and that there was talk in the port that 'several battleships including an aircraft carrier' had sailed south.

As 'A' Force's confidence grew, there were many, many more 'unconscious sources' who were not formally part of CHEESE's network, but inadvertently gave him useful tit-bits. A journalist who had been with Tito's partisans in Yugoslavia had replaced John Talbot, the Reuter's correspondent who had been taken prisoner with two photographers in June 1944. He said he was now attached to 3 Corps HQ, and was going to Alexandria. A London Scottish officer in the London Division mentioned he was joining 168 Brigade; an RB officer belonging to the 15th Motor Division was responsible for another report about the 33rd Motor Brigade. An 10th Armoured Brigade officer based at Suez worked on the staff of 3 Corps, to which his brigade belonged, was going to Alexandria to join the rest of his staff. A Greek officer had been on a course recently to learn English methods of extracting information from enemy PoWs; a 46th Division officer remarked that he would be leaving Alexandria in two weeks' time. A New Zealand nurse stated that the New Zealand troops in Cairo belonged to the 6th New Zealand Division. An 8th Armoured Division officer based in Cyrenaica said he had been in Kabrit for the past two weeks. A Gloucester Hussars officer who had been in Tobruk talked about the town's barrage balloons and claimed that a South African brigade was there, and that parachute troops were expected shortly.

Between 29 April and 10 September 1943 CHEESE sent seventy messages to Bari, of which five came from his 'ESR friend': Commando training centre in the Canal area; Commando training centre on the Little Bitter Lake: landing exercises; Passenger traffic to be restricted from 17 July; Troops embarked at Suez; Troops returned to Suez.

Two Greek officers in CHEESE's office who joined the ATB from Syria provided five messages: one was a captain working on Greek statistics; Transfer of Greek troops from Syria postponed; Captain on leave. Future plans delayed until Captain back from Syria; Greek division to be transferred soon.

A Greek interpreter friend is working at Divisional HQ. Leave expires 20 June. Possible date of invasion; Working at 56th Division HQ; arrival of Greek Division delayed.

During this period MISANTHROPE was busy, and contributed the content of nine messages:

> United Nations Parade. Greek armoured cars. Greek Division arriving from Syria; (from Alexandria) all invasion plans postponed; From Alexandria: Two battleships and one aircraft-carrier at Alexandria; (from ALEX) warships leave Alexandria; (from Alexandria) *Warspite* at Alexandria. (through a Greek officer) 1st Greek Brigade is in Syria; (through a South African corporal) 6th South African Armoured Division is in the Delta; de Gaullist troops have left Tobruk westwards; Major of airborne unit is on leave from Palestine.

CHEESE himself reported having observed:

> A convoy with GO in white on green circle; Increase of troops in Cairo; Decrease of troops in Cairo; New staff HQ in Antikhana; Troops with red berets and 'Airborne' on sleeve; Greek battleship at Port Said; Anti-aircraft guns in Canal area; Canadian aviators in Cairo; Armoured cars and lorries in Cairo. Totem white cross in blue circle with black horse. Greek drivers, returning to Kasaassine to refit.

Between 1 January and 29 June 1944 CHEESE transmitted a total of sixty-eight messages, of which eleven were identified as having been personal observations. In this category came

> The black cat sign of the London Division is in Alexandria; Sign of black cat

and white chequerboard; Many troops in Alexandria of the London Division and some wearing the sign of a green tree; Two large and three small cruisers, several destroyers and fifty mercantile ships; The King's Birthday Parade: The London Division including the London Scottish and Irish. Officer was heard to say probably last appearance in Cairo of the London Division. Units of the 15th Motor Division, 8th Armoured Division, GO sign, South Africans and New Zealanders; Indians and Australian Air Force; Still many Poles in Cairo; Many English troops disembarked at Alexandria; An officer in the 4th Division has been in Egypt one and a half months. Sign: quarter of a circle. Another division arrived with his. Order of Governate of Benghazi saying Arabs must be engaged urgently for construction of aerodromes in Cyrenaica. Trucks painted green and brown and bearing sign of white unicorn. Convoy of anti-aircraft guns going to Alexandria, painted brown and green. Order in office asking for officers speaking Bulgarian or Russian; Many Americans at Paynefield Aerodrome.

A further eleven messages were attributed to information gleaned from CHEESE's 'ESR friend'. He commented on such subjects as

An increase of military movement towards Tobruk; Think 10 English Armoured Division is at Suez; Military moves towards Egypt from Palestine; A division arrives from India at Suez; A division arrived from India is English and has sign of yellow hammer in a black circle; Movement towards Palestine including light and heavy anti-aircraft artillery and numbers of RAF trucks. Railway wagons at Suez to transport tanks to Port Said by 10 June. Tanks not arriving at Port Said till the end of June; Tanks belong to the 10th Armoured Division now to be at Port Said by 26 June; Lot of maritime activity at Suez.

Under the grouping 'learned in the office', CHEESE reported that 'General Paget has been to Cyrenaica and Mersa Matruh, Visited air troops at Gambit and armoured troops at Tobruk, also Greek sailors. Read order for officer to go overseas; going to HQ 16 Corps, he thinks destination will be India.'

Between 8 July and 28 December 1944 CHEESE sent fifty-five messages, most based on his own views, among them reports such as 'Have not seen 3 Corps here for some time; I think 15 Division has left Cairo but sometimes see trucks at Abbassia bearing sign of the white unicorn; I think HQ of 11th Army still here as we still see sign of seal balancing globe in the town; Have not seen sign of chequerboard for a long time. Increase in number of English soldiers here, most wear sign of yellow axe; No longer see sign of 3 Corps here, think it must have left; Speculation running high in office and town following Turkey's rupture of relations with the Reich; Signs of yellow axe and yellow hammer seen in Cairo, yellow axe is sign of 78th English Division; Head of Civil Affairs Bureau returned here after a tour of Libya; Think the airborne division may be English but contains Indian units; Have not noticed any reduction in numbers of New Zealand and South African troops here. I think 6 New Zealand and 7 South African Divisions still in Egypt; Among officers who took part in conference with General Paget were Generals Stone, Scobie and McConnell. Air Marshal Park and Admiral Rawlings; Several trucks in town bearing sign of 15th Division; At HQ yesterday three trucks with sign of head of red elephant on blue square; Section of my office which deals with former Italian islands is about to complete preparations for leaving; Number of British officers wearing sign of "Y"; Not seen sign of 8th Armoured Division for a long time; No longer see here sign of yellow axe but have recently seen several trucks with sign of white unicorn; See no more Poles in Cairo; Section which deals with Greek islands has left my office but is still in Egypt; Have heard nothing of an Indian Armoured Division; Only see few Indian troops here; Think HQ 3 Corps has left Egypt for Italy; The King has dismissed cabinet of Nahas from power and Ahmed Naher has formed a coalition cabinet; Much emotion in Greek circles following German evacuation of Athens; Heard nothing of battleships at Alexandria; Seen several English officers wearing sign of gold star on red and blue square. This is emblem of GHQ India; Seen Royal Artillery officer wearing flash "cinque ports" on sleeve; Think airborne division no longer in the Middle East as the parachutist sign not seen here now.'

Finally, there was the last tranche of signals, twelve of which were transmitted between 2 January and 10 February 1945. In his very last signal CHEESE reported that 'shipping between Turkey and Egypt will soon start again.' Thereafter, the channel fell silent, leaving the Abwehr completely in the dark about the fate of their master-spy.

CHAPTER FIVE

OPERATION HATRY

S IME's efforts to support CHEESE financially proved very frustrating, but the ingenious solution eventually decided upon was Operation HATRY, a scheme inspired by the financial conman Clarence Hatry who was imprisoned in London in 1929 and credited with being the catalyst for the crisis of confidence which resulted in the Wall Street Crash a few days later. SIME's version of HATRY was considered likely to be plausible to the Abwehr, and one based on a similar dilemma in London where a double agent codenamed TATE had run low on funds and had been replenished by the appropriately named Plan MIDAS, the expedient of having a Jewish intermediary circumvent the currency regulations by passing cash locally to a nominee when a similar sum had been deposited in his account abroad, in his case in the United States. HATRY, named after the famous financial fraudster, called for virtually the same model. An unscrupulous Jewish merchant in Cairo, Henri Cohen, was identified by CHEESE as a suitable candidate for the transaction, although the execution of the plan proved very complex.

The background was that CHEESE was essentially a mercenary and had been risking his life since his original recruitment by Levi in April 1941 when he had received £150, and he had been asking for further funds since 28 June 1941. His sixth message, on 14 August 1941, was a request for financial support, but all efforts to pass him the money had failed, and one of those attempts had resulted in the loss of a submarine, the *U-372* in August 1942.

The destruction of an entire U-boat employed by the Abwehr as a means of funding an individual spy, whatever his importance, must have been a heavy blow for both the Kreigsmarine, which was prevented from learning anything about the circumstances of the sinking through the deliberate isolation of the crew who were kept in quarantine for the remainder of the war, and for the Abwehr, which suffered the loss of a trusted courier and the money he was carrying. However, in December 1942 there was renewed evidence that the Abwehr had found a replacement courier, for earlier in the month CHEESE had been given 27 December as a firm delivery date, and on 4 January 1943 was promised that the courier would be in Cairo 'in the next few days'.

Paradoxically, because CHEESE had acquired employment at OETA, the pressure on him had been relieved somewhat as he now allegedly had a regular source of income, but nevertheless SIME was keen to learn more about the courier, and suspected that the man might be GULL, an agent who was already known to James Robertson. Based on a very casual interview he conducted on 3 January, GULL had a legitimate excuse for travelling to Istanbul where, according to TRIANGLE, he had been of interest to the Abwehr. Robertson judged GULL to be just a little too 'glib' in his cover story, and strongly suspected him to be the Abwehr's chosen route based on his personal communications which had been routinely intercepted by censorship.

> Without being directly questioned, he produced an explanation for the
> ambiguous telegrams which have been intercepted. Nothing in his story
> however excludes the possibility of his having been recruited by the

Abwehr for delivery of the money to CHEESE. He knows Cairo; his business cover is satisfactory. He is known to have expressed anti-British feelings while in Istanbul. It seems a likelihood that the Abwehr (whom we know from the reports of TRIANGLE to have had at least some interest in him) would have profited from the opportunity presented by his passage through Turkey to Egypt. It may be mentioned finally that, if there had been one flaw in his cover story, it is that it was too glibly told. GULL wishes to return to Istanbul.

Unfortunately, SIME faced an additional problem at the 'mousetrap', the flat at 20 Rue Galal, the site chosen by CHEESE for the money-drop, where the building was of such a nature that, according to the BGM, it would have been quite easy for the packet to be delivered to a different apartment. As SIME observed in a memo:

(a) The BGM reports that the topographical situation at 20 Rue Galal, is such that the money may possibly be delivered at the wrong flat. (b) If this happens the notional story to be told by CHEESE is simply that the money has not arrived. (c) Alternatively, the courier (or his agent) in doubt as to his address, may decide to leave his mission uncompleted. In this event the courier may cause enquiries to be made at 20 Rue Galal, though this is unlikely.

Furthermore, the block was inhabited by mainly Greeks and Italians, many of whom were thoroughly anti-British. SIME felt that if the courier could not be absolutely certain of identifying the correct flat he probably would not endanger himself by making enquiries, but would report his dilemma to the Abwehr, by which time SIME would have recommended a new address, thereby solving the problem.

SIME had taken considerable precautions to allow the money-drop to take place, and briefed MISANTHROPE on 11 October 1942 about the need to enable the transaction in preference to arresting any intermediary or courier. It was explained that

> to arrest the courier, while leaving possible accomplices at large, would give warning to the latter and at the same time cause them to suspect the integrity – perhaps even the existence – of Paul Nicosoff. She will therefore be told that, although she will have to prepare herself by learning the following 'part', it will be her role not willingly to reveal information about herself or Paul, but rather to remain constantly on the defensive. This will be naturally explained by the extreme nervousness of both herself and Paul. She will refer more than once to the recent execution of five Axis agents in Aleppo; she may also mention the arrest of two German spies on a houseboat and the spate of arrests they brought in their train.
>
> If pressed to introduce the courier to Paul, she will quote explicit instructions from him against this, and will plead his great nervousness. She will also advance the argument that a meeting between Paul and the courier would double the danger for both – as in fact it would.

SIME's plan for the meeting between CHEESE's representative and the Abwehr's courier were planned to the last detail:

> Rendezvous is the Café Bel Air on the Pyramids Road. The BGM (playing the part of the '*amie*') will be recognisable to the courier by the fact of her wearing a white costume with [a] red belt, and carrying a red handbag. Courier will also be in possession of a description of her. The agreed password will be exchanged. The enemy has been asked for a description of the courier.
>
> The BGM will be instructed in accordance with the brief already drawn up (of 11 October 1942) with such addenda as may have subsequently become necessary. This will be the responsibility of Captain Robertson. Details of the action to be taken by her at the rendezvous and subsequently will be imparted to her by Lieutenant-Colonel Jenkins or Captain Robertson – but

in any event after full consultation with the latter officer. At 2000 hrs on the agreed date the BGM will install herself at a table in the Café Bel Air. She will arrive in a taxi, which will wait outside. The chauffeur and his companion will be agents of DSO.

As a fallback, SIME anyway went through the motions of recruiting GULL as an ordinary agent, remaining entirely silent about the suspicions concerning his true role.

If the courier is GULL, he will have been briefed by us with a military questionnaire which should effectively eradicate from the minds of the Germans any idea that we may suspect GULL, or have any knowledge of his mission, or of the intended recipient of the money.

Thus, on 24 December, the Abwehr informed CHEESE that it had been impossible to change the agreed arrangements, and that the courier intended to make the delivery on Sunday 27 December. This turn of events led SIME to speculate that the courier had left Turkey before he could be warned, or perhaps that there was another network in Cairo already which had been entrusted with the task. In any circumstances it was thought likely that the courier might employ a 'conscious or unconscious Egyptian messenger' to make the final delivery, the moment of greatest vulnerability. The situation was further complicated by the unconnected police raid which had scared off CHEESE and left SIME wondering about how to handle the new tenant, Pietro Fuimo, and his family. Should they be indoctrinated into the operation and told to receive the Abwehr's package of money? In the end, Robertson opted to instruct Fuimo to accept any packet from a stranger and receive a gratuity of £30 for his trouble but, as it happened, nobody turned up. Fuimo, who had been interned for fifteen months as an enemy alien, had been released in

January 1942 because of 'his intense anti-Fascist feelings'. Nevertheless, in September 1942, Robertson contemplated his re-internment as a security precaution to prevent any leakage relating to Nicossof, whom he briefed about under the alias 'Paul Orloff', the name under which he could receive letters at the National Hotel.

On 6 January 1943 CHEESE announced that he had found a much better money drop, at Souk el Tewfikieh 6. Specifically, the address was apartment 16, on the fourth floor, with an entrance next to the Café Soleil where a flat had been rented, at additional cost to him, by his *amie*, who would take up residence there on 14 January.

A further, unexpected complication occurred when the BGM, destined for her walk-on part as MISANTHROPE, genuinely fell ill in March 1943, and announced that 'her services would not be available until at least April'. This problem arose just when the Abwehr had instructed CHEESE to keep the flat at Souk el Tewfikieh 6, a demand that SIME had suggested 'may be taken to indicate that a further attempt will be made to deliver the money'. These two challenges led James Robertson to set out the options:

- Plan 1: To recruit a person either (a) male to play the part of a friend of CHEESE or (b) female to play the part of CHEESE's '*amie*' who will be fully instructed in the part he or she has to play (including, necessarily, the whole story of CHEESE) and who will thus be qualified to answer questions about CHEESE and, if necessary, to frequent the company of the enemy courier and his acquaintances.

- Plan 2: SIME Special Section propose the following plan. (a) A person known to DSO Egypt, but not known by the uninitiated to have any connection with him, to be selected. (b) The address of this person to be communicated to the enemy who will be informed that CHEESE has a reliable friend to whom a message can be delivered, but who knows nothing of CHEESE's activities on behalf of the Abwehr. This intermediary will, in fact, will be little more than a human 'postbox'.

PROs and CONs:

PLAN 1.

PRO: This plan provides protection against any attempt by the enemy to use the 'money-intermediary' as a means of verifying the genuineness of CHEESE.

CON:
(a) It involves a considerable rick to security in that it necessitates placing a person outside the 30 Committee organisation in full knowledge of the true CHEESE situation.

(b) It is not necessary or in accordance with the notional CHEESE story, for the intermediary who receives the money to give away much (if any) information about CHEESE. CHEESE's nervousness and anxiety to conceal his whereabouts and identity have been made clearly apparent. It is therefore more in keeping with the notional picture of him that he should keep the intermediary as far as possible in the dark about himself, and that (fearing a British trap – especially after the police raid on 20 rue Galal) he should also instruct the intermediary to avoid answering questions.

(c) There can be no certainty as to the particulars of CHEESE given to the Abwehr by Renato Levi. Even if Levi's description of CHEESE given to Zaehringer was as he told us it would be, there can be no knowing what he has said since. It follows that in authorising the intermediary to give a description of CHEESE, some risk must be run that this will be entirely at variance with a description given by the inventive Levi at any time since his visit to Egypt.

(d) The qualifications required in any person who is to play the part of CHEESE's friend are so high as to be almost unobtainable. The BGM must be regarded as an exception not to be repeated. Their requirements are: firstly, absolute discretion, even when possibly kept idle and impatient over a long period; secondly, very considerable cover of memory, resources and acting ability. The finding of such a person cannot be guaranteed. The BGM has herself been asked for some time to look out for a suitable person, but has failed to produce one.

(e) Even if found, an agent earmarked for this purpose cannot be used for any other intelligence work, owing to the risk of compromise in the event of the enemy messenger (or his deputy) having been resident in Egypt for some time and thus having the opportunity to obtain information about the agent – either before or after the delivery of the money.

(f) If once the intermediary submits to being questioned, he or she may then inevitably may be drawn into further meetings with the enemy courier and his circle. The danger of CHEESE being unmasked will be directly proportional to the frequency of contacts between the intermediary and the enemy courier or his associates.

PLAN 2

PRO:
(a) Simplicity
The factual and the notional story in regard to the intermediary are almost identical; in such case he is told by a friend to accept delivery of a package, to inform the friend of delivery, to answer no questions, and to ask none.

(b) Security
From the 30 Committee point of view, the intermediary will have no

knowledge of the real significance of the apparently simple task he has to perform.

(c) Security from the point of view of both CHEESE and the enemy

The exchange of an agreed password (which CHEESE should ask for – compare Café Bel Air scheme of October–November 1942) will ensure the safety of the transaction, which should be equally unwelcome to both CHEESE and to the enemy courier.

(d) Fidelity in the notional picture of CHEESE

(See Paragraph (b) under PLAN 1, 'CON' above.)

FINAL DECISION

The 30 Committee has already given a ruling against the recruitment of fleshly bodies to represent the notional characters who feature in the life-stories of special agents. The question is now open to a final decision, in the light of the above PROs and CONs.

The last straw was a ruling by the 30 Committee that the introduction of 'fleshly bodies' to substitute for notional agents carried an unacceptable risk of leakage, so the whole scheme was abandoned.

A few months later the SIS station in Istanbul shed further light on this episode when Nicholas Elliott on 10 May 1943 reported that one of his informants had revealed the contents of a letter dated 16 April which the source had read on 5 May, concerning the delivery of E£415 to a certain ARMAVIR at 20 Rue Golol in Cairo. According to Elliott's contact, the person pressing for the delivery was a Swiss. Elliott, evidently unaware of SIME's previous adventures in the Rue Golol, offered to let his man act as an intermediary, confident that the

Swiss would not press him for details of precisely how he intended the money to reach Egypt.

On 15 May Elliott elaborated that he had been approached by an Armenian businessman who claimed to act as an intermediary for an established Abwehr network in Cairo and Alexandria, and alleged that the Cairo cell was 'in wireless communication with Istanbul thence to Berlin'. His direct contact was a man he was only prepared to identify as 'the Swiss' who, he believed, was subordinate to the German naval attaché, von der Marwitz. He had been asked to pass E£415 to a certain ARMAVIR at 'Madame MARIE, Cairo, Rue Golol 20, stated to be in the neighbourhood of Neiogan Tawgig.'

The Armenian went on to say that the chosen courier, using the route Gaziantepe–Aleppo–Egypt, was a priest whom he had met on 5 May upon his return from the Middle East, and who had produced a letter written on a piece of linen he cut from his coat. The Armenian, who wanted E£2,000 plus further large sums for more information, offered the note to Elliott who had it copied, and it was dated 'Alexandria, 20 April 1943' and appeared to be an accounting for E£6,250.

Elliott's enquiries in Istanbul suggested that the priest was probably an Italian missionary, Filippo Talvacchia, who had arrived in the city on 4 May on an Italian passport, No. 6280, and had stated that he had left Italy on 29 January. According to the Armenian, he would travel again on or about 17 May, carrying a letter addressed to NAHICHEVAN.

At a further meeting, on 17 May, Elliott's informant revealed that he had learned of two other bank transfers arranged by an Armenian cloth importer, M. Harliyah, to a recipient named Habib. One had occurred on about 15 December for £1,000, and the other on 20 January for £500, through the National Bank of Egypt in Cairo.

On 25 May Elliott had more to report:

Swiss has given INFAMOUS $1,700, the equivalent of £415. On return of courier from Aleppo INFAMOUS is to hand money to him. Courier will then return money to certain ABBAS who is organisation's paymaster in Middle East. ABBAS (who is probably identical with the second courier) … will arrange transfer of this money to ARMAVIR. Most important, latter's name not known to source. ABBAS has account Ottoman Bank Aleppo and INFAMOUS believes money will be transferred by him probably to Cairo. INFAMOUS considers reason Swiss has decided to send money by courier is that he has thereby been able to make substantial personal profit on our money exchange.

On the assumption that this information was true, it appeared that the Abwehr had succeeded in finding a method of sending cash to Cairo disguised as ostensibly innocent commercial transactions, so SIS set about recruiting Harliyah, who was suitably opportunistic to seize the chance of making plenty of money. His price proved too steep for SIS, but as a sign of his goodwill and capabilities he confided enough detail to Elliott about his past activities to enable SIS to confirm that he had indeed orchestrated the transfers already discovered. Elliott promised to seek advice about Harliyah's proposal, without letting slip the fact that he had already checked his credentials, and then dropped the issue.

Meanwhile, SIME in Cairo was hatching HATRY, an ingenious plot which involved a merchant in Cairo, Henri Cohen, releasing E£1,400 to a nominee in August 1943 once his contact in Istanbul, Emile Nicolesco, had confirmed receipt of the equivalent sum. In effect this manoeuver enabled Cohen to transfer a large sum of money to a neutral country, something that the Egyptian currency restrictions prevented him from doing legitimately. The scheme had the added advantage that it did not require the employment of any courier or intermediary whose behaviour might draw suspicion from the British authorities.

On 28 August 1941 the Abwehr promised £2,000 and thereafter there were further assurances, but in reality nothing was received during 1942 and it was not until March 1943 that eventually a delivery was made, but to the wrong address. This underlying security served to sap CHEESE's confidence, and prevented him from devoting his talent and energy to the espionage business. As James Robertson noted with some eloquence,

> Continued lack of funds was felt on the one hand to be hampering CHEESE as a spy, since not only was he unable to travel, but he was even unable to spend money on the entertainment of individuals of a type likely to supply him with information, while on the other his position was being endangered by the increasing improbability that he would in reality continue to work for an indefinite period without reward. It was therefore decided that since it appeared that the enemy was unable to work out a plan for the payment of this valuable agent, SIME would be obliged to take the initiative and prepare a method by which the agent could receive his just reward. The result of this decision was the institution of Plan HATRY which was launched at the end of August and put into effect by the Abwehr in mid-November, the delay between that date and the actual receipt of the money in January 1944 being due to circumstances beyond SIME's control.
>
> For the effective execution of Plan HATRY, which is based on a normal, black market transaction carried out in Istanbul, we were to some extent indebted to a SIME agent, GODSEND, who is himself a banker who dabbles from time to time in the inky waters of the international currency market, at considerable profit to himself. GODSEND was informed that we were anxious to investigate methods by which the Germans could effect payment to their agents in the Middle East and a notional suspect was put forward who had, we alleged, confided to another of our agents that he expected to receive funds from the enemy as a result of a private clearing transaction; we intended to make use of this transaction to provide concrete evidence

against the suspect and as a possible means of identifying other hostile agents. GODSEND informed us that such a transaction could easily be carried out since he himself knew a wealthy resident of Egypt named Cohen who was always ready to make use of any loopholes in the currency regulations for the purposes of transferring funds to his daughter in Switzerland.

GODSEND was therefore instructed to inform Cohen that he knew of a merchant who was willing to pay over a sum to the value of 30,000 Swiss francs in Istanbul against the counter value in Egyptian pounds. Upon receipt of this information Cohen wrote a letter to his agent in Istanbul (by name Nicolesco) dated 10 August 1943 telling him that he might expect a visit from a certain 'M Baron' who would pay over the sum of 30,000 Swiss francs (or a lesser sum) stating that it was 'for Andrea', this being the Christian name of Cohen's daughter. Nicolesco was to indicate that he had received this money by dispatching a telegram to Cohen offering a certain number of tons of decorticated almonds, the number of tons representing the number of thousands of Swiss francs paid in by M Baron. This letter was taken from Cohen by GODSEND on the plea that he knew a 'safe-hand' who would deliver it to Istanbul, and it was in fact delivered to Nicolesco through DSO Turkey on 24 August 1943.

Meanwhile, in an attempt to prevent Cohen and Nicolesco knowing too much of SIME's activities, the latter was instructed to inform the former that on receipt of Nicolesco's telegram he was to pay the money direct into the account of a cotton broker in Alexandria who was also cooperating with SIME and to whom a suitable tale had been told. In order to enable us to receive the money from the cotton broker without being obliged to have recourse to GODSEND, censorship were instructed to intercept all telegrams from Nicolesco to Cohen, but in point of fact both these arrangements failed in practice since GODSEND – unable to restrain his commercial instincts – took the money (plus a business commission) straight from Cohen and brought it to this office while censorship failed to intercept the vital telegram.

CHEESE passed the plan to the enemy in two messages on 30 August and

31 August respectively, stating that he had a friend who knew a financier who frequently bought Swiss francs in Istanbul for his daughter in Switzerland. The friend had arranged with the financier that the latter's agent Nicolesco should accept any sum up to thirty thousand Swiss francs from M Baron for Andrea and on receipt of a confirmatory telegram from Nicolesco would receive and pass to CHEESE the counter value of the sum paid in. He intimated that he would not be content with less than 25,000 Swiss francs and pointed out that no one, neither his friend nor the financier, realised that the affair was other than a private clearing agreement in payment of a debt.

The wheels of the Abwehr began to move on 6 September when they stated that the plan was being examined on 13 September, and on 15 September they asked for confirmation of Nicolesco's name and address, while on 30 September they stated that they hoped that the transfer would be effected soon and asked for confirmation of the name BARON and the words 'for Andrea'. At this stage matters became unduly protracted and owing to the fact that our wireless operator (CHEESE on the key) became seriously ill, and we were able to transmit at irregular intervals only. On 20 October we were told that arrangements were nearly complete and that the transfer would be made 'soon', and at our next contact on 5 November we pointed out that a fortnight did not coincide with our interpretation of that word!

Our operator's health then became worse and we were unable to transmit again until 10 December when a message from CHEESE stated that he was urgently in need of funds to meet his doctor's bill crossed with a message stating that the transfer had been carried out. We were unable again to transmit until 21 December and on that day CHEESE's message stating that the money had not yet reached him crossed with the most definite message we had as yet received from the Abwehr stating that the sum of 25,000 Swiss francs had been sent to Nicolesco against a written receipt dated 12 November.

A further factual complication arose at this stage in that GODSEND had gone to Palestine for Christmas and we had no way of contacting and questioning Cohen through him as to whether he had had any news from Nicolesco. CHEESE was therefore obliged to inform the enemy that he could not make any investigations into the non-arrival of the money pending the return of his friend in the early days of the new year.

GODSEND returned from Palestine on 3 January 1944 and contacted Cohen on our instructions the following day. The latter stated that he had received a letter from Nicolesco dated 6 November 1943 stating that he had not yet received the expected visit from 'M Baron' and had further received a telegram from his daughter at the end of November which, as it had included the phrase 'good news from Uncle Emile' he had assumed to mean that she had received money from Nicolesco, whose Christian name is Emile. GODSEND, knowing that Cohen had been absent from Cairo owing to ill health during most of November, asked him to investigate the files in his office to see if any telegram had arrived which he had not dealt with personally. It was then found that a telegram from Nicolesco on 10 November making an offer of twenty-five tons of decorticated almonds, i.e. indicating that he had received 25,000 Swiss francs. The particular significance of this telegram was of course unknown to the staff of Cohen's office who naturally realised that they were not interested in the purchase of almonds and then filed away the telegram. It was at this point that GODSEND exceeded his instructions and promptly extracted the counter value from Cohen amounting to E£1,400 plus an additional E£150 as banker's commission. He then brought the total sum to this office and stated that he himself would pay it into the cotton broker's account. After the delay he was informed that we would prefer to make this payment ourselves, and we finally took delivery of E£1,625 on 6 January, CHEESE informing the enemy that being the sum that he himself would have received at the current rates of exchange.

It is clear that had censorship been successful in intercepting the 'almond' telegram, CHEESE would have received his reward some six weeks earlier but in view of the fragmentary nature of his recent operations due to sickness, no great harm has been done and we have accomplished not only our primary object, the payment of CHEESE, but we have also opened the door for future payments either to CHEESE himself or to other agents under our control.

No sooner had the Abwehr's money arrived, which included payment intended for the SAVAGES too, than Raymund Maundell circulated ISLD and 'A' Force with a division of the spoils, issuing an invitation to collect each organisation's share from his personal safe. His statement for the distribution divided the loot into Sterling, gold, dollars and Egyptian pounds, which amounted to $8,600, £80 on Sterling, £30 in gold and E£1,400. Of this 10 per cent went to 'A' Force, 45 per cent was allocated to SIME and the remainder was retained.

Not surprisingly, in the opening weeks of 1944 there was an air of self-congratulation at SIME, with the end of the war in Europe eagerly anticipated. A manifestation of this atmosphere was a hugely entertaining letter dated 11 January from Rex Hamer addressed to Terence Robertson.

> I am instructed by Brigadier Clarke CBE to extend his congratulations to the Mad Hatter's Tea Party and to all persons who, working in the spirit of Clarence Hatry and under the guidance of the manifold involutions of the 30 Committee's collective genius have provided so brilliant an example of that system of relief and rehabilitation which upon an even grander scale will be one of the finest features of the future co-operation of the United Nations.
>
> The approvisionment of CHEESE after so prolonged a period of penury cannot but be the happiest augury for the future of your efforts and Brigadier Clarke will consider it his duty to recommend to Dr Smart-Alick that, at the next Narkover Speech Day, the 'Governor's Prize for Peculation and Financial Manipulation' be awarded to T. C. Robertson and the Sensburg-Kennenkuhn award for Practical Chemistry be granted to the Committee

Jointly (under the 'Cribbing and Combined Study' statute) for their successful laboratory work in 'producing and maintaining for over two years an odourless and inexpensive cheese'.

CHAPTER SIX

1943

S IME and ISLD had the benefit of a steady stream of interrogation reports from the Combined Services Detailed
Interrogation Centre (CSDIC), the organisation designated
as MI14, which screened recently captured enemy prisoners and used
a variety of techniques, including the employment of agents provocateur and concealed microphones, to extract useful information.
Another valuable source was Imperial Censorship which monitored
the mails and commercial cables.

To coordinate these disparate ventures was the Middle East
Intelligence Centre, headed by Illtyd Clayton, the Joint Intelligence
Committee (Middle East), and eventually the 30 Committee which
from March 1943, chaired by Oliver Thynne, supervised the region's
double agents, with five subcommittees based at various times in
Beirut (31 Committee), Baghdad (32 Committee, which included a
34 Committee in Tehran), Nicosia (33 Committee), Asmara, Tehran, Istanbul, Nairobi, Tripoli, and Algiers, and liaised closely with
'A' Force, the deception planners led by Dudley Clarke. In July 1942
Thynne was replaced by Michael Crichton, who was himself succeeded by Terence Kenyon in July 1943. A 31 Committee based

in Beirut would be chaired by a former headmaster, Rex Hamer, until July 1943 with a membership of John Wills, the 3rd Viscount Astor (from the Naval Intelligence Division), and Peter Chandor and Michael Ionides from ISLD. A 32 Committee in Baghdad was chaired by David Mure with support from the ISLD representative, Frank Giffey, who would be replaced by Reg Wharry. Altogether, some forty different double agents would be manipulated by the 30 Committee and its offshoots.

One of the major challenges to be addressed by these committees, which amounted to channels authorising the transfer of information (much of it authentic) to the enemy, was the issue of proportions. How much genuine material should be disclosed to sugar-coat the false? In February 1943 'A' Force undertook a study to assess CHEESE's relative veracity and reviewed the content of forty-two messages transmitted since October 1942. Of this total, only eight items were considered 100 perfect false, although a further eleven were more than 80 per cent untrue. For example, four items were sent in October 1942 which were completely untrue: 'Units of the 9th Australian Division were in the line; General Martel had passed through Cairo en route to Baghdad; General Casey had arrived from Iraq; Polish officers to Iran'. On the other hand, all the reported content of an OETA officer's desk diary, reported on 12 January 1943, was quite true.

> The above statistics in themselves can prove nothing. One of the reasons being that the percentage reality is only our estimate and consequently affected by bad memory and incomplete knowledge! Certain trends however emerge and are interesting. It must be borne in mind that no 'domestic' messages are included in the above analysis and that all domestic material is 100 per cent false. It appears that before and after putting over a 100 per cent falsehood we have usually given items with a high percentage of veracity. Although this is very reasonable and correct we should guard against too

obvious build-ups and reestablishments in future which on a close analysis by the enemy might look suspicious. The strong influence which CHEESE's notional story has upon the quality, and more particularly, the quantity of traffic is very noticeable. Although this may at times be a nuisance from the operational point of view, it is essential that the notional picture should be followed faithfully and with the greatest care. Care must be taken when CHEESE opens up again to maintain a steady flow of chicken-food which could be obtained from OETA sources. If and whenever possible a programme should be mapped out for CHEESE for about ten days ahead and based on the strategic addendum of 'A' Force instructions.

By June 1943, when Terence Robertson visited London and saw MI5's Guy Liddell, he reported that 'A' Force was running three double agents, being CHEESE and SAVAGES in Egypt, and a pair of Greek Cypriots codenamed LEMONS posing as refugees, and run by Philip Druiff in Cyprus. In fact the radio operator, LITTLE LEMON, who had a very pale appearance, had denounced his leader, BIG LEMON, to the British, and he was enrolled as a double agent. LITTLE LEMON continued to transmit deceptive information to the Germans until September 1944, and among his notional sources was a genuine troupe of chorus girls working in Nicosia cabarets, consisting of a Belgian codenamed MARIA; a Bulgarian, MARKI; a Romanian, SWING-TIT; an Austrian, TRUDI; and a Hungarian, GABBIE.

SAVAGES consisted of a Cypriot, who notionally was operating a transmitter from Cairo, and a pair of Greeks based in Cyprus, who had been arrested upon their arrival on the island in July 1942, the skipper of their boat having abandoned their original plan to sail to Syria. The Cypriot reported that he had found a job in the Allied Liaison Branch at GHQ in Cairo, a position that was intended to improve his status.

Liddell noted in his (redacted) diaries that whereas double agents in England often had a counter-intelligence purpose, to identify other enemy spies, those in the Middle East were run exclusively as a means of conveying deception. They

> were begun by ISLD [XXXXXXXXXXXXX] but their case officer was pro-
> vided by SIME and received (I speak at second-hand) far more assistance
> from DSO Syria than from any representative of ISLD in Syria. KISS was,
> I suppose, controlled by CICI, but his case officer was provided by SIME
> and the B Section of ISLD. The ISLD representative in Persia was incapa-
> ble of making any valuable contribution to his working. The guiding hand
> controlling all the double agents was Major Terence Robertson of SIME
> Special Section, and he, not ISLD, trained case offices for similar work
> in Italy and Greece. There were two ISLD agents, SMOOTH and CRUDE
> started by [XXXXXXX] and covering Syria well. But the most important
> agents were run by SIME representatives, namely DOLEFUL, handed over
> to DSO Turkey by the Turks, and BLACKGUARD, handed over to DSO
> Turkey by B Section ISLD representative in Istanbul (this may be wrong
> but he was certainly run by the Defence Security Officer). DOLEFUL con-
> tinued to work for the Turks and also most certainly for the Germans; and
> BLACKGUARD was used primarily to penetrate the Abwehr (ISLD's job)
> and might perhaps have been better run (ISLD certainly thought so). But
> the fact remains that DSO ran them, not ISLD.

KISS was the codename for an Iranian who had been recruited by the Abwehr before the war in Hamburg, but had been sent to Teh-ran on a mission and was denounced to Security Intelligence Middle East by BLACKGUARD, another Iranian who had been employed as an announcer on Radio Berlin. Unusually, KISS was run jointly by Combined Intelligence Centre Iraq (CICI) with their NKVD coun-terparts to pass deception material to the enemy, but collapsed in March 1945 because of Soviet suspicions.

Having volunteered to work for SIS, BLACKGUARD was sent to Istanbul by the Abwehr on a mission to recruit agents for assignments in Egypt, Persia and India. One of his coups, in July 1944, was to convey a transmitter to another double agent, FATHER, based in India. FATHER was a Belgian pilot, Henri Arents, who had been run as a double agent since his arrival in England from Lisbon in June 1941. In August 1944 he had been posted to Calcutta, and elaborate arrangements were made by the Abwehr to supply him with a transmitter, codenamed DUCK. The delivery was made through BLACKGUARD, and the radio link was established by a police radio operator, member of the Delhi Intelligence Bureau. During his February 1944 interrogation, Erich Vermehren confirmed that the Einz Marine branch of the Abwehr held this particular source in high regard.

DOLEFUL was Ahmed, a Turkish wagon-lits attendant on the Tagus Express who had been recommended by the Turkish Security Bureau. His entirely notional sub-source, SCEPTIC, was later identified by Vermehren as a trusted agent known to the Germans as HELMUTH.

SMOOTH was a Turkish customs officer in Antioch who supplied information to his German controllers allegedly supplied by HUMBLE, invented by Michael Ionides, who was the notional proprietor of a fruit and vegetable shop in Aleppo. In turn, HUMBLE supposedly was in touch with KNOCK, a salesman in medical supplies who travelled frequently to and from Iran and Iraq. SMOOTH was run by ISLD's Michael Ionides, who was able to use him to identify two important Abwehr spies in Alexandretta, Turkey: Paula Koch, then the matron of the German hospital in Beirut, and her Armenian brother-in-law Joseph Ayvazian, who was married to her younger sister. HUMBLE's performance was so good that the Germans authorised him to recruit two more sub-agents, WIT and WAIT.

Ionides also dreamed up ALERT, supposedly an orderly working in a British army who was motivated to spy for the Abwehr by the rape of his mother in the Great War by an Australian sergeant-major. ALERT sent his information in letters to CRUDE, a German source employed as a *kavas* (janitor) in the British consulate-general in Istanbul and codenamed HAZARD by the Abwehr.

Axis reliance on controlled sources increased in February 1943 when the DSO in Palestine arrested Ellie Haggar, the son of Egypt's chief of police, who had been studying in France in 1939 and had been recruited by the Abwehr. Betrayed by TRIANGLE, Haggar spent the remainder of the war in prison.

By November 1943, with his status restored but still ostensibly penniless, CHEESE succumbed to illness, and moved to Alexandria to convalesce, which gave 'A' Force the opportunity to expand the Cairo network that had been left in hands of MARIE, a member of Nicossof's Greek menage. Equally notional, MARIE was supposedly MISANTHROPE's '*amie* direct', a Greek woman aged about thirty, 'young enough to attract Allied officers and old enough to be steady from the espionage angle' and fluent in French with some English. Allegedly 'AD', as she was referred to, had met CHEESE some six months earlier while in the company of a British officer, and a few days later he had introduced himself to her when she was alone at Groppi's Americaine, the most popular bar in Cairo. He professed that she would prefer a Levantine like himself to a 'cold Anglo-Saxon' and although she already had 'a regular lover of local extraction to whom she remained faithful in thought though not in deed'.

Nicossof's plan was to recruit a new source in Alexandria and a SIME case officer. Captain G. R. C. Davis, recorded that

> he feels as far as finance is concerned that they owe him an answer. He will stress his need of money, but he will be inclined to wait and see what he gets on the next transmission before he really releases the considerable head of steam he has acquired during his sick leave. He is in two minds whether

to play up his illness to dispel any ideas the Germans may have that he is malingering or whether to trade as far as possible on the penniless situation in which he finds himself as a result of being ill. If he does the latter the Germans may think he is in fact malingering, when he is still keen but fed up with their incompetence.

The dilemma for SIME was how to properly interpret the Abwehr's demonstrable inability to fund their star source. CHEESE had successfully re-established himself as a source of proven reliability, yet the Germans had not found a channel to fund him. The contradiction was so manifest that SIME began to wonder whether its security apparatus was rather more efficient than they had dared hope.

It is possible that we underestimated the success of our security measures in the Middle East, and consequently underestimated the enemy's difficulties in getting, or even attempting to get, a large sum of money to a spy in Egypt.

By January 1944 MARIE had established herself as a useful sub-agent, her 'contacts with the members of the Allied forces have proved of considerable value as a source of information'. With CHEESE having recently received E£1,400 from the Abwehr, she was asked on 28 January to develop a network in Alexandria, and on 4 February she replied that she had visited Nicossof in Alexandria and he had agreed to consider the proposal. Her other mission, requested by the Abwehr, was that she should report on Vichy sailors around the port.

Initially CHEESE had been quite reluctant, acknowledging that a sub-source would require more money from the Germans, and raised several issues of security. A suitable candidate would have to travel frequently to Cairo to deliver his information if it was still to be relevant, and this could not be entrusted to the mail as CHEESE had no experience of secret ink. Having almost decided against the idea, CHEESE by chance encountered an old acquaintance in a café who had moved to Alexandria from Cairo, a businessman aged about forty who was 'an enthusiastic woman-chaser'. The two men met several times before CHEESE moved back to Cairo on 7 February and in his second transmission after his return, on 9 February, CHEESE described his nominee, whom he referred to as 'A', as a man who had espoused support for Germany's 'sincere will to create a New Order out of European chaos', and said he was due to meet him again on the following day. He advised on 11 February that 'A' would require 'substantial sums of money' but would take no further action until he had received his masters' approval.

The great Allied undertaking of 1943 was HUSKY, the invasion of Sicily for which a cover-plan, BARCLAY, was devised to keep the Germans persuaded of a continuing threat in the eastern Mediterranean, and specifically to provide evidence that the 12th Army was in Cairo, preparing for a move to Syria, and then the Balkans. The 12th Army, of course, was one of Clarke's inventions, and was alleged to comprise of twelve divisions, but in fact it was only ever five real divisions, with a further three, greatly inflated, divisions. Thus the 12th Army became one of 'A' Force's mainstays, and was accepted by the enemy. In February and March 1944, when three of its real divisions were sent to Italy, they were replaced by notional divisions, and by April the 12th Army consisted of just two divisions and three brigades but, according to the official historian Sir Michael Howard, 'none of them in any condition to take to the field'.

As well as the entirely fictitious reports generated by CHEESE, the plan was supported by some genuine troop deployments. The plan worked, to the extent that the German reinforced the Balkans with an additional ten divisions, and when the landings happened in Sicily there were only two German divisions there, which were taken entirely by surprise.

In a review of CHEESE's contribution to BARCLAY, dated 25 March 1944, 'A' Force reported to SIME's Major Robertson that

1.   CHEESE transmissions over the three months of BARCLAY on 50 out of 92 days, i.e. more often than every other day.

2.   During a typical 'negative' month (September 1943) he transmitted on 15 days.

3.   The average number of words per message was 59. September 1942.

4.   During the present period (ZEPPELIN) he has transmitted 14 times in 51 days with an average of 74 words (NB: Not a fair comparison in view of the 'technical amelioration' period but his average is only once every three days lately).

An analysis completed by 'A' Force immediately following HUSKY concluded that prior to BARCLAY the German forces amounted to six divisions in Yugoslavia, with one in Greece and one in Crete. By June reinforcements changed these figures to nine divisions in Greece, and seven in Yugoslavia:

> It seems fair, therefore, to claim a net ten divisions as having been added to the German Balkan Armies during the period of the operation of the BARCLAY plan. The garrison in Southern France has been increased simultaneously by two to three German divisions while two more had been sent to occupy Sardinia and Corsica.

Throughout 1943 'A' Force undertook studies to determine the degree of their campaign's success, and it emerged that one reason for the enemy's greater reliance on double agents, and perhaps in part an explanation for CHEESE's recovery in the eyes of the Abwehr, was the domination of the skies exercised by the RAF. Total air superiority meant that the Luftwaffe was unable to fly aerial reconnaissance missions, which heightened Rommel's reliance on other sources of intelligence, the principal two being the interception and analysis of signals, and the networks of Abwehr agents. Thus, ironically, the Afrika Korps became increasingly dependent upon human sources that were under British control, because the Luftwaffe was incapable of completing flights over enemy lines. Indeed, as Allied wireless communications' security improved, prompted by clear proof in ULTRA summaries of poor radio procedures, the Germans came to place heavy reliance on the Abwehr.

During the summer of 1943 CHEESE's traffic reached a remarkable volume. Ten of his messages repeated items he had spotted in the newspapers:

> Walter Kirk has been appointed ambassador to the Greek government; General Sikorski is in Cairo; The news of Churchill's arrival was false; The Belgian GOC Order of the Day; General Sikorski inspects Polish troops; King George VI was in North Africa; The Greek King returns from the Lebanon; The Yugoslav government is moving to Cairo at the end of August.

Fifteen of CHEESE's messages originated from what were termed 'casual sources' which included a Greek corporal from the 3rd Corps in Syria who was staying in Cairo. A 'journalist I know' said that at a press conference General Montgomery had announced that the 8th Army would carry the campaign to the end. A telegraph officer had mentioned aircraft in Cyrenaica; His interpreter talked of troop movements on the Derna-Tobruk road, also aircraft and ships in Tobruk, and a convoy with 'GO' on a green circle. Two Greek sergeants in a café were heard to say that Greek troops were to be transferred from

Syria from 18 May, and that they were convinced that Greece was the next target.

A sailor on leave said there were 'more than fifty ships in Alexandria'; 'An English soldier I know' announced there would be 'night manoeuvers till 1 July'; a sergeant in the Warwickshire Yeomanry said the regiment was conducting landing exercises at Kabrit. 'A doctor I know' was credited with noting that the Arab Medical Congress had been postponed until 1 August, and that the Syrian frontier would be closed on 14 July.

In more general reporting from 'Greek circles', CHEESE reported that they had been astonished by the landings in Sicily and anticipated the approaching invasion of Greece or the islands. Some Greek officers said the RAF Regiment was leaving, and that no attack on Greece would take place without the Straits of Otranto. They also referred to aerodromes at Lecce. A New Zealand sergeant was described as a member of the 2nd New Zealand Division, and part of the 12th Army. He said that a unit leaving Cairo was part of the 16 Corps. Another acquaintance, a Greek sergeant pilot, mentioned that he had seen landing craft along the coast of Cyrenaica. The Chief Clerk of the Greek legation talked of landing exercises, morale among the Greek troops, anticipating operations in the autumn.

Between October and December 1943 CHEESE sent six messages based on own observations, which reported

> Polish airmen but no troops here; An increase of South African troops here. Few Greek soldiers but many sailors in Alexandria. Still many South Africans in Cairo; Trucks with a fig-leaf sign; Trucks with a sign of a blue band on yellow with white felucca imposed; Large number of paratroops in Cairo; Cars bearing 'GO' sign; More cars in Cairo bearing 12th Army sign.

Although not having claimed to have seen them personally, CHEESE also stated that 'many Poles arrived recently near Cairo, wearing sign of green fir tree on red and white'.

CHEESE also relied on newspaper articles for eight messages:

> Ten Italian warships arrived in Alexandria; The King of Greece is now in Syria; An advertisement for radio mechanics; The arrival of the King of Yugoslavia and government in Egypt; Photos of Indian troops in Italy; General Smuts in Cairo visiting troops of the 6th South African Armoured Division; The occupation of Cos; The Americans built Payne Field aerodrome; Indian troops of the Jodphur Sardar Regiment now in Italy.

Three of CHEESE's messages reflected rumours that were alleged to be in current circulation:

> The war in Italy will be shortened by a landing near Bologna; There will be no invasion of Greece this year; The Indian division which sailed from Port Said has gone to Italy.

CHEESE also sent two messages based on information he had received from a source described as his 'ESR friend': 'An Indian division recently left Port Said, probably for Italy; Goods trains guarded by airborne troops went towards Palestine.'

Another of his sources was a corporal in the 6th South African Armoured Division who was credited with messages mentioning that 'his camp was on the other side of the Pyramids; he belongs to the Durban Regiment; he thinks that the 1st South African Division has returned to the Cape.'

A New Zealand sergeant asserted that his unit was part of 16 Corps which was soon to leave Cairo. His unit in the 2nd Division left Cairo for Byrg el Arab.

The net effect of this deluge of detailed information was to demonstrate the wide range of CHEESE's informants, and the detailed nature of their reports. These were the building-bricks of the Allied Middle East order-of-battle under construction by Fremde Heere West, and they were really nothing more than a plausible fiction. What the Allied deception planners did not yet suspect was CHEESE's growing primacy within the Abwehr. In a relative vacuum of sources, and under pressure from OKW, the enemy's apparatus was coming to not just believe in the CHEESE organisation, but to rely on it when making critical strategic decisions.

CHAPTER SEVEN

1944

T he great event of 1944 was D-Day, to which CHEESE made a significant contribution. Having pioneered the concept of strategic deception, 'A' Force, which had by now grown to a staff of forty-one officers and seventy-six NCOs, was asked to develop FORTITUDE, the cover-plan for the invasion. Accordingly, in December 1943, Clarke's deputy, Noel Wild, was posted to Norfolk House in St James's Square to head 'Ops B', the SHAEF deception cell.

The deception scheme for the largest amphibious landing ever contemplated in military history was suitably comprehensive, supported by a Whitehall bureaucracy that, dictated by the need for secrecy, was top-level, highly influential but compact in size. Soon after the War Cabinet and the Chiefs of Staff had approved the creation of a London Controlling Section (LCS) to coordinate all deception plans, a sub-committee, codenamed TWIST, was established as an inter-departmental coordination agency with a membership of ten, drawn from MI5 (T. A. Robertson, Anthony Blunt and J. C. Masterman) and SIS (Frank Foley and Martin Lloyd) with representatives from the LCS (Ronald Wingate and Harold Petavel), the Foreign Office (Sir

Reginald Hoare), the Naval Intelligence Division (Ewen Montagu) and Lionel Hale from Economic Intelligence. At the end of February 1943 TWIST supervised what amounted to a full dress-rehearsal for D-Day by drafting a blueprint to protect HUSKY, the planned invasion of Sicily with 'an invasion of the Balkans. This version the Germans also took to be highly credible; they assumed that a base was being built on Cyprus for the invasion of Crete and Rhodes and then of the Balkan Peninsula.'

The threat to Crete and Rhodes, as a prelude to a supposed offensive in the Balkans, was the foundation of the deception strategy which, in the following months, would become more elaborate.

Around November 1943, British troops, notably the 50th and 51st Divisions, began to move from the Mediterranean to Britain. In order to disguise the true objectives of this move, the TWIST Committee proposed spreading rumours that this transfer was taking place so that battle-hardened troops could pass on their battle experience to younger soldiers at home.

In January 1944 a plan relating to the eastern Mediterranean was drafted by the LCS, which was approved by the TWIST Committee in February and the accompanying memorandum noted that

since major cross-Channel landings will not be possible before the end of the summer, the Allies' main military efforts in the spring of 1944 will be directed against the Balkans. The following operations will be carried out:

(a) An attack by British and American troops on the Dalmatian coast

(b) An attack by British troops on Greece

(c) Landing operations by the Russians on the Bulgarian-Romanian coast

Turkey will be invited to join the Allies; this will increase available operational resources, including airfields, to be used to seize the Aegean islands as a precondition to an invasion of Greece. Pressure on the German satellites to break away from Germany will be intensified.

The Anglo-American operations in Italy will continue. Landing operations will be carried out in the northwest and northeast. If these are successful, the 15th Army Group will move east through Istria to support operations in the Balkans.

Simultaneously, the LCS memorandum cited a recent newspaper article published in London about a genuine event, the appointment of General Wilson which had been interpreted to reinforce the overall strategy.

On 2 January of this year, the well-known journalist [James] Garvin wrote in the *Sunday Express* that the appointment of Wilson to the post of Commander in Chief, Mediterranean, dispelled the last remaining doubts that a front was going to be opened in the Balkans in the air, at sea and on land. This event was bound to have a decisive influence on Turkish policy [he wrote]. Moreover, 'when the Western powers make contact with the Soviet armies via the Balkans, the last hour of Hitlerism has come'.

One part of the OVERLORD cover-plan was ZEPPELIN which was required to keep a threat from the Mediterranean alive until at least D+25.[2] ZEPPELIN comprised of TURPITUDE, which concentrated on the Balkans, and anticipated a future Allied offensive in the Adriatic, and VENDETTA, which was designed to pin down the ten German divisions in the South of France and encourage them not to move north to reinforce the Normandy defences. This latter task was

---

2   Twenty-five days after D-Day: 1 July

undertaken by the imaginary 12th Army and the authentic US 7th Army from Algiers, but the Balkan ruse fell largely to CHEESE who described the preparations for operations in Greece, and detailed the training in amphibious landings being given to Greek troops in Egypt. This aspect of the deception kept twenty German divisions tied up in the Balkans, troops that otherwise might have been available for a counter-attack in Normandy.

In January 1944 the DSO in Damascus, Douglas Roberts, provided SIME's Captain McElwee with some very unwelcome news.

> Joseph Weiser, an Austrian Jew, and a member of a gang of money counterfeiters and passport traffickers, who was interned in June 1942 at Mieh Mieh, told the Field Security sergeant attached to the camp last May … that a certain Renato Levi who was supposed to have worked for the British in Genoa, received a number of forged passes from a person called Silbermann. Levi paid a very large sum for these passes, and he had had this money changed by Heim and Silbermann. Weiser was of the opinion that these passes were from a South American state, probably Cuba.

Further enquiries by SIME revealed that the counterfeiters were mainly Jewish refugees who had set up a business in Milan before the war to sell forged visas and travel documents of all kinds. When Italy joined the war the gang moved to Turkey where in 1941 Weiser had betrayed his confederates to the police in Istanbul. As a result Alfred Heim had been sentenced to three years' imprisonment for forgery. His 32-year-old mistress, Elfrieda Berger, whom he had allegedly lived off, then went to live with another member of the gang, Anton Raab, who moved to Palestine, and she finally made her way to Berlin. Another conspirator, Robert Silbermann, was a friend of Heim's and had lived at the Hotel Modern in Milan. According to Weiser's testimony in June 1942, Silbermann travelled on a forged

Norwegian passport and had moved to Sofia with Lotte, described as his German Ayrian wife.

Other members of the gang were identified as Martin Sands and Jacob Weiss, who were interned with Weiser at Mieh Mieh, and four others: Joseph Buchegger, Eugen Kienast, Arno Gutentag and Rudolf Bodner. Their significance was that this was the same group that had been involved with Fulvio Melcher, Levi's radio operator, who had been arrested with them in 1940. SIME's fear was that perhaps inadvertently the gang had implicated Levi and led the Abwehr to conclude that their supposed star agent had been compromised by his previous relationship with the British in Genoa.

The first news from Levi himself consisted of a letter dated 10 February 1944 which was addressed to the British Passport Office in Istanbul, and eventually relayed to SIME in Cairo. Headed as having come from 'care of Captain Cooley, 7th Division Headquarters', Levi described his harrowing experience.

> As I have not been able to communicate with you since I last left Istanbul on 4 June 1941 for Italy on my return from Egypt, I feel it is my duty, now that it is possible for me to do so, to let you know the cause of my silence up to date.
>
> You have only to look up my file to know that I went to Egypt and was returning to Italy. There is no need for me to let you have any further as to what had been arranged in Cairo with Captain Jones of the Intelligence Department Headquarters. My reports which you will find in my file contain any information you may require. At your embassy I was generally interviewed by [XXXXXXX] at the Passport Register Office.
>
> I arrived in Italy without any difficulty on 12 June 1941 after having travelled through Burgas, Sofia, Belgrade, Vienna, Munich and the Brenner Pass on to Venice. I have nothing of importance to report in reference to my voyage to Italy, except that on my arrival in Vienna, I was handed a message to go on to Munich and report at Marien Theresien Strasse No. 4. Here I was

interviewed by Major Travaglio to whom I handed my report as arranged with Captain Jones and [XXXXXXXXXXXX].

On 14 June 1941, [the] date of my arrival in Rome, I immediately got in touch with Colonel Helfferich, Chief of the German Wehrmacht Nachrichtendienst for Italy, who had his headquarters at the Ministry of War in Via XX Settembre. After having given Colonel Helfferich detailed information in reference to my trip to Egypt, he highly congratulated me for the successful work I had been able to carry out. On his request I also handed him a written statement similar to the one I gave to Major Travaglio in Munich. Colonel Helfferich there informed me that they had not yet been able to connect Rome and Naples with Cairo, although according to my report, which had been sent ahead through the German embassy in Istanbul, they should have been able to do so since the 26 May 1941, which was the date fixed by Cairo headquarters. He told me that he was very pleased I was back, so that I could immediately try to get in touch with Cairo through Istanbul, find out what had happened in order to obtain contact as early as possible. He further instructed me that should I not succeed I was to return again to Egypt to make sure the thing would be set going.

Unfortunately each trial remained unsuccessful for another two or three weeks when connection was finally obtained following instructions received by wire from Cairo via Istanbul in reply to my second telegram. I was then requested to report immediately to Colonel Helfferich. He gave me a wonderful reception. He told me of being extremely pleased that such an important and dangerous mission had been successfully carried out. I was asked whether I was prepared to undertake another trip to Egypt, as it was most urgent now that news could be got through, that someone should go once again in order to bring the necessary funds to the men I had engaged and organise a chain of new agents in different parts of Palestine and Egypt for the supply of any valuable information which was badly needed by the German HQ, otherwise the work done by me would become practically useless. To reply, I pretended that I had no desire to undertake a second trip as it carried too great a risk and I could easily be suspected if I was seen again in Egypt. I told him I rather preferred if he could send someone else. I would be very pleased if he could oblige me by giving me a different mission. He pointed out that unfortunately I was the person he knew capable to go through such an important task successfully and insisted on me going back once more successfully with the promise that on my return I would be highly compensated. I finally accepted, pretending I was a great deal displeased. He wanted me to leave in 48 hours, but I insisted on fifteen days' leave before going back in order to see my family and settle certain private business matters which badly needed my personal attention. I was finally granted fifteen days' leave, while the date of departure from Italy was fixed for 5 August 1941.

Before taking leave from Colonel Helfferich, I was handed the necessary instructions which included a long list of information required by them, a new cipher code, timetable and a large sum of money in American and English currency which would have been wanted for the purpose. I was also given a few names of persons living in Haifa, Cairo and Alexandria with whom I should have got in touch, as valuable help could have been obtained from them. One person particularly was recommended to me, for he should have put me in touch with a high Egyptian Government official.

After this interview I left for Genoa to meet my family.

On the 2 August 1941, quite unexpectedly, six persons attached to the Italian CS (Contro Espionaggio) came to see me at my house. I was told they had received instructions to search my house, which was immediately carried out without giving me any explanation. A few private papers of no importance, besides the documents handed to me in Rome, were seized, including the funds which had been given to me by Colonel Helfferich. I was then requested to accompany them to a waiting car with which I was brought straight to the gaol, Mnrassi, in Genoa.

The same night I was accompanied handcuffed by two Carabinieri to the railway station, put on the train to Rome where I arrived the following day after a journey of eighteen hours and was brought immediately to the prison Regna Caoli. I would like to point out that during the whole trip, not even for a minute was I ever relieved of my handcuffs.

A few days later started my first interrogatory and [I] was finally charged. The charge brought against me was that I had cooperated with the British Intelligence Service in Belgrade (Yugoslavia) and in Cairo. No mention was made then or at any other time interrogations about Istanbul.

The first question put to me was 'why the radio receiving and transmitting set erected by me in Cairo was at the moment working under the control of the British authorities?' My reply was that I was greatly surprised and stated that I had never had any connections with the British Intelligence Service, but only with the British embassy in Belgrade and Istanbul for purely personal reasons with reference to my British passport to obtain the necessary visas in order to be able to reach Palestine and Egypt. I further stated that if his statement referring to the radio transmitting set was true, either the man I had engaged had not been acting secretly enough and had been arrested, or they themselves, for a lack of funds, must have sold the show to the British authorities for the purpose of making money. As no questions were put to me by any of my interrogators referring to my activities in France from December 1939 to June 1940 while I was working under instructions by the Deuxième Bureau by order of Major Knowles of the British embassy in Paris, I stuck firmly to the story arranged in Cairo and acknowledged in Istanbul by Captain Whittal. I supported my defence by stating that should I have had any connection with the British Intelligence Service I would not have insisted with Colonel Helfferich on being granted fifteen days' leave, but would have without delay left Italy in 48 hours as had been requested by him.

I was not permitted any lawyer for my defence although my family had already appointed one.

The judge who had my case in hand told me that probably I would be tried by the Tribunale Speziale (Special Court). This to my great relief did not happen and, after a great many interrogations made over a period of several months, he did not think there was sufficient evidence available for me to be brought before the special court. However, instead of being released, the judge on 17 October decided to sentence me to five years to be served as a political prisoner on the island of Tremiti (Adriatic Sea) and provided at the same for the confiscation of $3,801 and £100 found in my private safe which belonged to me.

Owing to ill-health (due to the hardships I was forced to bear on the island) I was permitted on 11 May 1943 to enter the Civil Riuniti Hospital at Foggia, for treatment. On 19 August 1943, due to heavy air bombardments which made it unsafe to stay any longer in Foggia, I was transferred to the military hospital at San Severo. On 21 August the medical officer in charge instructed the Carabinieri Police of the town to take charge of me, saying that he could not keep me any longer owing to shortage of beds, so that the Carabinieri Police, not knowing what to do with me, being unable to send me back to the Island, brought me to the prison of San Severo, when they ordered that I should be kept to await the pleasure of the Questura at Foggia.

On 17 October 1943, a few weeks after the occupation of San Severo by the British troops, by the AMGOT CAO officer Captain Cooley who the following day engaged me to act as his interpreter and clerk. I gladly accepted the position offered to me, which up to date I am holding.

This is all I have to say regarding my activity since I left Istanbul on 4 June 1941 and I would be pleased if you will let me know whether you require my services any longer.

I wish to point out that on my release from gaol in San Severo, I was finable to produce my British Passport or other documents to prove my identity as a British subject. I would be much obliged if you would confirm same to the AMGOT authorities for whom I am now working and further clarify my personal position with them regarding my future duties.

I wish to state that taking into consideration my past activity it would give me great pleasure if you would arrange to have me transferred to the

Intelligence Section, even if I am to be officially attached to the British Army. Please note that I can speak and write correctly in German, French and Italian.

Before closing I would like to state that, since my arrest on 2 August 1941 up to the date of my release on 17 October 1943, apart from personal suffering which I [was] forced to bear in gaol and on the island as a political prisoner, I have concurred a large financial loss in the way of sums of money in foreign currency confiscated as previously mentioned, and other large sums paid out by my family for the defence of any trial, and for my personal expenses while on the island and in hospital. No allowance was ever made to me by the Italian Government as generally was the custom with the other political prisoners. Consideration should also be taken that, for the above period, I had no means to earn any money with which to provide my family, who, fortunately could be provided for by my bankers in Genoa from my personal account. I await your further instructions.

Upon receipt of Levi's four-page letter SIME was faced with a considerable dilemma and the priority was to establish firstly whether CHEESE had been blown and, if so, on what date. There was also the underlying fear that Levi had himself been playing some complex game of his own, perhaps as a triple agent, and a lengthy analysis was undertaken to establish the truth. Another anxiety was that if the Germans learned that Levi had been liberated, and was in British hands, they might assume that CHEESE had been compromised. All these were considered by James Robertson in a four-page memorandum dated 26 February 1944:

1. Renato Levi's background and his original major role in creating CHEESE have been discussed in previous reports. On 19 February 1944 SIME received a letter dated 10 February 1944 from Levi at present apparently employed as an interpreter-clerk by Civil Affairs Branch in Italy. This letter

is the first communication between Levi and ourselves since he left Istanbul for Rome at the beginning of June 1941.

2. The following is a summary of own account of his activities from June 1941 up to the present time (February 1944).

1941
_____

4 June: Left Istanbul for Rome.

12 June: Arrived Italy, reporting en route to Major Travaglio in Munich.

14 June: Arrived Rome. Reported to Helfferich who congratulated Levi for his good work, and told him that wireless communication had not yet been established with Cairo.

July: Wireless communication finally established after attempts and following an exchange of telegrams between Cairo and Rome via Istanbul.

Helfferich was delighted and was very keen that Levi should return to Egypt to pay his agents and organise a further network in Palestine and Egypt. Levi pretended he had no wish to return to Egypt, but finally yielded to Helfferich's insistent demands and agreed to return, the date of his departure fixed for 9 August 1941. Helfferich gave Levi detailed directive of information required, a new cipher and traffic plan and a 'large sum' in English and American currency. Helffferich also gave him a list of a few persons living in Haifa, Cairo and Alexandria to be contacted and who would give valuable aid. One person in particular was mentioned who could put Levi in touch with a high government official.

Levi took leave of Helfferich and proceeded to Genoa on fifteen days' leave to see his family and settle his private affairs.

2 August: Arrested by Italians in Genoa. Removed to Rome.

August – September – October: A few days after arrest interrogation commenced. He was charged with having cooperated with British Intelligence in Belgrade and Cairo. No questions were put to him concerning his work for the Deuxième Bureau in France. The first question put to Levi was 'why the radio and receiving set erected by me in Cairo was working under the control of the British authorities?' Levi denied the charge of cooperation with the British authorities and stated that if the set was really under British control the reason was probably that Levi's men had been caught by the British or else they had sold their information to the British authorities. Levi stuck to his story through several interrogations, spread over a period of two and a half months. The case was regarded as non-proven and Levi was not charged before the Tribunal Speziale.

17 October: Levi sentenced to five years imprisonment to be served as a political prisoner on the island of Tremiti and to the confiscation of $3,801 and £100.

1943

15 May: Released from Tremiti owing to ill-health, transferred to civil hospital at Foggia.

19 August: Owing to heavy air bombardments, transferred to military hospital at San Severo.

21 August: Owing to shortage of beds in the hospital Levi was transferred to the prison of San Severo.

17 October: A few weeks after the British occupation Levi was released by

Civil Affairs Branch officer Captain Cooley who engaged Levi as an interpreter and clerk.

B COMMENTS ON LEVI'S LETTER

3. While Renato's narrative tallies in the main with the scanty information which has reached us from most secret sources there still remain a number of points which require clarification:

4. It is evident from Levi's narrative that he was imprisoned on *suspicion* and escaped with a comparatively light sentence for treason because there was no concrete proof against him. Levi states that he was arrested on 2 August 1941, a few days after he had taken leave of Helfferich in Rome, with the understanding that Levi should return to Egypt on 5 August 1941. It is reasonable to suppose therefore that Helfferich (or the Italians?) gave the order for Levi's arrest on information received during the ten days or so prior to 2 August 1941. (Levi does not give exact dates).

    An examination of CHEESE traffic of this period shows that on 21 July CHEESE was told 'tell George that Levi will arrive soon with funds. In the meantime get information.' This is consistent with Levi's own intended return to Cairo, and one may perhaps assume that until 21 July CHEESE was unsuspected. There were only two other wireless contacts between the date and the date of Levi's arrest, the evidence therefore points to the probability that the serious suspicions of the Germans or Italians were aroused by the subject matter or phrasing of one or more of the three messages sent by us on 21 and 24 and 31 July 1941. It is known from most secret sources (original not at present available in Cairo) that the hand of the British Intelligence Service was regarded by the Germans as apparent in November 1941.

5. It is difficult therefore to reconcile the fact that CHEESE was apparently

brulé at the end of July 1941, and certainly at some stage in November 1941, with the theory we held prior to the receipt of Levi's letter that 'CHEESE was the main source by which successful deception was achieved resulting in complete strategic surprise at the outset of the Western Desert Campaign.' (19 November 1941) i.e. about three and a half months after Levi had been arrested.

6. The information in Levi's letter throws no further light on the question as to how the re-establishment of CHEESE was effected.

7. At the beginning of April 1943 we received information from a most secret source that he was to be released from imprisonment, and Rossetti was asked by Scirombo of the Italian Intelligence Service what should be done with him. There was an obscure reference to his being transferred to the Germans. Rossetti requested that Levi be sent to Sofia to be at Rossetti's disposal. In mid-May 1943 Rossetti in Istanbul asked Athens if Levi could be brought to Sofia. Ten days later he again asked Athens what had happened to Levi.

   We received no further information on this subject and, if Levi's statement is true, he never was actually released from prison except to go to hospital for medical treatment in May 1943. It may well be that the Germans were considering releasing Levi for use as a courier to pay CHEESE, but finally decided against it.

CONCLUSIONS

8. It is suggested that Levi should be interrogated closely on the following points:

(a) The exact date on which he took leave of Helfferich to go to Genoa.

(b) The exact details of his interrogations.

(c) Whether he heard any mention of a possible release from prison in April/May 1943.

(d) Whether it is likely to be known that he is now in Allied hands.

(e) Why did he not communicate earlier with British Intelligence in Cairo?

9. On the basis of the evidence at present available, the contents of the Levi letter do not in any way interfere with or alter the position with regard to our present use of CHEESE.

Thus Robertson concluded that there was no reason to believe that CHEESE had been compromised, but the priority was for SIME to talk to Levi direct, and his travel under the alias 'Mr Rose' was arranged so he arrived in Cairo early in March 1944 to undergo a series of lengthy interviews, the first of which was conducted on 3 March, as recorded by James Robertson in a three-page memorandum:

1. The purpose of this preliminary conversation was primarily to establish:

(a) Reasons for arrest in August 1941.

(b) To determine the attitude of the German and Italian Secret Services towards Levi both before his arrest, and during the subsequent period of the CHEESE operation.

(c) To decide whether or not the return of Levi and the information obtained from him has in any way added to or detracted from the reliability of the CHEESE link.

It is hoped that the following interim report will throw some light on the above questions. Levi is still being interrogated daily and a full report and appreciation will follow.

2.   Attitude of Travaglio and other Abwehr officers towards Levi before his arrest

On about 15 June 1941 Levi met Rossetti in Naples and the latter said that he had been hearing 'adverse reports' about Levi. (Levi believes that his name had been blackened by an Abwehr agent in Belgrade who was afraid that Levi might have reported his inefficiency to the Abwehr and was therefore trying to get his story in first.)

When Rossetti added that Levi's name had been coupled with that of the British Intelligence Service, Levi pretended to be deeply hurt, and handing his passport to Rossetti, said, 'I can do no more work for you till this matter is clarified.' At this Rossetti protested that he had complete confidence in Levi, handed him back his passport, and stated that Dr Travaglio would meet Levi in Venice the following week, and would go into the matter personally.

It is to be noted that Rossetti did not at any time actually say that had been accused of working for the British.

Levi met Travaglio in Venice as arranged. Travaglio was most friendly and insisted that the whole affair should be forgotten until they had had a week's leave. Levi (remaining however on his dignity) agreed and they spent a pleasant week on the lido, Levi posing as Travaglio's clerk.

At this stage, another Abwehr official, bearing like Travaglio the title 'Dr' joined the party. Over drinks Travaglio said that they would now settle the matter once and for all.

The unidentified Abwehr official then produced a long list of questions, of which the first was 'Do you know a man called JEAN?'

Levi at first denied this, but when he perceived that his questioner knew for certain that he had known JEAN, he admitted to an acquaintance-ship with him. It was then revealed to him that JEAN – who had formerly worked for Travaglio in Holland – had stated categorically that Levi had been working simultaneously with himself for the Deuxième Bureau. Levi states that it was clear at this point that the Abwehr had positive evidence that he had been a Deuxième Bureau agent. He nevertheless parried every thrust until, to his surprise, Travaglio suddenly appeared tired of the inter-rogation, and, stating that he had absolute proof that Levi was 100 per cent loyal and that he had absolute confidence in him said, 'give me the paper and I will sign it.'

Levi believes that Travaglio – whom he describes as a rather weak charac-ter who admitted himself not to be a good Nazi – saved him on this occasion in order to avoid the discovery by his superiors that he had been fooled, not only by the double agent JEAN, but also by Levi.

3. Arrest and interrogation of Levi

When Levi was arrested in August 1941 no formal charge was ever made against him. On 5 August a senior civilian official of the Italian CS Depart-ment said to him, 'What about this radio set that you are supposed to have organised so well being under British control?' Levi replied to this, 'I know nothing about it.'

Throughout the interrogation Levi was not questioned at all about the story which had been concocted in Cairo and subsequently told to Zähringer in Istanbul about Paul Nicossof and the acquisition and estab-lishment of the wireless set in Egypt. He is convinced that the Italians in fact knew practically nothing about his activities in Cairo, and this indicates that the Germans had no share in the responsibility for his arrest.

The interrogation took place in a friendly atmosphere, a few ques-tions being put to him every few days. The subject of the wireless set was not brought up again after the first remark that is quoted above. He was questioned about a number of photographs which had been found in his possession, the majority of which were of Mena House 'lovelies'. He was also questioned about a cabaret girl whom he had taken with him to Istanbul on the first stage of his journey to Egypt (and who, in complete innocence had been arrested at the same time as himself in 1941). He was asked, in addition, about his activities in Belgrade, all of which he was easily able to explain. It was apparent throughout that the Italian officers had little or no 'ammunition' to use against him in the interrogation.

It is particularly noteworthy that when, after about four days of interrogation, Levi asked how long the affair would take, and urged that enquiries be made from Travaglio and from Rossetti, he was informed that this had already been done and that the information received from both Abwehr officers was excellent. They were even prepared to take Levi back into employment as soon as the matter at issue had been settled.

At this, Levi asked why, when the service for which he had been working had nothing against him, and even wanted him back, he was still detained. He was then told that for reasons which it was not possible to explain, this question could not be correctly answered. The enquiries up to that time however, were all in Levi's favour. It was merely a question of slight suspicion (*leggero sospetto*) which, owing to the position which Levi held, had caused his arrest, and had to be cleared up before his release. He was urged not to worry, as it was only a question of a few days before he obtained his freedom.

4. Attitude of the Italians and Germans towards Levi during the period of his imprisonment

During 1942 Levi's relations met Travaglio in Genoa, and asked for his favourable intervention. He replied that the matter was out of his hands and that he could not help. Rossetti, in contrast, showed himself favourably disposed towards Levi, and it was as a result of a letter written to

Rossetti and Scirombo that Levi was granted leave in mid-August 1942 to go to Mont Cattini.

When he went on leave Levi was informed by two Brigadieri of the CS (Rome Section) that the cause for which he had been imprisoned was not really of very great importance and that the decision against him had only been reached as a result of one man's vote. The CS official responsible for this casting vote remains unidentified.

In November 1942 a Sardinian named Pirie was released from the island and subsequently arrested in Cagliari. Among the documents found on this man was Levi's address, which Levi had given him simply in order to help him find work after his release. As a result a CS official already known to Levi was sent expressly from Rome to interview him on the island. Nothing was discovered against him, and at the questioning approached him on the subject of his release. The official replied that Levi was only on the island for a reason which he was unable to explain to him. Later on, one of the guards informed Levi that the Rome official said to him that he ought in reality to be released.

5. The story told to Zähringer in Istanbul

After his various experiences Levi had some difficulty in remembering the details of the story he told Zähringer nearly three years ago. He was emphatic however that the picture he had painted of CHEESE was almost exactly that which had been agreed upon in Cairo. He gave no physical description of CHEESE, as he was not asked for it. All he said about him was [that he was] a Syrian, supposed to be a former Merchant Service wireless operator. CHEESE's motive for working he gave as mainly financial. He had found CHEESE through the intermediary of an Italian who had been responsible for producing the wireless set after sufficient financial inducement.

It seems certain that if the Abwehr have any picture of CHEESE at all in their minds, it must be an extremely vague one.

6. Present acquaintances in Cairo

The only persons likely to recognise at the present time are George Khouri (interned); the porter at the National Hotel (whom will avoid) and the journalist Habib Jamati (about whose present whereabouts enquiries are being made, and out of whose way Levi will also be instructed to keep.)

7. Conclusions

(a) On the basis of the evidence so far available there seems much to support Levi's own theory that he was imprisoned by the Italians as the result of the jealousy of the Italian Secret Service against the Abwehr. Levi thinks that the most jealous of all was probably Scirombo, who had seen his own original espionage plans for Egypt go completely to ground, so that the 'Germans had to take over and compensate for his own failure.'

(b) It is clear that at least one Abwehr official (Travaglio) must have known that Levi was, or had been, a double agent. There is no evidence however that Travaglio or anyone else knew him to be a British double agent, and whatever the Abwehr knew it is clear from the visit to the Lido in June 1941 that Travaglio was sufficiently scared of the Gestapo or the Russian Front to keep his views to himself.

(c) It may be surmised that Levi's continued detention, when nothing at all had been proved against him, was probably due to Travaglio's guilty knowledge. It made no difference to the CHEESE link whether Levi was in prison or not; and as long as he was in prison, an Italian prison, there was less likelihood of Travaglio's dishonesty becoming apparent.

The final result of SIME's debriefing was a lengthy *History of Renato Levi from June 1941 to March 1944* compiled by Eric Pope and amounting to twenty-three pages, with an appendix of a further four pages containing personality sketches of various Abwehr officers. Uppermost in the minds of the SIME analysts was whether it was safe to continue using CHEESE as a channel of disinformation to the enemy, and this judgment could only be reached after the most exhaustive scrutiny of the chronology of events which began with Levi's unexpected arrest in Genoa.

The following detailed narrative of Mr Rose's return to Italy in 1941, his arrest and imprisonment by the Italians, and his final liberation by British forces, is based on a written statement made by Levi and on a series of conversations held with Levi since his arrival in Cairo from Italy on 1 March.

I ROSE RETURNS TO ITALY – FIRST ACCUSATION – WIRELESS COMMUNICATION ESTABLISHED WITH CAIRO

1. Levi left Egypt on 4 June 1941, travelling to Italy via Burgas, Sofia, Belgrade Vienna, Munich and Venice. On arrival in Vienna, he was instructed to proceed to Munich to report to Major Travaglio at Marien Theresien Strasse No. 4. This Levi did, telling Travaglio the story previously arranged with the British authorities in Cairo and Istanbul. Levi continued to Rome where he arrived on 14 June 1941 and immediately got in touch with Colonel Helfferich, whom Levi describes as Chief of the German Wehrmacht Nachrichtendienst in Italy, and whose office was in the Italian Ministry of War in the Via XX Settembre.

   Levi verbally explained in detail the result of his mission to Egypt, and was warmly congratulated by Helfferich who requested him to make a written report. Helfferich informed Levi that up to that time wireless contact between Cairo and Rome or Naples had not yet been established; Helfferich was accordingly very pleased that Levi had returned as he could pursue enquiries via Istanbul with a view to establishing contact with the minimum delay. Should these efforts prove abortive, [he] would then return to Egypt to make a further attempt.

2. Levi proceeded to Naples, where he was interviewed on about 16/17 June 1941. During the course of conversation Rossetti mentioned that he had been hearing 'adverse reports' about Levi concerning his association with the British Intelligence Service. Levi believes that his name had been blackened by a minor Abwehr agent in Belgrade who was nervous that Levi might report his inefficiency and therefore tried to get his story about Levi in first.

   Levi gave a suitable display of injured innocence and handed his passport to Rossetti stating that he could do no further work for the Germans until his name had been cleared. Rossetti reacted as Levi had intended that he should, by returning the passport to Levi protesting all the while that he had complete confidence in him. He went on to inform Levi that Travaglio would meet Levi in Venice the following week to clear up the matter.

3. Levi met Travaglio in Venice as arranged. Travaglio was extremely friendly and gave Levi a warm welcome, insisting that they should forget the accusation against him until they had taken a week's leave together. Levi remained slightly on his dignity, pointing out that a very serious charge had been levelled at him and that he wished to clear his name. Travaglio persuaded Levi that he had nothing to worry about and the two spent a pleasant holiday together on the Lido, Levi posing as Travaglio's clerk.

4. One week later a German whose name Levi does not recall but who he believes was an Abwehr official, appeared on the scene. After introductions, drinks were ordered and Travaglio said that they would settle the case against him once and for all. The visiting official asked Levi several questions, of which the first was whether or not Levi knew a certain individual called JEAN. Levi replied that he did not remember him, whereupon the

official, to refresh Levi's memory, reminded Levi of the man with microscopic handwriting. Levi had no alternative at this point but to admit to an acquaintance with JEAN. The official stated that JEAN had been arrested in Paris, having been working all along for the Deuxième Bureau. Levi feigned astonishment at this information. The official then asked Levi whether JEAN had brought Levi a letter to Genoa. Levi admitted this but turned to Travaglio and asked Travaglio to confirm that had passed on this letter to him. Travaglio confirmed this (in point of fact JEAN had brought two letters, one for Travaglio, the other a secret communication for Levi from the Deuxième Bureau in Paris.)

5. The official then stated that JEAN had made a statement to the effect that Levi himself had been employed by the Deuxième Bureau and had paid frequent visits to the British Embassy in Paris. [Levi] defended himself indignantly: he admitted going to the British Embassy, but this had been merely for routine passport formalities. He insisted that he had had absolutely no contact with the Deuxième Bureau, neither had he entertained any suspicion that JEAN was working for the French.

A further series of questions followed concerning JEAN's activities. From the nature of these questions it was apparent to Levi that the Abwehr official was very well informed concerning JEAN's activities on behalf of the Deuxième Bureau. Levi continued to deny any knowledge of these activities, but felt extremely uncomfortable because JEAN 'knew everything' about Levi and came to the conclusion that the Germans must have brought pressure to bear on JEAN who had probably mentioned Levi in the course of his interrogation. At any rate it was fairly clear to Levi at this point of the conversation that the Abwehr had definite evidence that Levi had been a Deuxième Bureau agent. Finally, to Levi's relief, as he believed that he was in a very awkward situation, Travaglio rallied to Levi's defence, stating that he was tired of the interrogation and that he had absolute proof that Levi was completely loyal; he, Travaglio, had complete confidence in Levi and stated that he would sign a document to that effect. This appeared to close the incident.

6. According to Levi, JEAN had worked for Travaglio in the Netherlands, although really serving the Deuxième Bureau. He was arrested by the Germans after their occupation of Holland, but at a later date JEAN had apparently re-established himself in Travaglio's confidence and the latter (then in Italy) re-engaged him.

Levi recalls that JEAN's second arrest occurred through a certain Karl (Charles) Kurt (alias Charles Masson), an Alsatian German (technically a French subject) who was arrested in Paris in 1938 by the French authorities, and, after a prolonged trial, sentenced to death for espionage.

Levi was introduced to Kurt in Rome about October 1940. In the course of conversation Kurt told Levi that he had been betrayed by a Frenchman (unnamed) who was a Deuxième Bureau agent but who pretended to be working for the Germans. Fourteen other persons who formed a German espionage network in Metropolitan and Colonial France were arrested at the same time as a result of this Frenchman's activities. Kurt himself had had a 'miraculous' escape. According to his own statement, he was being removed by the Vichy French authorities soon after the armistice from the German-occupied zone to the non-occupied zone, together with some petty criminals. At the frontier Kurt shouted out to some German troops, who stepped on the train and removed Kurt and some political prisoners whom the Vichy French authorities had tried to smuggle into the non-occupied zone as ordinary criminals. Kurt was later sent to Italy to work with Travaglio.

At a later meeting with Kurt and Travaglio in Rome (about October 1940) Travaglio read out a message he had received from Paris stating that a certain JEAN had presented himself to the German authorities in Paris alleging that he belonged to Travaglio's Section. Travaglio's opinion was asked concerning JEAN's disposal. Travaglio told Kurt and Levi that he did not recall who JEAN was and asked whether he remembered him. Levi pretended that the name meant nothing to him but Kurt chipped in suddenly and asked Travaglio whether this JEAN might be a person whose reports were all written in microscopic handwriting. Travaglio turned to Levi and asked Levi if he remembered such a person. Levi replied that it must have been the person that Travaglio had engaged in Genoa some time ago and who had previously been employed by Travaglio in the Netherlands. It was agreed that this must be the man. Kurt became extremely agitated and asked Travaglio to give immediate instructions for JEAN's arrest and execution, because it was JEAN who had been responsible for the arrest of Kurt and fourteen other German agents. Kurt said that he could give definite proof that JEAN had been working all along for the Deuxième Bureau. Levi interrupted at this point and told Travaglio that it would be advisable to take further enquiries before giving definite instructions for JEAN's arrest. Kurt insisted with some heat that there was no need for this as he was absolutely certain that JEAN was a traitor. Travaglio accordingly ordered Levi to draft a message for transmission to Paris containing instructions for JEAN's arrest. Levi was to have this message transmitted to Paris from Bari, when he returned to that city.

The next day Kurt left Rome for Milan leaving Levi and Travaglio together. Levi interceded on behalf of JEAN and told Travaglio that, after careful consideration, he did not think that JEAN could be the person mentioned by Kurt. Travaglio, who respected Levi's opinions, accordingly cancelled the message Levi had drafted the previous day and instructed Levi to send a message solely stating that he, Travaglio, no longer required JEAN's services. Levi states that JEAN's final arrest, despite this message, may have been due to Kurt's insistence with the German authorities in Milan; alternatively, Levi's message may have arrived too late and the German authorities in Paris may have arrested JEAN on their own initiative. Some time later Travaglio was told that JEAN had been sent to a concentration camp in Germany.

When Kurt returned to Rome a week later he and Levi reported together to Helfferich. Kurt was given definite instructions for the future. As far as Levi can remember, it was planned that Kurt should make his way alone, by whatever route he chose, to reach Palestine or possibly Syria, to work his way into pipeline territory where he could organise sabotage. Kurt refused to take a wireless set with him, as he asserted that he could construct his own set by buying the component parts locally.

Levi states that Kurt stood very highly in the Germans' estimation and was very well paid by them. Kurt is of medium height, stoutish, heavily built, brown hair, usually well dressed, [an] expert wireless operator [who] 'looks like a Frenchman'.

Levi met Kurt again in Rome in June or July 1941 and gathered that the original plans for Kurt to go to the Middle East had not materialised. Kurt told him, however, that he was flying to Tripoli (Libya) with another agent and that they were to be dropped somewhere behind the British lines in the Western Desert, equipped with wireless sets. A few days later Levi saw Kurt and asked him how it was that he had returned so soon from Tripoli. Kurt explained that he and the other agent had been arrested by the German authorities on arrival in Tripoli and had been flown back to Italy in hand-cuffs. Levi got the impression that this incident had been caused through Travaglio (for whom Kurt was working) trespassing in territory which was the responsibility of a different Abwehr Section. Kurt was apparently highly amused over the whole business.

7. Levi believes that on the occasion of the Venice meeting in June 1941 Trav-aglio saved him in order to avoid the discovery by his superiors that he (Travaglio) had been fooled, not only by the double agent JEAN, but also by Levi.

8. Wireless contact between Italy and Cairo was finally established in July 1941 after a series of trials and following an exchange of telegrams between

Cairo and Rome via Istanbul in accordance with the pre-arranged plan. Helfferich sent for Levi and was apparently highly delighted with the successful establishment of wireless communication. He pressed Levi to return to Egypt to pay the agents he had recruited and to organise a further espionage network in Palestine and Egypt. Levi feigned complete disinterest in this scheme, but gradually yielded to Helfferich's insistent demands and agreed to return to British occupied territory. The date of Levi's departure was fixed provisionally for 6 August 1941, although Helfferich would have preferred him to have left earlier. Levi insisted, however, on being granted some leave to return to Genoa 'and settle outstanding family and private affairs'. Before leaving Rome for Genoa on about 16/17 July 1941, he was given a detailed directive by Helfferich for his new mission. This included the type of information required, a new cipher and traffic plan and a 'large sum' in American and British currency. He was also given the names of certain individuals living in Haifa, Cairo and Alexandria who could be relied upon to provide assistance. The name of one person in particular was stressed, who could put him in touch with a high Egyptian Government official. Levi cannot remember these names.

9. Towards the end of July 1941, during the period which Levi spent in Genoa, prior to his intended departure for the Middle East, an incident occurred which Levi considers may have a bearing on his arrest. An individual arrived at the same hotel in which Levi was staying in and introduced himself as Captain Alessi of the Italian Air Force. He was wearing civilian clothes and told that he had been sent to him by Rossetti's secretary, Annabella. Alessi did not give Levi any written message from Annabella but, judging from his conversation, he was apparently fairly well-informed of the German's affairs. Alessi also mentioned that his visit to Genoa was partially in connection with a private business transaction.

Levi and Alessi became friendly and went out together on several occasions. Alessi explained his intention of going abroad to work for the same section as Levi and asked him for advice. On one occasion he asked Levi abruptly whether he could keep a secret. Levi assured him that anything he said would go no further, whereupon Alessi told Levi point-blank that he did not like the Nazis or Fascists and wanted Levi to help him by backing up his attempts to go abroad. Alessi stated that, once out of Italy, his real intention was to stay away for the duration of the war. (While out with on previous occasions Alessi had often spoken favourably of the Americans and stated that he was a personal friend of an American official in the American Embassy in Rome.)

Levi asked Alessi why he was not on active service, to which he replied that he had had some trouble with a Fascist official and had left the Air Force of his own accord, for personal reasons. He did not pursue this any further. Up to this point of their acquaintanceship, Levi had been favourably impressed with Alessi, and had not entertained any suspicions that Alessi was an agent provocateur. Alessi's self-confessed anti-Nazi anti-fascist attitude, however, naturally aroused Levi's doubts. Accordingly, he was in the difficult position of having to frame his reply to Alessi in such a way that he would not incriminate himself in the event of Alessi being an agent provocateur, but at the same time not scare Alessi away in case his anti-Fascist attitude was a genuine one, in which event Levi realised that he might be of considerable value to the Allies once in Allied-occupied territory. Levi accordingly told Alessi that, whatever he had said, he could rest assured that it would not go 'any further', whether or not Alessi was sincere in what he had told Levi. Levi did not care what Alessi did once he got abroad. Levi pointed out that as far as he was concerned, he could not be of any assistance in expediting Alessi's departure as this matter would depend on a decision upon Naples. All he could do would be to inform Naples that he had had a conversation with Alessi and that as far as he, Levi, was concerned, they could engage Alessi in whatever way they thought best.

Alessi thanked Levi for his advice and begged him to exert his influence on Rossetti through Annabella with a view to getting him sent away as soon as possible. He asked whether he would help him once he was abroad, and whether they could arrange some rendezvous, in view of the fact that he was hoping to leave about the same time as Levi (early August 1941). Levi replied that if they should he might be able to assist him in obtaining visas for Palestine or Egypt by introducing Alessi to the British authorities in Turkey as a Jewish refugee. Levi told Alessi that should he assist him in this way, he would not be concerned as to whether Alessi did his duty towards the Germans or not, as Levi had taken it upon himself to spy upon other agents, or to gossip to the Germans about their activities. Levi amplified this by stating that if, on return to Egypt, he found out that the people he had engaged had 'gone wrong', he would not create trouble for them, although it was arguable that his duty would be to report it immediately to his German masters.

Levi told Alessi that he had always done his duty up to that time and even assuming, for the purpose of argument, that he might not be 100 per cent friendly towards the Nazis or the Fascists, this would not make any difference to his work. He would look upon it as a question of doing his duty for an employer he disliked. All this did not mean, of course, that Levi did actually dislike the Nazis or the Fascists – he was merely looking at it from Alessi's angle.

Some time after this interview, Levi spoke to Annabella on the telephone and told her of Alessi's visit. She knew about him and asked Levi to arrange an appointment for her to meet Alessi somewhere in Rome. Levi gave her Alessi's address in that city. Annabella told Levi that she thought Alessi might be very useful and that it might be profitable if Levi and Alessi teamed up. Levi replied that he preferred to work alone as far as possible.

Before Alessi left Genoa on about 25 July 1941, Levi asked him not to betray him to the British should he (Alessi) throw in his lot with the other side once he got abroad. Alessi assured him that he would respect his attitude exactly as Levi respected his, and would continue to do so if he succeeded in getting away from 'this blasted country'. He would certainly not betray Levi.

Levi describes Alessi as follows: about 6 feet tall, fair hair, English looking, possibly blueish eyes, good looking, pleasing personality, good manners and well educated, considerable savoir faire, obviously a man of the world, always smartly dressed. Spoke fluent French, English and Italian, Anglo-Saxon drinking habits (fond of whisky, gin, cocktails, etc.)

10. In the late evening of 1 August 1941, the day before his arrest, Levi received a telephone call from Annabella in Rome, who wished to know on behalf of Rossetti when he was going to leave for the Middle East. Apparently Rossetti wanted him to leave as soon as possible. Levi explained to Annabella that there had been a slight delay owing to passport formalities.

II LEVI'S ARREST, IMPRISONMENT AND FINAL RELEASE BY BRITISH FORCES

11. On the night of 2 August 1941, Levi was arrested in his hotel in Genoa by officials of the Italian CS. He was removed the same night from Genoa to Rome, and on 3 August was imprisoned in the gaol of Coeli in Rome.

He was interrogated for the first time on 5 August 1941. No formal charge was made against him.

The first question the CS official who conducted this and subsequent interrogations asked him was '*che cosa sapete dell aparecchio che avete ire piantato cheimplantato a Cairo eora trasmette sotto il controllo Inglese?*' ('What do you know about the wireless set you placed in Cairo and which now transmits under British control?')

Levi feigned complete amazement and said he knew absolutely nothing about the matter. Leaving this point, the official asked why he had been in touch with the British Embassy in Belgrade. Levi replied that this was no secret, since he had been obliged to visit the British Embassy in connection with passport formalities.

He had reported these visits in writing to the German authorities at the time. The official jokingly urged Levi not to be foolish, as they knew all about him and it would be best for him if he told the whole truth. He promised to save Levi and send him home if he made a clean breast of it. Levi was not deceived by this clumsy approach and insisted that he knew absolutely nothing about the whole affair, and that he was extremely surprised at the accusation as, apart from passport formalities, he had never had any truck with the British authorities or been approached by them with any suggestion that he should undertake intelligence work on their behalf. The official said that, if this were true, how then did Levi account for the fact that the wireless set was now in British hands? (*'Ebbene ditemi ome lo pensate vol sia la ragione che l'apparreochio si trova ora in mani Inglese?'*)

Levi replied that he could not understand how this could have happened. The only reasons he could suggest were that the agents he had engaged had not taken sufficient security precautions and had been caught by the British authorities, who had assumed control of the wireless set, or, alternatively, his agents may have come forward with their story in the hope of a liberal regard. The official closed the interview without putting any further questions to Levi. Before leaving he told Levi in reply to the latter's query as to when he would be released, that he need not worry, as it would merely be a question of a few days.

12. The same official returned to see Levi about two days later (approximately 7 August 1941), and asked under how many passports he had been travelling. Levi replied that as far as he could remember he had only used an English passport outside Italy and a German one in Italy itself.

The official then asked Levi about the Dutch passport in his possession. Levi did not understand what was meant and replied that he had never had in his possession or travelled under a Dutch passport. The official told him to wait as he was going away and would be back again within a few minutes with proof. He returned fifteen minutes later and told him that the girl who was going to travel with him confirmed that on one occasion she had seen three passports among Levi's possessions, one a greenish colour (Dutch), another blue (British), and a third brown (German). Levi then recalled that he had at one time had a Dutch passport in his possession but that it did not belong to him and he had held it merely because he had had it specially made for an agent who was supposed to be going to France on behalf of the Germans. It so happened that the Christian name on this passport was the same as Levi (Renato).

Levi told the official that he could confirm this statement by referring to Rossetti. (This matter dated back to the time when Levi was working for the Deuxième Bureau and as far as Levi could remember the passport was never actually used.)

13. The girl whom the official had referred to as having seen these passports was a certain Azeglia Socci, a cabaret artiste who had been Levi's girl-friend for some time. Levi had made arrangements to take her back with him to Turkey on his intended return to the Middle East. The reason for this was that he had told the Germans in Istanbul that the excuse he had given to the British authorities in Istanbul for returning to Italy was that he wished to get his wife out of Italy. Therefore Levi argued that he would have to bring some female back to Istanbul as tangible evidence to pro-duce to the British authorities to show that he had in fact returned to Italy for the purpose he had stated.

The official asked whether Socci knew of his secret activities. Levi replied that he did not think she did, as the only thing he had told her was that he was going abroad on a buying mission for the Italian government. The official said that he thought Socci knew pretty well what Levi was actu-ally doing and pressed Levi to tell him whether or not he had confided in her. Levi denied this emphatically. He had realised by now from the ques-tions the official had put to him that Azeglia was also locked up in the same gaol. She had been arrested at the same time as Levi but he was under the impression at the time that she had been released immediately. He had been told this by his guard when he was removed from Genoa to Rome. Levi told the official that he could not understand why Socci had been arrested and was still detained. He begged the official to release her immediately, swore that she was not implicated in any way whatsoever in his affairs, and further, that she was not the type of girl who could be used for secret service work, being pleasant but stupid. The official promised Levi that he would release her the same day and would see to it personally that she arrived safely in Genoa. The interview then ended.

Ten days later Levi received a letter from Socci in which she stated that she had been released on the date of Levi's last interrogation. She had been very well treated by the official, who instructed the CS department to give her 100 lire for the journey and arranged to have her accompanied to Genoa by a CS official.

14. During the next week Levi made at least two written appeals to the CS department protesting against his arrest and requesting his immediate release. He received no reply. About mid-August 1941, and one week after his second interrogation, the official came to see Levi for the third time. On this occasion he brought with him a number of documents and a collection of photographs (mostly negatives); these had been taken from Levi's private flat in Genoa which had been searched some time after his arrest. The documents were merely private letters with no bearing on intelligence activities and were immediately dismissed by the official as irrelevant. The photographs were all miniatures, arranged and numbered in an album. The official questioned Levi closely concerning these photographs, which were merely innocent amateur efforts and in no way incriminating. The individuals appearing in these photographs were nearly all girlfriends of the cabaret artiste type whom Levi had met in the course of his travels, and whose names he could not remember. After two hours' interrogation, with the official writing down answers, the interview ended. (The official took the opportunity of purloining the gem of Levi's collection – an enlargement of a magnificent nude.)

15. The official's fourth visit took place about five days later (approximately 20 August 1941). Before the official put any questions, [Levi] protested strongly against his continued detention, and asked how long it would be before he could be released. He begged the official to make urgent enquiries through Travaglio and Rossetti. The official stated that he had already done this and that both Travaglio and Rossetti had given the most excellent references. They were even prepared to re-employ Levi as soon as the matter at issue had been settled. Levi asked for some explanation, at least, for his continued detention in view of the fact that his own employers had nothing against him and even wished to re-employ him. The official replied that he could not give a complete answer to this question but he could assure Levi that the enquiries which had been conducted up to that time had been entirely in Levi's favour. It was merely a question of a slight suspicion (*leggero sospetto*). Owing to the important position which [Levi] had held, this suspicion had to be cleared up before he could be released. The official urged Levi not to worry, and to keep his spirits high, as it was only a question of a few days before he obtained his freedom. Levi stresses the fact that throughout these interviews the official concerned was extremely courteous and genuinely friendly. For example, on this occasion he noticed that Levi was suffering from an outbreak of spots on his body and showed concern over them, explained that these were probably due to the filthiness of the cells in which he had been confined. The official turned round to his clerk and said that they must finish the affair as soon as possible (implying that Levi was having an undeservedly rough time).

16. During this interrogation Levi was asked the circumstances in which he first came to work for Travaglio. Levi explained that he was introduced to Travaglio by one of the latter's agents in Milan. This agent had struck up an acquaintanceship with Levi in Genoa and after a couple of weeks had proposed to Levi that Levi should do a job of work for a friend of his (the agent's), without indicating the exact nature of the work in question.

At this point the official suddenly asked Levi whether he had been better paid by the German or British authorities – which were the more generous? Levi did not fall into this obvious trap, replying that as far as the Germans were concerned he could not complain, as they had always given him everything he had asked for; as for the British, he had no idea how they paid their agents as he had never had any dealings with them. The official retorted – 'You really do not want to tell us the truth about your relations with these people?' Levi replied earnestly that it was absurd to insist upon this point; he had repeatedly stated the truth. If he 'were not believed he suggested that they had better hasten the enquiry, put him up against a wall, and have done with the whole business as soon as possible'. The official laughed at this and told Levi that it was not as bad as all that and he should not take it all so seriously. Levi told the official that he was very worried because he had received no news from his family in Genoa; and so he had no money to pay for his personal requirements, although some money should have arrived. He begged the official to authorise the delivery of mail and money. The official promised that he would look into the matter immediately, and should there be any mail or money, Levi would have it the next day. He told Levi to write a letter to his family and that he would personally arrange for this to be posted. He gave the chief warder instructions to supply Levi with paper and ink and authorised him to write one extra letter over and above the regulation two per week. The official gave Levi some cigarettes and matches and left. The following day his clerk posted the letter. Levi questioned him as to how the enquiry was proceeding. This clerk replied that he could assure Levi in all sincerity that his case was progressing very favourably.

17. A few days later (probably towards the end of August 1941), Levi was interrogated by three Italian CS officials whom he had not seen previously. This interrogation was very brief. Levi was merely asked to give the names of the hotels in which he had stayed during his recent visit to the Middle East, with the appropriate dates. The officials then left.

18. Roughly three weeks elapsed before Levi was again interrogated (about mid-September 1941). This long interval worried Levi to such an extent that he wrote several letters, one to Travaglio at his Munich address (10 Maria Kirchnerstrasse), and one to Rossetti, begging them to look into his case, as he was held on completely unproven charges. He also wrote a letter to the CS official who had conducted this first series of interrogations, requesting an urgent interview as he had important information to convey. (Levi used this device to make sure that the official would come.)

Two or three days after the dispatch of this last letter the official came to see Levi, apparently eager to hear what he had to say. Levi told him that it was very important that he should know when his case was finished; he could not understand what possible reason there was for his continued detention. Levi pointed out that he had written to the official to make sure he would come as he had not seen him for a few weeks. The official explained that he had been away on leave and Levi should be grateful to him for not having passed the case on to another official who might not have proved so sympathetic. Levi need not worry, however, as the official was going to bring the case to a conclusion within the next few days. He told Levi to write a complete and detailed account of his activities from the first day he entered the employ of the Germans up to the date of his arrest. Once this statement was written the official would try to finish the case.

The official left. Levi returned to his cell and wrote a 45-page statement which was collected two days later by the official's clerk.

A week passed, when Levi was interrogated by an Italian CS official whom he had not seen before.

19. This new official's manner was offensive and aggressive, in marked contrast to the kindly attitude of his colleague. He told Levi that he had come to take down a written and signed statement, then showed a type-written letter with a newspaper clipping attached to it, and asked him whether he recognised these documents. Levi stated that he had never seen them before

and asked whether he might read them to see to what they referred. The official did not allow him to read them but stated that they concerned the Minister Plenipotentiary of Thailand in Rome. The official asked whether he had ever been instructed by his German employers to make enquiries regarding this diplomat and, if not, how did he account for the fact that these documents had been found in his letter box in Genoa. Levi replied that he had never received any such instructions nor made such enquiries, and, furthermore, he could not understand how these papers could have been found in his letterbox; he knew of no one who had been given any such instructions.

The official cautioned Levi to tell the truth in his own interests. If he had in fact been instructed to make such enquiries, no harm had been done because the information was of benefit to the Axis. Levi insisted that he had no knowledge whatsoever about the matter and had never seen the papers before. He wrote and signed a statement to this effect.

20. The official then asked Levi to make a general statement, but to be as brief as possible as he did not have much time to spare. Levi told him that he would keep his statement to the point but was not prepared to make any statement at all unless he was allowed to say everything he wanted to. The official started to write down his statement, which began with the period when Levi started to work for the Germans, but cut him short and said that he was being too verbose and must shorten his lying testimony. The official stated that, if it depended on him, he would finish the whole matter by putting twelve bullets into Levi's back. Levi replied with some heat that as he was as innocent as the official himself they should share the gift the official had offered him (i.e. six bullets apiece). The official, visibly annoyed, rebuked Levi for impudence and told him that, anyhow, he would not get away with it. Levi proceeded with his statement until 1 p.m. when the official left, returning at 5 p.m. Before he left, Levi had occasion to be left alone for a moment with the clerk who, on his own accord and

without prompting, told Levi not to take any notice of what the official had said, to carry on as he had done up to then, and that everything was going smoothly. Levi's statement was completed in the evening, the official punctuating the proceedings with heavy sarcasm.

21. A few days later (probably early October 1941), Levi was again interrogated by the same official, who asked for particulars about the strong-box he owned and which was in the keeping of his bankers in Genoa. Levi explained that the only contents of this strong-box were purely private papers and family documents.

22. The day after this interview the official who had conducted the first series of interrogations came back to the gaol to see Levi and asked him whether he would be prepared to re-enter the service of the Germans if he were released. Levi replied that he would not mind doing so provided he were not sent back to Egypt or to British-occupied territory, because it was quite probable that in view of what had happened he was already brulé in those parts. He suggested that it might be a good idea to work again in France, as the Germans could give him the necessary protection there.

The official stated that the enquiry was now concluded and that, as far as he was concerned, he had no reason for detaining Levi any further; he would that same day issue orders for Levi's release. He was completely satisfied that Levi was innocent and thought that Levi would probably be asked to return to work for the Germans. The official took leave of Levi wishing him all the best.

23. The same afternoon Levi was summoned by the chief warder of his section of the gaol. He confirmed that the enquiry was finished and that Levi would now be transferred to another section of the gaol (non-political) where he could mix with other prisoners until the order for Levi's release was received from the political branch of the police. The CS, who had been

handling Levi's case, had apparently dismissed it before bringing it up for formal trial. Levi was placed in the third (transit) section of the gaol and was expecting to be released day-to-day. Up to that time Levi had been in solitary confinement in the section of the gaol reserved for political offenders. On the door of his cell was a label with instructions that he should be very strictly guarded and bearing the initials TS (*Tribunale Speziale*). This Tribunal tries all offences of a political, anti-fascist, or anti-national in character including espionage. During his first or second interrogation Levi had been told by the official that he would appear before the Tribunale Speziale. At a later date, however, he was told that it would probably not be necessary for him to be brought before this special court, but he was given no explanation.

24. On the 17 October 1941 Levi was visited by an official of the Publica Sicurrezza who served Levi a summons to appear before the Provincial Commission (*Commissione Provinciale*) at the Rome Prefecture on 18 October. Levi was escorted to the Prefecture with other prisoners. When his case came up for trial he was charged with anti-national activity (*Attività Anti Nazionali*) and was asked what he had to say in his defence. Levi stated that he had already said quite enough and that if the Court were not satisfied with his previous statements he had nothing further to add, except that he protested his innocence and stated that he had been unjustly charged before the Court. He was asked whether he was of Jewish faith and explained that he was of Jewish origin but Catholic by religion. He was then led back to gaol without being informed of the Court's verdict. This was communicated to him on the following day, in writing. The gist of it was that he was sentenced to five years confinement as a political prisoner for being socially dangerous (*socialmente pericoloso*).

25. On 29 October two minor CS officials in civilian clothes fetched Levi from gaol and told him that they had instructions to accompany him to

Genoa in order to inspect the contents of the strong-box at his bank. The trio travelled by train to Genoa. Levi was not handcuffed and was treated in a friendly way. On arrival in Genoa Levi was not permitted to speak to any persons other than his close relations, but his escort handled the matter tactfully. They examined the contents of his strong-box in Levi's presence, removing the British passport belonging to his son and an old one of Levi's, the validity of which had expired, together with a few documents of no value and foreign currency totaling $3,801 and £100. To Levi's astonishment, his stepfather allowed him all the documents and papers which had been seized by the CS at the time of Levi's original arrest. His stepfather said that that these documents, which included his German passport, had been brought back to Genoa personally by one of the two officials escorting Levi. Levi had a quick glance through these miscellaneous papers and does not think that the CS had retained any of the papers originally confiscated, with the exception of Levi's small address book and two or three photographic prints, none of which, according to Levi, contained incriminating material. Levi and escort returned to Rome on 30 October 1941. On arrival he was put back in the political section of the gaol.

26. On 10 November 1941 Levi was escorted from Rome to Manfredonia on the Adriatic coast, where he was put in gaol awaiting a ship to take him to the island of Tremiti, where his sentence was to be served. He remained in Manfredonia gaol until 20 November 1941. This gaol was of an indescribable filthiness, being built to accommodate ten prisoners whereas in fact there were six times that number under lock and key. Sanitary arrangements were almost non-existent. On 20 November 1941, in broad daylight, Levi, together with fifty-four other political prisoners, were marched in irons through the main streets of Manfredonia to the docks. During the seven-hour sea passage from Manfredonia to Tremiti the human cargo remained manacled together in the hold below decks.

27. At Tremiti Levi was allotted a bed in a section of the barracks allotted to prisoners who claimed to be Fascists. About one month later he managed to obtain a room of his own, for which privilege he had to pay. (Those prisoners who had private means paid all their own expenses; those who had no resources of their own were given a government grant of 9 lira daily.) Levi estimated that from the time of his arrest to the time of his release he and his family spent on his behalf some 200,000 lire (approximately £2,000 at the then rate of exchange). This money was dispensed on Levi's maintenance and food, bribes to prison officials, 'gifts' to officials to help Levi's case, and payment to a solicitor and accountant for looking after Levi's affairs.

28. Some time in December 1941 Levi wrote to Rossetti informing him that he was very disappointed over the whole affair and could not understand why the Germans had not intervened on Levi's behalf. Levi strongly protested his innocence, and begged Rossetti to do his best for him and to obtain permission for him to be given leave to go home and to settle his private family and business affairs. About the same time Levi also wrote to Scirombo, Helfferich and Travaglio in Munich, but does not think that this last letter reached Travaglio. For this correspondence Levi had to make out an official application naming all the persons with whom he wished to correspond in the future. Until such authority had been granted he was only authorised to correspond with his son, wife and stepfather. Three weeks after making his application, authority was granted for him to correspond with all the persons he had named, which included Helfferich, Scirombo, Rossetti, all Levi's relations and his girl-friend Socci, but not Travaglio.

On several other occasions, Levi wrote further letters to Helfferich, Scirombo, Rossetti and Travaglio asking for assistance. Levi cannot remember the exact dates of these letters. The only reply he received to these letters was from Rossetti. (See paragraph 29 below.)

29. On 31 January 1942 Levi was 'double' arrested for having consumed an extra
ration of bread, above his entitlement, and on 11 February 1942 was put into
gaol at Lucera on the mainland. Before sailing from Tremiti for the mainland a warder informed Levi confidentially that it was a pity he was under
arrest as his permit to go on leave had arrived from Rome the previous day.
A few days later, when Levi was in gaol at Lucera he received a letter from
ROSSETTI dated 16 January 1942. ROSSETTI stated that he had interviewed
Scirombo and obtained an assurance that Levi would be granted leave. Levi
thinks, but cannot be certain, that ROSSETTI also stated in this letter that
he would see what he could do to help Levi in other ways.

About April 1942, while Levi was serving a six months sentence in Lucera gaol, his stepfather and brother visited him. They told him that they
had visited the Questura at Foggia, had gone through Levi's papers and
had seen the authorisation for his leave. The Chief of Police had informed
Levi's stepfather that when Levi had served his sentence for the bread incident he would see that he was sent immediately on leave.

30. Towards the end of Levi's sentence, the Chief of Police at Foggia issued
instructions that on the date of expiry of the sentence Levi should be accompanied home on leave: unfortunately, however, a few days before his release
(31 July 1942) an order from Rome cancelled his leave indefinitely, with the
result that he was taken back to Tremiti. On arrival back in Tremiti Levi
obtained an interview with the Governor, a certain Coviello. Levi states
that Coviello was notorious for his harsh treatment of the political prisoners on the island and thinks that he was arrested by the British authorities
when we occupied the island – Levi heard this through Field Security
contacts. He describes Coviello as about 6ft 1in tall, broad, pitch-black
hair, aged about fifty.

Levi appealed to Coviello, asking him why his leave had been cancelled.
Coviello explained that this was due to the bread ration incident. He permitted Levi to make a written application requesting that his leave should

be regranted. Levi wrote out the application, but at the same time wrote to Scirombo, knowing that the latter had authorised his leave in the first instance. Levi explained the matter in detail and requested Scirombo to re-authorise the leave. A few days later (about mid-August 1942), Coviello received a telegram from Rome authorising Levi to proceed on leave to Montecattini (near Florence). Levi's first impulse was to refuse this leave, on the grounds that he had no relations in that town nor any private business to settle there, which therefore made it seem as though a mistake had been made in specifying Montecattini instead of Genoa. The Governor could not give an explanation and also thought some mistake had been made. Accordingly he telegraphed Rome, at Levi's expense, requesting confirmation. Rome confirmed that the leave was to be taken at Montecattini and that Levi could meet his family there but was not permitted to return to Genoa. Levi had no option but to accept this ruling.

31. A few days later a minor official of the CS department arrived from Foggia to escort Levi on leave. He was handed over to two other CS officials in Foggia and taken to Rome. Here he was passed on to two other officials of Warrant Officer rank who had orders to accompany him to Montecattini, guard him the whole time, and bring him back when his leave had expired. In order to obtain the maximum amount of freedom, Levi deliberately treated those officials well, paying for their accommodation in the same hotel he was staying in, as well as liberal entertainment expenses. They had absolutely no scruples about accepting these indirect bribes.

One of the two WOs told him that the reason for his confinement was not of very great importance, and that the final decision that he should be interned had depended upon the casting vote of one CS official (unnamed).

When Levi met his relations in Montecattini they told him that they had approached Travaglio in Genoa to enlist his aid in securing Levi's release. Travaglio informed them that he was unable to help as the matter was out of his hands.

32. After ten days' leave Levi was escorted back to Tremiti. During the rest of his confinement on the island, Levi was 'double' arrested on two occasions, the first time for undesirable political talk, and the second time for having bought a stolen chicken. On each of these occasions he was brought for trial to Manfredonia on the mainland. On both occasions the case against Levi was dismissed before coming up for trial as a result of the palm-greasing activities of Levi's legal representative, a 'smart' solicitor. Apparently it was a standing joke among the prisoners on the island that the authorities were wasting their time 'double' arresting as he would always find some way of getting away with it.

33. About November 1942 a Sardinian political prisoner named Pirie was released. Levi had given him his address in Genoa, with the object of helping him find work. Some time later Levi was summoned before the CS official who had conducted Levi's original interrogations. Levi gathered from his questions that Pirie had been re-arrested in Cagliari and that incriminating documents had been found on him. Levi's address had also been noted in his address book. Levi explained that he had merely hoped to assist Pirie in finding work. Levi took this opportunity of approaching the official on the subject of his continued detention and possibilities of being released. The official replied that Levi remained on the island for a reason which he could not explain. After the official left, one of the warders told Levi that the official had informed him that Levi ought really to be released.

34. About mid-March 1943, after making continued applications and bribing the medical official concerned, Levi obtained authority to be sent to the Civil Hospital at Foggia. He states that at that time he was seriously ill and needed treatment for cardiac trouble, which had been aggravated by the rigours of the island climate. He remained in this hospital for about a month and was then sent back to the island. On return he immediately resumed his attempts to return to hospital, as by this time the physical and psychological

strain of living on the island was bearing heavily on him and he realised that if he did not get away again he would have a serious breakdown.

(During his stay on the island several people went out of their minds and others deliberately committed offences against the regulations in order to be given sentences to be served in civil jails on the mainland.)

Levi succeeded in returning to the hospital at Foggia for the second time in mid-May 1943 on the pretext that his teeth badly needed attention. He remained in hospital until 19 August 1943. During this period and also during his first visit to the hospital, he received visits from his relations in Genoa, his stepfather being a very frequent visitor. The latter had been trying to arrange for Levi's transfer from the island to the mainland and had hopes of arranging this through the Police Commissioner of Foggia, with whom he was on good terms.

A few days before 19 August the Police Commissioner fetched Levi from hospital and took him to the provincial doctor, who had been 'fixed' by Levi's stepfather and who wrote out a certificate recommending on medical grounds that Levi should be transferred to the mainland.

35. On 19 August 1943 Foggia was heavily bombed by the USAAF and the hospital was rendered unserviceable. The majority of the fifty political prisoners from Tremiti who were in hospital at this time took the opportunity of escaping during the general chaos and confusion of the bombing. Levi himself, with three or four other prisoners, remained behind to assist the medical staff in dealing with the wounded. The hospital was ordered to close down and transfer all patients to the civil hospital at San Severo. Levi assisted in the evacuation of the patients and left with the last truck, which arrived in San Severo in the early hours of 20 August 1943. There was no accommodation available in the civil hospital for the political prisoners, who were put in the military hospital. They were not guarded as all the carabinieri had run away, and could have escaped without difficulty, but they considered that as they had no documents of identity it

would be advisable to remain in the military hospital and await orders for their release. They were expecting such orders to come through at any time following Mussolini's resignation one month earlier. The chief medical officer, however, on learning that there were some political prisoners among his newly-arrived patients, instructed the local carabinieri to remove them. The carabinieri did not know where to accommodate them, and, owing to the complete disruption of communications, had no means of sending them back to the island; they were accordingly handcuffed and put into the local gaol at San Severo. Levi remained here from 22 August 1943 until 17 October 1943 when he was released by Captain Cooley, AMG officer in San Severo.

36. Captain Cooley employed Levi as an interpreter-clerk. Levi states that in December 1943 he wrote a letter addressed to the British Military Intelligence authorities in Cairo giving a brief outline of events since returning to Italy. He gave this letter to Captain Cooley with a request that it should be forwarded. Some time elapsed, and by chance Levi found this letter which had remained in Captain Cooley's office and had not been forwarded, accordingly Levi took steps to write a further letter, the onward transmission of which he arranged privately through contact in the Army Post Office, and which was received by the British authorities in Cairo on 18 February 1944.

III COMMENTS

37. The pattern of Levi's narrative provides very considerable evidence that the Italians, and not the Germans, were responsible for his arrest and confinement.

Levi himself believes that his arrest was due to Italian Secret Service jealousy of the Abwehr, Scirombo being the most jealous of all, having seen his own espionage organisation in Egypt fail miserably, with the result that the Germans had to step in. This may well be true.

38. It seems likely that Alessi (although apparently employed by the Germans) was assigned the task by the Italians of making a check on Levi's loyalty. His behaviour and approach to Levi were typical of the agent provocateur. The 'slight suspicion' on which Levi was arrested by the Italians may have been merely that he was too lukewarm in his devotion to the Axis, having failed to 'inform' on Alessi. The questions put to Levi concerning the wireless set being in British hands may have been shots in the dark with little or no basis of concrete suspicion.

39. It is probable that the Germans had no knowledge of the Italians' intention to make trouble for Levi since Annabella telephoned him the day prior to his arrest to enquire on Rossetti's behalf when he would be leaving to return to the Middle East.

40. Three weeks after his arrest, Levi was told by the Italian official conducting his interrogation that both Travaglio and Rossetti had given him excellent references and were prepared to re-employ him once his case was settled. Again, in October 1941, Levi was asked whether he would be prepared to re-enter the service of the Germans if he were released.

    According to reports from Most Secret sources, Rossetti (in Istanbul) received information from Scirombo in early April 1943 that Levi was to be released. Rossetti requested that Levi should be sent to Sofia or Athens and put at his disposal. Evidently the decision to release Levi was cancelled, as on 27 May 1943 Rossetti was asking Athens what had happened to Levi.

41. We know from Most Secret sources (original not at present available in Cairo) that in November 1941 the hand of the British Intelligence Service was regarded by the Germans as apparent in the CHEESE traffic. This

would not necessarily compromise Levi in German eyes as they might well consider that Levi's agents had been captured or their organisation penetrated by the British authorities after they had been functioning for several months. Hence the fact that the Germans were apparently perfectly prepared, and even eager, to re-employ Levi.

42. The fact that the Germans apparently brought no serious pressure to bear on the Italians to secure Levi's release is understandable. As far as they were concerned he had accomplished his main task by establishing wireless communications between Italy and Egypt. While with his past experience and British passport he would have been useful to them for further missions, the security of the wireless link already established was strengthened at their end with Levi out of the way in gaol. Travaglio too probably preferred to see Levi in prison since he realised, no doubt, that the longer Levi continued to be employed by the Germans, the greater the possibility that his activities as a double agent would come to light. This in turn would present Travaglio himself in an unfavourable light as an incompetent who had been deceived by two double agents, JEAN and Levi. While Travaglio, to save his own skin, was perfectly prepared to defend Levi in June 1941 against the charge of having been a Deuxième Bureau double agent, there would be no reason why he should exert himself on Levi's behalf if Levi were in trouble for other and less serious reasons, which would appear to have been the case when Levi was arrested by the Italians.

43. The present interrogation of Levi has thrown no light on the problem of the manner in which the re-establishment of CHEESE was effected after November 1941.

44. It is apparent that Levi conducted himself with considerable fortitude during the course of his interrogations and while confined for two years in circumstances which broke the health and spirit of other prisoners on the island.

He does not appear to be in the least embittered by his experiences and is genuinely willing to undertake any further work which may be offered him.

• • •

Since the above notes were written Levi has given the following additional information on the habits of the Abwehr officials in Italy:

45. Levi often acted as unofficial agent for black market exchange transactions on behalf of Rossetti, Annabella and Travaglio, particularly the latter. These Abwehr officials were supplied with American dollars with which to finance their agents. Instead of paying them in dollars, however, Rossetti and Travaglio would have the dollars changed into Italian lira on the black market obtaining almost twice as many lira to the dollar as was possible at the official rate of exchange, thus making substantial private gains. On one occasion in 1940 Levi was arrested in Genoa by the Italian police when attempting to change several thousand dollars on the black market on behalf of Rossetti. He was released after a few hours as Rossetti interceded with the Italian authorities and apparently convinced them that Levi had really been carrying out a secret investigation into black market activities. On another occasion Rossetti insisted that the Italian Police should release two Italians who had been arrested while carrying out similar black market transactions on behalf of the Germans.

Levi's detailed knowledge of the fact that German Abwehr officials in Italy were exploiting their official position and funds to make considerable sums of money for themselves by illegal black bourse activities may have been a strong factor influencing both Travaglio and Rossetti against making serious efforts to obtain Levi's release.

During this period of debriefing, Levi was accommodated in Cairo and measures were taken to prevent the arrival of 'Mr Rose' from being noticed by anyone who had known him previously. When questioned about this, Levi identified just three people who might remember him. They were: the porter at the National Hotel; George Khouri, who was still in an internment camp; and a journalist, Habib Jamati, to whom Levi had been introduced by Khouri, and SIME attempted to trace. Meanwhile James Robertson conducted a preliminary interview with Levi and decided that he had probably been imprisoned because of some rivalry between the Abwehr and Count Scirombo, one factor being that the entire Italian espionage system in Egypt had apparently gone to ground as soon as war had been declared in June 1940, a debacle that required the Germans to step in to rectify the situation. Robertson also speculated that Travaglio had been content to let Levi languish in an Italian prison where he would be unable to create problems for him with the Gestapo, on the basis that he had realised that Levi must have been a double agent, most probably for the French only. 'There is no evidence however, that Travaglio or anyone else knew him to be a *British* double agent, and whatever the Abwehr knew, it is clear from the visit to the Lido in June 1941 that Travaglio was sufficiently scared of the Gestapo or the Russian Front to keep his ideas to himself'.

CHAPTER EIGHT

PLAN JACOBITE

I n May 1944, ISLD put up a proposal to SIME and 'A' Force suggesting a scheme, codenamed Plan JACOBITE, which would greatly expand CHEESE's operations, and have him establish a network in Greece. JACOBITE envisaged that the original organisation in Cairo would be left in the hands of MISANTHROPE, now codenamed MARIE, and that CHEESE should travel to Greece so he could fulfil a counter-espionage mission and peddle false information about Allied activities across the Balkans coordinated by a sub-group of the 30 Committee designated the 39 Committee. The proposal to the Abwehr was transmitted by CHEESE on 29 August, together with a request for an address in Athens where he could collect a transmitter. As Douglas Roberts noted on 8 September,

> From what we know of CHEESE's past history we are inclined to think it probable that the Germans will make some effort to comply with his proposal. In preparation for this provisional plans have been made during the past two months for the case officer to proceed eventually to Athens in order to be responsible for making use of the wireless set which we hope the enemy will leave behind for CHEESE. He will be accompanied, in the event of the

255

plan materialising, by our wireless operator, the latter being essential for the continuation of the link since his operating style has been well known to the Germans over the course of the past three years. After the transfer of CHEESE, it is our intention to continue to maintain the link from Cairo by making notional use of CHEESE's (of course imaginary) young woman friend, who is already well known to the Germans as a reliable sub-agent and who is believed by them to be a fairly competent wireless operator. For this purpose we have a second operator available in SIME.

If – as may occur very shortly – this plan is brought to fruition by our receipt from the Germans of definite instructions in regard to the address in Athens, I think it would be a pity not to make use of it, especially if it is remembered that CHEESE has served the enemy for three years and is likely therefore to be welcomed by them should he prove able to continue his service in another territory. The officer in charge of the case has had two years' experience in double agent work and is most competent at his job.

By September all the various interested British agencies had agreed to the scheme, and, on 23 September, Roberts, who had by then succeeded Maunsell at SIME, wrote to ISLD's Colonel Hill-Dillon to confirm that the Abwehr had also embraced the notion and had even buried a wireless set and a cache of gold in the Athens suburb of Psychiko. The project, which became known as the ODYSSEY, was originally intended for Pope as case officer and Rowley Shears as radio operator to move to Athens, but SIME decided that a new case officer, fluent in Greek, was required, a recommendation that was adopted. Accordingly, very detailed directions were relayed from Cairo to Athens so the treasure could be recovered. As a security precaution the Abwehr declined to send CHEESE an exact address but instead on 4 October gave him some extremely detailed instructions about where to find the buried transmitter and £10 in gold in the capital's northern suburbs.

You go from the capital in the direction of Kifisia main road to Psychiko. Along the Kifisia road you will find a street called Pericleous on your right. Follow the street until the corner of Kyteropis Street and pay attention to the white house forming the corner of the two above-mentioned streets. The garden door of this house is in Pericleous Street and has a plate with the name Mitsopoulosis. From the corner where the white house is following Evtkopis Street in the same direction as the main road, that is to say, to the North. Now watch carefully on your left. From the approach to this white house, after a distance of about 40 metres, there is an isolated fig tree, then after 250 metres there are three pits resembling a kind of disused quarry. The last one, that is the biggest, has a sort of entrance or sunken path from the West formed by two big rocks covered with earth. This is the secret place. On entering the secret place immediately to the right on the ground there is a very white stone engraved with the letters XXX. Buried underneath, at about 30 centimetres, there is a black parcel, it is the cover of a little portable suitcase containing the instrument and the papers. The key is attached. You had better cut this rubber cover on the spot with your knife.

Now pass into the entrance and turn left. At a distance of about five paces you will see on the ground a stone formed by the rock resembling an artificial plaque. This stone is marked by a triangle engraved on it. Directly underneath this sign you will find a box containing 10 English pounds in gold.

Late in October 1944 the newly reopened SIS station in Athens was given the task of digging up the promised radio, an adventure which was summarised by one of the officers involved on 26 October:

We arrived on 23 October, a Monday, and immediately on entering the hotel recognised Brigadier Dudley Clarke. At a meeting the same evening it was decided that a search should be made as soon as possible. I offered to go out at first light on the 24th.

Wearing civilian clothes I went out in a car lent by MI9 to a spot on the main Kifisia road. You will recall that I came away from GHQ more or less briefed to look on the left of this road for Pericleous Street and not on the right. This delayed me a little. But the German instructions proved extremely exact in every detail. I am returning to you the aerial photograph which I brought away from Cairo on which I have marked the streets Pericleous and Evtkopis, the white house and the three pits. I have put a spot of ink near the rock-like gates of the last pit – and you can even see the young fig tree at forty metres from the house.

I got out of my car and after some walking about looking at street names, I found Pericleous Street on the right-hand side of the road. My concern was not about the possibility of being accosted by another agent or being surprised by a booby-trap but about the ELAS bands who were roving the area and the streets of Athens arresting people they didn't like. Pericleous Street brought me to a white house bearing the name Mitsopoulosis. I turned left and sure enough I found myself in Evtkopis Street. At forty metres I found the fig tree and two hundred and fifty metres further on the largest of three pits. They were certainly not quarries – mere diggings which people tended to use as refuse dumps for old tins.

It was now quite light but I decided that I could take the risk of going into the pit despite the proximity of houses on three sides. Going through the motions of obeying nature's call, I left the street. The pit had, on the west side, exactly the entrance described, rather like a Minoan gate, twelve feet high.

You can see the gate in the photograph. On my right I found the white rock marked with an X, and taking five paces, I found the tablet-like rock marked with a triangle. In very high spirits I returned to the main road, found my car and went back to shave.

I reported to 39 Committee the complete success of my recce.

I decided to dig that morning and as a Greek speaker, Captain Lafontaine, offered to come with me and to remain in the car, I took only a clasp knife, a torch and my automatic. We left Athens by 0200 hours on 25 October. I was digging by 0230. After digging for the set for about three-quarters of an hour

I had made a hole about eighteen inches deep and two feet wide under the X marked on the rock. Our instructions were to dig 30 centimetres, about one foot. Then I heard a tin kicked. I passed through the gate and flattened myself against the sides of the shallow pit into which the gate leads. I waited five minutes. Again I heard a metallic click much nearer. It may have been an animal but I decided to return to the road. I made a detour and found the car. We drove a mile further along the Kifisia road and stopped. I decided to wait until the sky lightened and dig without having to use a torch.

I returned at about 0430 and dug beneath the X mark to a depth of two feet. Disappointed, I pushed back the earth and tried for the gold below the triangle. I reached a depth of eighteen inches and again had to fill in the hole. But it was still early enough to try once more. I returned to the car, obtained Captain Lafontaine's help and return to the spot. We dug up both holes again to a good two feet in depth. We covered our traces before we returned to the car.

I felt now that my next attempt had to be made as soon as possible, and had to be, to some extent, final. I asked Rowley Shears to put on civilian clothes and come with me at 2200 on the 25th. Captain Lafontaine again remained in the car. Rowley and I dug to a depth of three feet square using pick and shovel. We found nothing and refilled the pits made.

The committee here has decided that it is not useful to continue digging and that security will be endangered by any further attempts. I did think of sounding the whole pit with a mine detecting apparatus – but I cannot believe that the German who was so exact in every detail of his instructions can made a mistake either in estimating the depth at which the set is buried, or the exact spot.

The possibilities are,

1. that the set was never buried. Either because the NCO detailed to bury it kept the gold and sold the set after making the markings on the rock, or else because the Germans had to leave prematurely,

2. that instructions were left with some post-occupational agent to buy a set for CHEESE after the departure of the Germans but that following the recent arrests of many stay-behind agents, these instructions have not yet been carried out,

3. that the Odyssey was a hoax – but I cannot believe this, particularly now that I have received your inward traffic of 22 October, [or]

4. that the set and the gold were stolen. But the ground at both places was solid and did not appear to have been disturbed. I noticed that the grass over the 'gold' spot did come away very easily and rootlessly. Otherwise my opinion is that the soil had not been touched for at least a month. We have had a lot of rain here lately – in fact my first dig took place in rain which drenched my clothes.

THE FUTURE

Obviously MISANTHROPE will have to report that CHEESE had written saying that he had had no luck. And we must wait for reactions. I am absolutely certain that I have found the right place, as you will when you look at the enclosed photograph which is remarkably clear. Mideast should scrap the Stadtplan of that area – it's worse than useless. But it is possible that, despite the accuracy of the instructions in every other respect, the set may not have been buried 'directement' below the markings.

It is certainly not possible to continue digging for the present. The 'reaction' may encourage us to try harder in which case we can think again. But it would be a bad policy to continue merely because we can. CHEESE could make a set but the story would stink. The Hun knows well how little technical material is available here. CHEESE would have to claim that he had cut the crystals himself.

This report was to be a huge disappointment as ISLD reported to Cairo the same day.

> Attempts to find CHEESE set and money unsuccessful. Place definitely located but both cupboards bare, with no sign of having been disturbed. Consequently EFFIGY and PEDANT of greater importance to DOWAGER. These cases now being developed. CHEESE will send letter to MARIE explaining position, on receipt of which suggest she inform employers and ask if they have any further instructions for CHEESE.

This crushing blow implied that CHEESE had reached the end of his usefulness, perhaps had even been abandoned by the Abwehr, which had established at least two stay-behind sources in Athens, EFFIGY and PEDANT, who were considered more valuable and were supporting a deception scheme codenamed DOWAGER (formerly GALVESTON). Unfortunately PEDANT, who communicated in Greek to the Abstelle in Vienna, supervised by Geoffrey Hinton, had to 'lie low' for a period but EFFIGY, who transmitted direct to Berlin in French, was unaffected. Certainly, from ISLD's viewpoint, the situation was clear, and B Section would be fully occupied with running them as double agents.

On 12 January 1945 CHEESE and, more specifically MISANTHROPE, were placed in jeopardy by the arrest in Greece by the local Deuxième Bureau of a German spy, Konstantinos Kossiadis, whose contact details had been supplied to her by the Abwehr just four days earlier as the person who had been entrusted with CHEESE's transmitter.

Kossiadis led his captors to an Abwehr IH I safe-house where a wireless transmitter was recovered. The capture of Kossiadis resulted in the detention of five other members of his stay-behind network, and the fear was, as articulated by British counter-intelligence officer Captain G. D. Klingopolos, on 24 January, that

a slight suspicion will certainly fall on CHEESE as a result of these arrests
– if the Germans ever learn of them. The wireless agents so far captured
were not working. But so many thousands of people have been arrested
or transported in the last few weeks that suspicion will certainly be slight.
After a lapse of some weeks MISANTHROPE should be able to report that
CHEESE has searched in vain for the occupant of the empty house who was
not known to the permanent inhabitants of the district.

This message prompted a reply from Eric Pope on 29 January who reassured Klingopolos by pointing out that MISANTHROPE had informed the Abwehr that she had passed on the safe-house's address to CHEESE on 26 January, long after the contentious arrest. Pope also disclosed that SIME intended that MISANTHROPE's final transmission to the Abwehr would take place on about 10 February when it was planned that she would announce that CHEESE had failed to find Kossiadis and therefore, his mission having been frustrated, he intended to return immediately to Egypt, and that in the meantime she would cease transmitting. As Pope explained, 'This will be MISANTHROPE's last message. She will not come up again – leaving the Germans completely in the dark as to what has happened to CHEESE and to her.'

The decision to liquidate CHEESE was taken at a 30 Committee meeting held on 7 January when it was proposed that on around 10 February MISANTHROPE would relay a message from CHEESE reporting that he had failed to find the wireless buried at Chillabdariou Street in Athens, and then on 15 February announced that, 'having got the wind up' because of a warning from her sub-source ELIF, she was going to cease all activity for a month.

The news that the CHEESE case was to be closed down by SIME on 17 February 1945 was an event that prompted MI5 to express the wish for the radio link to be maintained, as Guy Liddell wrote to Pope from London on 4 March.

Alec Kellar and I have discussed this exhaustively; I, for my part, have talked it over with John Marriott (who is now head of the section formerly run by Colonel T. A. Robertson) and we are in agreement that it is in general worthwhile to continue running any double agents who are in wireless contact with the Germans as long as the latter are prepared to reply to our signals (that is to say, unless there is any very strong reason – such as, for example, the possibility of compromising other agents) for closing down other than the approaching end of hostilities.

I am hoping to discuss with the department responsible for post-armistice security in Germany the question of possible future underground SD activities and, as soon as I have been able to acquire more information on this subject I will let you know. In the meantime the following points are perhaps worth your consideration.

Firstly, it may be taken for granted that elements of the SD will go underground; among their objects in so doing will be the continuation of the use of agents for the purpose of rendering the task of the occupying Allies as difficult and uncomfortable as possible. In so doing they will probably endeavour to create dissention between the various Allies: it will be, of course, especially within the boundaries of the former Reich that they will attempt to achieve this aim, but it will no doubt suit their purpose if they can make trouble further afield (in passing it is worth noting that if KISS survives after the Armistice, he may appear to them to be especially suitable as a tool for any activities of this kind). Quite apart from making trouble of this kind, it also seems likely that the German underground, whatever form it may take, will be anxious to acquire information from the outside world – the more so now that its necessarily mole-like activities will cut it off from normal contact with the countries outside the former Reich. For such purpose, agents of the type of CHEESE, if they continue in being, might well be useful both (in appearance) to the Germans and (in fact) to us.

It may, of course, be argued that any underground SD organisation will find it impossible in practice to maintain wireless communications owing to the danger of their being D/F'd by the occupying Allies. It seems to me however, that there are certain remote regions of Germany where, by nature of the terrain, it would be extremely difficult to locate a sufficiently mobile wireless station. There is also another side to this argument in that, by maintaining communication through CHEESE, or any similar agent, we can provide the Allied security authorities in Germany with a target for their D/F experts and thereby perhaps assist them to locate concealed German headquarters.

It is proposed to enter into this whole question in greater detail when we have SIME's opinion.

As Pope later explained, the decision agreed by both the head of SIME and the Chairman of the 30 Committee allowed for the possibility that CHEESE might be revived, and he acknowledged that the Germans had continued to try and re-establish the link throughout March. He had arranged for the CHEESE/MISANTHROPE control station in Germany to be monitored after the traffic had been closed down on 10 February, and although no signals were reported in the period until 3 March, Pope suspected that there had been undetected transmissions, because, as he noted,

I have had Mackenzie listening since 2 March. He has heard the Germans calling on 2, 5 and 7 March, but not since 7 March. I think it likely that the Germans will go on calling intermittently for some time.

Pope went on to explain that

our method of closing down the link was intended to allow for the possibility of reviving it should the necessity arise, and also, incidentally, to ensure that the Germans should go on calling us for some time. The 30 Committee have discussed your proposal to revive CHEESE at some length. The security considerations which prompted 'A' Force to press for the closing of the case are still valid and, in the opinion of Head of SIME and the 30 Committee, it is undesirable to revive it.

CHAPTER NINE

MAX AND MORITZ

A further, unanticipated complication in the CHEESE case was the discovery, in early 1942, that an Abwehr source, codenamed MORITZ, was supplying information which appeared to originate in Cairo to the KO in Sofia. This remained a signals analysis problem for cryptanalysts in England until July 1942 when Johannes Eppler and Heinrich Sandstede were arrested and admitted to SIME, their interrogators, in July 1942 that they had been assigned those codenames for their wireless traffic, but they had never been able to achieve a single transmission. So who was MORITZ, and was there another enemy spy-ring in Egypt capable of contradicting CHEESE?

The mystery surrounding MAX and MORITZ would last for years, but its origins are to be found in the ISOS traffic on the Sofia to Vienna circuit, with the call-signs SCHWERT and VERA, relaying information from the Middle East and, apparently, Cairo. During the period of interception, in 1942 and 1943, almost a thousand messages were intercepted and decrypted. Between December 1941 and March 1942 forty messages from MORITZ were read, and in August 1942 SIS's Section V reviewed the texts and, having rejected the possibility that they were based on signals intelligence, judged them to have 'a professional flavour, being up to date, terse, well-arranged and definite', noting that the information came from 'Syria through Iraq and Persia to Egypt and Libya' but concluding that 'there were no clues to the sources of the MORITZ reports.' The content varied in quality from patently false to uncannily accurate. For example, on 23 October 1942 there was a signal with a completely authentic content, although the raid mentioned had not yet been released to the press:

> MORITZ reports – 100 British Lancaster bombers attacked Genoa port in northern Italy last night. Reports indicate accurate hits against warships and supplies at the port.

On the following day there was another message in a similar vein;

> MORITZ reports – General Montgomery is leading a new British operation, Operation LIGHTFOOT near el Alamein, west of Alexandria. The Germans have begun to retreat westwards.

At a particularly critical moment in the North African campaign, on 9 November 1942,

> MORITZ reports – Last night American forces invaded North Africa in Operation TORCH. The British launched Operation SUPERCHARGE from the east and advanced towards Tunis. The double offensives against the Germans from east and west will trap them and destroy Rommel's entire Korps.

The very next day, 10 November 1942,

> MORITZ reports – Warships crossed the Suez Canal from the south. They will join the marine forces in the Mediterranean Sea.

Later the same month an inaccurate message dated 30 November 1942 stated:

> MORITZ reports – Yesterday and today American bombers attacked Bizerte, Tunis, from the air. Air raids against German targets in Bizerte will continue.

A few days later, on 8 December 1942, there was an accurate text:

> MORITZ reports – Large British forces are making preparations for an offensive near Sirte Bay in Libya.

These messages, which would include five purporting to give a daily commentary on the British attack on Tobruk, and suggesting that Rommel's DAK was on the verge of collapse, prompted a review of the material to identify clues to the identity of the network or spy responsible for gathering the information.

> The most striking feature of the MORITZ reports was that they were at the same time detailed and for the most part so inaccurate that they seemed to be reasonably explained either as a deliberate attempt to deceive the Germans or as a concoction put out for mercenary reasons.

The resulting analysis concluded that a transmitter in the Spanish embassy in Ankara codenamed ANKER, was in daily contact with SCHWERT, the Abstelle in Sofia, using a hand cipher. The exact same messages were then relayed from Sofia to VERA in Vienna on an Enigma channel at the same time each afternoon, except Sundays. Each of the transmissions consisted of four or five messages from MAX, and just one or two from MORITZ. VERA, the Vienna Abstelle headed by the Graf Rudolf Marogna-Redwitz, then passed the messages on to BURG, the Abwehr's headquarters in Berlin. Within half an hour, BURG was circulating the reports to Fremde Heere Ost at the Boyen Fortress in Lötzen, eastern Prussia, and to the OKW headquarters in Rome. The circuit had opened in October 1940 and had broadcast a final signal on 13 February 1945.

A lengthy study of the traffic conducted by the Radio Security Service (RSS) revealed that MAX and MORITZ were part of an Abwehr dienstelle headed by a certain Fritz Klatt, a name that turnd out to be an alias adopted by a Czech Jew, Richard Kauder, whose network of more than seventy agents, of whom around a dozen were Jews, accounted for much of the Sofia Abstelle's activities. Kauder operated from a company that he owned, the Mittermeyer Import-Export Company, based at 55 Skoolev Street, not far from Otto Wagner's KO at 57 Patriarch Aphtimey Street.

The RSS study, conducted by Gilbert Ryle, posed a series of questions. How could Klatt's network submit reports from Cairo to Sofia on the same day? Some of the messages referred to events that had taken place across the Middle East the previous day. One significant characteristic of the traffic was the frequent misspellings of names, and the use of Russian names, for example Galiopolia for Heliopolis. Similarly, fighter aircraft were described as *isterbaitle*. Broadly, the information from the Middle East did not pose a serious threat to the Allies, and much of it could have been gleaned by the Germans from other sources. The reporting was long on generalities but short on specifics, so the decision was taken to inform the Soviets of the existence of MAX and MORITZ, and the news was delivered at a meeting convened with Stalin in Moscow by the SIS representative, Cecil Barclay, on 19 April 1943, in the presence of the ambassador, Archie Clark Kerr. Curiously, the Soviets seemed disinterested, despite a further conference with the DMI, General Fyodor Kuznetsov, on 29 July, and the traffic continued, apparently unaffected, so the British concluded that the entire organisation was operating under the

NKVD's supervision and therefore was part of some elaborate deception campaign.

That verdict had been reached after the most intensive scrutiny conducted by both MI5 and Section V which included a veracity check on forty-nine messages decrypted in June and July 1943, of which only five were thought to have any value. Thirty-three were shown to be useless, and eleven could not be subjected to any comparison.

Research into MAX and MORITZ escalated after the war when captured Abwehr officers underwent interrogation by the Allies in an effort to identify the organisation's sources. MAX turned out to be General Anton Turkul, a Ukrainian who had fought against the Bolsheviks in the Russian Civil War with the whites, and had later settled in comfortable exile in Paris where he had become an informant for Dick Ellis at the SIS station. When interviewed, Turkul revealed that the codenames MAX and MORITZ were not individual agents, but codenames for groups of geographically based networks, MAX being the Ukraine and Russia, and MORITZ being Turkey and the Middle East. He alleged that the names had been inspired by Wilhelm Busch's illustrated rhyming tales, *Max and Moritz: A Story of Seven Boyish Pranks*, published in 1865, and admitted that he had worked for the NKVD for years, and that Kauder had quickly realised that his own organisation was actually sponsored by the Soviets.

Kauder was freed from prison in Vienna by American troops in May 1945 and under interrogation he admitted that his entire organisation had been run by the NKVD, but he had decided, for reasons of self-preservation (because he was already in fear of the Gestapo), not to tell the Abwehr. He was later transferred to Camp King in Oberrursel where he was questioned by Klop Ustinov, and then in 1946 by Gilbert Ryle.

Kauder's candour helped solve the mystery of MAX and MORITZ and provided eloquent proof that if the NKVD was ruthless enough to accept hideous sacrifices to enhance the status of a valued double agent, the Abwehr across the Mediterranean region was inherently corrupt.

CHAPTER TEN

FINALE

After the war Count Scirombo was interrogated, and he shed new light on the CHEESE case. He confirmed that Levi's original recruitment had been conducted jointly by SIM and the Abwehr. Without realising the double agent's true role, Scirombo confirmed that Levi had been sent to Egypt posing as a Jewish refugee seeking to escape religious persecution. He also said that Levi's sub-agent had communicated first with a SIM wireless station at Forte Braschi, but control had later been switched to an exclusively German facility in Athens.

Scirombo claimed that Levi had raised suspicions when it was learned that he had visited the British delegation in Belgrade while on his way to Turkey. The decision then had been taken to question Levi through an informant who happened to be one of his friends. This had been the encounter with the Italian air force officer, Captain Alessi, and Scirombo said that Levi had

talked very freely to the informer and told him all the details of the mission
he had undertaken on behalf of SIM and the German Intelligence Service.

He added that he was expecting shortly to receive instructions to return to Egypt, but had no intention of doing so.

The Germans endeavoured to bring pressure to bear on SIM to obtain Levi's release. They pointed out that Levi had accomplished a very successful mission and, in an effort to convince [the] subject, showed him copies of the messages which were being received from the agent in Cairo. Subject states that the quality of the traffic was excellent and the information given on Allied troop movements were checked and found to be accurate. The agent quoted as one of the principal sources of information was an Allied NCO working in a military headquarters situated near the Italian consulate in Cairo. Subject also remembers seeing messages requesting funds. In spite of all this SIM refused to adhere to the repeated requests from the German Intelligence Service for Levi's release and the latter remained in a concentration camp until the Armistice when subject supposes he was set free by the Germans. (Note: subject has no idea of his present whereabouts.) In December 1943, when subject was evacuated from Athens by the Germans, the wireless contact established by Levi in Cairo was still functioning.

Another loose end was represented by Johannes Eppler and Heinrich Sandstede who, in February 1943 had come to the end of their usefulness. Accordingly, SIME asked Herbert Hart, of MI5's B1(b) section, whether there was any point in sending them to London.

In our view all the intelligence these characters have to give has probably been extracted from them already, and even if it has not we have no better facilities for extracting it than Mid East, with their knowledge of local conditions, background, etc. We therefore have no objection to their being dealt with locally.

Consequently, Eppler and his partner were detained as prisoners of war in Egypt until March 1946 when Eppler and Sandstede were repatriated to Germany. The first details of their story emerged in 1958 when the war correspondent Leonard Mosley published *The Cat and the Mouse*, a highly inaccurate account in which he claimed that Eppler had achieved radio contact with Rommel's headquarters, and had employed a book code based on Daphne du Maurier's *Rebecca*. In fact, of course, the code was based on *The Unwarranted Death*.

Another version of Eppler's arrest emerged in 1965 when Colonel A. W. Sansom, who had served with the Field Security Wing in Cairo in 1942, published *I Spied Spies* and claimed that he had masterminded the raid on the German agents. According to him, the first clue that a spy had reached Egypt was when New Zealand troops had overrun the Bir Hachim intercept site and found two PoWs, who did not speak English, in possession of a copy of *Rebecca* that had been sold in a Lisbon shop.

> I sent a cable to London and asked them to investigate. The answer gave me the first, as yet insignificant, lead on Eppler. At least now I knew for certain that this must have been the code book of an agent and that the man concerned was certainly in this country. It wasn't much – but it was a start.

In Eppler's own account, *Rommel ruft Kairo* which appeared first in 1960, with an English language edition, *Operation Condor*, released in 1977, he provided a very different tale, diametrically contradicting his CSDIC statements. He claimed that he had been recruited by the Abwehr in Beirut in May 1937, and since that date had undertaken numerous missions across eastern Europe and the Middle East, acted as an interpreter for Adolf Hitler, and operated as a spy in Alexandria long before his final participation in Operation CONDOR. Furthermore, he and his companion had established good radio contact with

Rommel's headquarters, and his belly-dancing girlfriend Hekmat Fahmy had been a very active co-conspirator.

> From Hekmat's sources I had received some essential information about the Allies' growing military superiority: at that very hour 100,000 mines were being taken up to the Alamein Front, and a new defence line between the sea and the Qattara Depression was being organised. Hundreds of brand-new American tanks were ploughing through the sand on their way to the front. I knew that the Allies' material superiority was growing steadily – that the enemy was swimming in fuel and up to his ears in tanks and artillery – and that all this would shortly be thrown against Rommel's army. Our work had all been a complete waste of effort.
>
> Hekmat had wasted her time and risked her life in vain worming secrets out of British officers. In vain had I been nosing about at the Turf Club, the meeting place of Allied staff officers. In vain had I crept round the perimeter of the Eighth Army supply depot at Abassia to take down details of what was being loaded and unloaded there. Someone back home, having established that the two radio operators had been captured at Rommel's headquarters, had cut off our line of communications and had stopped acknowledging our radio signals. Then we received this message: 'stop! mission aborted. beware of British decoy information. don't reply. we'll lie low.'

Eppler's story effectively ended at his arrest, and he drew a discreet veil over his subsequent experiences, omitting his role as a prosecution witness in the various trials that took place, for example, of Anwar el Sadati. Nor did Eppler expand on the subject before his death in 1999. Sadati, of course, succeeded Gamal Abdel Nasser as president of Egypt in October 1970, and was assassinated in October 1981.

There is much in Eppler's somewhat self-serving autobiography that is contradicted by his SIME dossier, and there are other claims, for example that he discovered from his money-changer that he had been given counterfeit sterling notes by the Abwehr, that do not appear in the file, as one might have expected.

Eppler's interrogator, Harold Shergold, who was the first CSDIC officer to be decorated during the war, joined SIS in 1947, attended the Cambridge University's Russian course and used his interrogation skills on Oleg Penkovsky and George Blake in 1961. He retired in 1980.

Another of the Abwehr's spies, Paul E. Fackenheim, survived the war and in 1985, when he was then living in Henstedt-Ulzberg, near Hamburg, was the subject of a biography, *Arrows of the Almighty*, by Michael Bar-Zohar. Apparently unaware of the influence, or even existence of TRIANGLE, and without the benefit of Fackenheim's yet to be declassified MI5 file, Bar-Zohar speculated that Fackenheim's mission had been deliberately betrayed by a mole, Hauptsturmfuhrer Kronberg, the senior Sicherheitsdienst officer in Athens, motivated by inter-agency rivalry and jealousy of the Abwehr, even before KOCH had embarked on his flight.

Of the German spymasters, Rolf von der Marwitz was interned in Turkey in August 1944 and was repatriated in November 1946. He retired to Wiesbaden and died, aged seventy-seven, in September 1966. Erich Vermehren adopted a new identity, 'Eric de Saventheim', and went to live in Switzerland. He died in Bonn in April 2005. Paul Leverkühn survived his imprisonment by the Gestapo and served as a lawyer at the International War Crimes Tribunal at Nuremberg. He later resumed his law practice, was elected to the Bundestag, and died in March 1960. Willi Hamburger changed his name to Wilhelm Hendricks and after his release from American custody became a well-known journalist in Vienna, where he died in 2011.

Having been released from a PoW camp at Weilheim in Bavaria in June 1945, Walter Sensburg was arrested in Salzburg by the American Counter-Intelligence Corps in August 1945 and interrogated at length. He proved very cooperative and provided a detailed account of the Athens Abstelle which he had commanded from November 1941. He also described his star agent, ROBERTO as having

transmitted valuable information on Allied forces in Egypt and North Africa. ROBERTO was the sole Ast Athens agent reporting from Egypt. For this reason all the evaluation agencies showed interest in ROBERTO. ROBERTO's principal assignment was reconnaissance on Allied forces in the Cairo area, for which work he was briefed regularly and in detail. The briefs came from the evaluation sections of Fremde Heere West through Abwehr I in Berlin and the i/c of O/Bef So, first in Saloniki and then in Belgrade. Further enquiries sometimes had to be made by I-H Ast Athens, where ROBERTO's messages were checked before being forwarded to evaluation offices at higher headquarters, ROBERTO's reports to Ast Athens covered:

1. The appearance of new unit designations.

2. Troop and staff movements in Cairo, at the front, and in Syria.

3. Organisation of a Greek brigade in Egypt.

4. Names of CGs and COs.

ROBERTO once reported he had recruited one or two collaborators, but these were soon dropped, since the Ast was unable to supply the necessary funds to ROBERTO. Later ROBERTO indicated he was receiving most of his information from two unidentified persons, a woman friend and a corporal. Details are not known to Sensburg.

The twice-weekly wireless communication between Ast Athens and ROBERTO was sometimes interrupted by atmospheric disturbances; occasionally ROBERTO was silent because of dissatisfaction over pay. Generally wireless communication was satisfactory.

ROBERTO's reliability was doubted by the Ast Athens station, since the much better equipped station sometimes had to cope with transmission or reception difficulties, while at the other end ROBERTO reported no difficulties whatsoever. Although these suspicions were widely shared, no proof of ROBERTO's unreliability ever came to light.

Sensburg has no definite information on payments to ROBERTO. He knows only that Rittmeister Graf Schwerin, of Abwehr I Berlin, was sent to North Africa with the mission of paying ROBERTO after the expected occupation of Cairo.

When Rossetti left Athens in summer 1943, Schenk took over supervision of ROBERTO. Schenk, transferred to KO Bulgara after the dissolution of Ast Athens, continued to oversee ROBERTO from there.

Naturally, his interrogators ensured that Sensburg never suspected that ROBERTO had always been under British control but, over many hours of questioning, Sensburg proved very cooperative and provided an account of all his agents across the Middle East. Because the responsibility for intelligence collection in the region was shared with the rather smaller KO Istanbul, about which so much was already known because of Vermehren and Hamburger, Sensburg served to fill in the gaps. His description of the Abstelle's assets made fascinating reading, especially when his version of events coincided with cases with which SIME was already very familiar, and involved that recurring character, Clemens Rossetti. Among his list of sources were two failures: MIMI had been parachuted into Palestine or Egypt in late 1941 with a transmitter, but was never heard of again. Similarly, GEORGES had been 'dropped' into 'Egypt, Palestine or Syria at the end of 1941 or the beginning of 1942' and disappeared. MOZART,

a completely capable linguist and musician, was enlisted by Rossetti in Italy and received only tactical training. In late 1942 he went to Turkey, but Ast

Athens received no military information from him. KO Turkey probably took over MOZART when Rossetti was transferred there after Ast Athens' dissolution. REMY received tactical and probably wireless training. Sensburg recalls vaguely that REMY essayed a trip to Egypt, via Turkey in 1943, but that he obtained a visa only for Turkey. Ast Athens never received any information from the man. Sensburg assumes he was taken over by KO Turkey when Ast Athens was dissolved.

Sensburg also mentioned Paul Fackenheim, revealing that originally he had been trained 'to be parachuted into England, but adverse flying conditions necessitated abandonment of the scheme'. He also confirmed that after he had been dropped near Haifa on a military reconnaissance mission, KOCH had fallen silent.

According to Senesburg, his Abstellen relied on two agent recruiters, Ludwig Stoeckel, codenamed MARIO, who had previously worked in Lyons but had been brought to Athens by Rossetti because of his strong family connections in Greece, and Rosa Zardiniti, who may have been assisted by her son. These handlers acted as intermediaries between Snesburg and the Abstette's networks, of which the largest would have been the Georgians, a trio of three Russian political refugees recruited by Rossetti in Rome and codenamed MARCO, KANT and TELL. They arrived in Athens in May or June 1942 and having undergone training were about to be deployed in the Middle East when they were recalled to Berlin and then sent to Warsaw. Sensburg did not encounter them again. There were also two other distinct groups. One was known as MUSTA-SASCHA-PARIS, also recruited by Rossetti, which was to go to 'Cyprus or Egypt. Before preparations were completed, Ast Athens was dissolved and Schenk continued to supervise the three agents from KO Bulgaria. Schenk thought highly of the MUSTA-SASCHA-PARIS contact. Sensburg is uninformed as to their subsequent activities.'

Sensburg also talked of the AGFA group, a pair of Afghan princes related to ex-King Amanullah. One was codenamed APOLLO and the other was Obeid Ullah, and they had been recruited by Rossetti in Rome, however, although the agents reached Athens in preparation for a mission to Turkey, and then to Syria, Palestine or Egypt, the scheme stalled for lack of travel papers, followed by a ban from Berlin on any activity that might embarrass the Afghan government. Accordingly, the AGFA project was shelved indefinitely.

SIME was particularly interested in the ALT group, of whom Sensburg recalled ARTHUR and TOM, both of whom had Cypriot backgrounds.

> In late 1942 or early 1943 the group left Piraeus in a fishing craft for Cyprus to recconnoitre Allied forces in Cyprus and the Middle East. Later the group was to proceed to Egypt with the same mission. Although wireless communication between the ALT mission and Ast Athens was effected, Sensburg does not recall any messages with military information from Egypt.

He also listed the MOHR-BELAMI group, which consisted of 'two Armenians and a wireless operator'.

> The group left Greece for the Syrian coast in a fishing craft with the mission of reconnoitering Allied forces, mainly air forces, in the Middle East. The group was unsuccessful and never established wireless communication with Ast Athens. The Ast later learned that the participants in the mission had been arrested on espionage charges and that at least one of them had been executed.

Sensburg also mentioned two women upon whom he had relied. One was Anna Dettlach, codenamed POLA, who had been trained in Brussels, given a forged Scandinavian passport in the name of Larsen and sent to Athens in the autumn of 1941 for a mission to Turkey, where she had been married before the war.

> In late 1941 POLA was sent to Turkey where she was to approach high Allied
> officers in an effort to obtain certain military documents. From Turkey she
> was to go to Cairo on the same mission. She was unable to procure the
> desired documents however, and never reached Cairo.

The other woman was a Belgian, codenamed LUX, who was transferred to Athens in 'the spring of 1942 with a recommendation of being thoroughly reliable' and was tasked 'by Sensburg to make contact with persons having exploitable connections in the Middle East. None of the persons engaged by LUX proved qualified for agent work.'

A review of Sensburg's total agent rosta suggested that he had achieved very mixed results. Of the agents he was responsible for supervising, only a few were deployed operationally and none of them succeeded in reaching Egypt where, of course, they might have been in a position to contradict CHEESE. As a result, CHEESE's reporting was accepted by the Abwehr, and Heere Fremde West, unchallenged. The Allied assessment of Sensburg's record of failure would be reinforced by other Abwehr detainees who were arrested making their way back to what was left of their homeland.

Despite requests for Otto Mayer to be returned to Yugoslavia to face a trial for alleged war crimes, and an undertaking to this effect given by the SOE representative at Tito's headquarters, he was released from Camp 020 in July 1945 and returned to Germany.

Otto Wagner, the Abwehr chief in Sofia, was detained in the French zone of occupation in Germany and interrogated at Bad Wildungen. Richard Klauder and Anton Turkel were questioned at Camp King, Frankurt. Richard Klauder died in Salzburg in July 1960 and General Turkel died in Munich in 1958.

Of the other British double agents run in the Middle East, TWIST proved to be one of the most resilient. Employed by the Italian consulate in Istanbul, TWIST volunteered his services to SIS in May 1942 but in October 1943 TRIANGLE revealed that he had also made himself available to the Abwehr to whom he had admitted his relationship with the British. SIS continued to run him, even when he disclosed in April 1944 that the SD had approached him too. In June he produced an SD questionnaire relating to Allied military intentions in the region, but the channel closed in August when the Turkish authorities interned the entire German diplomatic staff. Undeterred, SIS tried to have TWIST offer himself to the Japanese, but that plan failed when all Japan's envoys were expelled.

Of the Americans, Hal Lehrman worked for the *New York Times*, *Newsweek* and the *Herald Tribune* after the war and was elected president of the Overseas Press Club. He died in November 1988 and left his papers to the Kroch Library at Cornell University, from whence he had graduated in 1932.

Edgar Yolland, identified by Vermehren as having been recruited as a German spy, renounced his US citizenship in an apparent deal with the ambassador. Steinhardt and OSS reported that he was expelled from Turkey sometime before April 1945 and later tried to acquire a British passport.

Perhaps the most tragic epilogue of the CHEESE story is what happened to Evan Simpson. In 1946, having returned to Oxford for his MA, Simpson released *Time Table for Victory: A Brief and Popular Account of the Railways & Railway-owned Dockyards of Great Britain & Northern Ireland During the Six Years' War of 1939–45*, giving no clue as to how his own very considerable talent for invention had been applied during the recent conflict. Next, in 1948, he wrote *The Network: It Could Happen Here*, and then *Time after Earthquake: An adventure among Greek Islands in August 1953*. On 27 December 1953, four months after having witnessed the earthquake as part of a relief mission to the Ionian Islands, Simpson succumbed to depression and shot himself with a rifle. According to his widow, who gave evidence at an inquest held at Henley-on-Thames, he had taken his own life in woods near his home, Neal's Farm, at Checkendon in south Oxfordshire. She explained that her husband suffered from fits of depression and that when he did 'his creative power to write was destroyed'.

Two years after his death Simpson's publisher released *The Darkness*, a fictionalised account of Christ's crucifixion, as reported to the Roman security office in the form of intelligence bulletins.

Dudley Clarke, the founder of 'A' Force and the principal architect of modern wartime strategic deception, received permission to publish a sanitised version of his autobiography, *Seven Assignments*, in 1948, but was not allowed to mention CHEESE, nor proceed with his wartime memoirs, *The Secret War*. In his typically modest foreword, Clarke wrote that

> The secret war of which these pages tell was a war of wits – of fantasy and imagination fought out on an almost private basis between the supreme heads of Hitler's intelligence (and Mussolini's) and a small band of men and women – British, American and French – operating from the opposite shores of the Mediterranean Sea. The author had the honour of leading that team through five crowded, urgent years – years which brought moreover, a rare privilege to a professional soldier. For the secret war was waged rather to conserve than to destroy; the stakes were the lives of frontline troops, and the organisation which fought it was able to count its gains from the number of casualties it could avert.

Having retired from the army in 1947, he worked at Conservative Central Office, wrote a thriller, *Golden Arrow* in 1955 and died in 1977. The extent to which his stratagems and phantom armies really duped the Axis only became clear when Allied analysts had the chance to study captured enemy documents. The material recovered in France proved beyond any doubt that the Fremde Heere West was completely taken in by FORTITUDE, and, for weeks after D-Day, continued to believe that the main amphibious landings, spearheaded by the (fictitious) First United States Army Group would occur in the Pas-de-Calais. Likewise in the eastern Mediterranean, the Axis clung to the conviction, created in 1942, that the Allies intended to attack 'the soft under-belly of Europe' through the Balkans, and a memorandum drafted by the Hungarian army's chief of staff General Ferenc Szombathelyi in February 1943, immediately after he had attended a strategy conference addressed by Hitler, predicted landings in the Balkans later the same year. This flawed assessment led to the escalation of German forces in the region, which in March 1944 amounted to twenty-nine first-rate divisions, At the end of that month, in anticipation of a non-existent threat to Hungary, fourteen German divisions entered and occupied the country, including the battle-hardened II SS Panzer Corps, consisting of the 9th SS Panzer Division Hohenstaufen and 10th SS Panzer Division Frundsberg, which had been transferred from France for the purpose.

These Axis forces, therefore, were not available to defend Normandy, nor to participate in an armoured counter-attack on the invaders. Captured documents demonstrated that of the twenty-six imaginary divisions in the eastern Mediterranean dreamed up by 'A' Force, twenty-one were positively identified by enemy analysts and entered on their order-of-battle assessments.

Finally, CHEESE himself disappears from MI5's files after the decision has been taken to compensate him financially for what he had endured during his incarceration. On 4 April 1945 Captain Pierre Grandguillot of 'A' Force, formerly a Davis Cup tennis player, urged Eric Pope to treat Levi with the generosity he deserved, pointing out that this was probably the cost of his silence. Pope then advocated that CHEESE, who had expressed a wish to rejoin his wife and son in Genoa as soon as the city was occupied by the Allies, should be paid £1,300 in reward plus £2,000 in compensation for his imprisonment, being the equivalent of the 200,000 lira claimed.

> Stress should be laid on the great skill and ingenuity with which Levi ran his case in the early days, without which it could never have been developed. The point should not be overlooked that Levi may be tempted at some future date, if not treated generously enough, to make money by selling his story to the press. It would be most unfortunate if it came out prematurely and in a manner we could not control. This is thought to be a strong argument for generous treatment and for an explanation that it is given partly as the price for secrecy.

Having been paid, CHEESE drops from view as far as Whitehall is concerned, but it is believed that he returned to Italy to collect his wife and son, and then travelled to Australia, having chartered a banana-boat and filled it with a cargo of Turkish carpets which he then sold in Australia. He died in Italy in 1954, never having fully recovered from the malnutrition he experienced while in prison, the details of his remarkable adventure apparently buried forever in MI5's secret archive.

It was not until David Mure, who served in 'A' Force and chaired the 31 Committee in Beirut, published his memoirs *Practise to Deceive*, in 1977, that a slightly garbled account of the CHEESE case was made public for the first time following a fleeting reference by J. C. Masterman in *The Double Cross System of the War of 1939–45* as 'a famous double agent of the Middle East … apparently blown in 1941 but was built up again and became once more effective in the summer of 1942'.

Unfortunately Mure, without access to official records, unaware of Levi's true name or background and heavily reliant on postwar conversations with Noel Wild, gave a rather fanciful account of a double agent codenamed ORLANDO, and tried to correct the error three years later in *Master of Deception* by describing another spy, codenamed MOSES. In fact, of course, Mure had conflated several different real and notional agents and succeeded in muddying the waters.

The policy of successive postwar governments was to maintain secrecy about clandestine operations in case similar strategies might be needed in a future conflict, and unauthorised disclosures, or the speculation of individuals such as David Mure, were strongly discouraged by the authorities. Accordingly, almost nothing was said publicly about CHEESE and, even when his MI5 dossier was declassified, considerable efforts were made to redact any clues to his true identity. The secrecy surrounding his case was perpetuated only after details had been released about other wartime double agents because he had been run by SIME, an organisation that was wound up in 1958. Although MI5 would continue to have a peacetime existence right up to the present day, the British withdrawal from Palestine and Egypt eliminated the need for a large regional security apparatus and SIME simply disappeared, most of its remaining staff being absorbed by either MI5 or ISLD's parent, the Secret Intelligence Service. However, the files in SIME's registry, the essential, functioning heart of any intelligence structure, were not all repatriated to London, and most were consigned to the War Office and to the care of British Middle East Headquarters in Nicosia. Accordingly, what survives is a disparate collection of ostensibly unrelated files, together with various reports that, read separately, give little idea of what was accomplished.

Levi himself, of course, was one of the war's most remarkable spies and, working in relative isolation, was wholly dependent on his own mainly notional spy-ring. Furthermore, his handlers had absolutely no previous experience of the management of double agents, and essentially wrote the handbook on strategic deception, a concept that was entirely novel at that time. By the end of the war CHEESE had demonstrably fabricated a plausible but bogus Allied order-of-battle and, equally impressively, had conveyed it to the enemy. By any standards, this was an astonishing achievement, and the fact that the entire operation was kept under wraps for so long is equally remarkable.

Often, in the shadowy world of espionage, it is hard to discern cause and effect, to find a definite link between a message conveyed by an agent, and its verifiable consequence. In the case of MINCEMEAT, MI5's celebrated deception scheme undertaken in April 1943, it was possible to recover some enemy signals that suggested certain troop deployments had been made to the Balkans as a direct consequence of a German acceptance of the false material found on the body of a bogus military courier, 'Major William Martin RM'. Equally, documents captured after the war proved that a message from GARBO on 5 June 1944, the day before D-Day, had persuaded the Nazi High Command to cancel the transfer of the 1st SS Panzer Division from the Franco-Belgian border to Normandy. Such compelling evidence is rare, yet we now know from intercepted signals, captured enemy documents *and* the interrogation of prisoners, that CHEESE accomplished more, over a longer period, than any other single Allied agent. Although, ironically, Renato Levi himself knew little of what had been undertaken in his name, especially during the months of his imprisonment, CHEESE undermined the accuracy of the Axis assessments of Allied strength, and helped save the Suez Canal and much of the region from capture and occupation.

CIPHER DEVISED FOR CHEESE

The cipher may best be described as an extension of the familiar 'Playfair' system.

The keyword is written down (omitting any repeated letters) as the beginning of a square of five letters by five. This square is then filled in by writing down the rest of the alphabet omitting all letters already used. In order to reduce the alphabet from twenty-six letters to twenty-five it is also necessary to omit the 'K'. Thus, if the keyword is ELEMENTS the square will be:

E	L	M	N	T
S	A	B	C	D
F	G	H	I	J
O	P	Q	R	U
V	W	X	Y	Z

Each letter of the 'clear' is represented by a pair of cipher letters. The first letter of the pair may be any letter in the same vertical line as the letter to be enciphered: the second is any letter in the same horizontal line. Thus LD represents A, UM represents T, etc.

It will be noted that the cipher differs from (and has one great advantage over) Playfair in that there are sixteen alternative ways of encyphering any given letter. E can be enciphered as SL, SM, SN, ST, FL, FM, FN, FT, OL, OM, ON, OT, VL, VM, VN or VT.

'K' being omitted from the square, is the signal for numerals. The first two lines of the square, following K, become the figures 1 (E), 2 (L) etc., up to 10 (D). The signal for 'numbers off' is the letter O encoded, i.e. AH, WJ or the equivalent. The letters standing for numerals must also be encoded: 1 is not represented by E but by SL, OT or its equivalent.

It was arranged that the third word of each message should be the keyword for the next. Thus if a message (say on Monday) began with the words 'Argent pas encore arrive…' the square for Thursday's message would be as follows:

E	N	C	O	R
A	B	D	F	G
H	I	J	L	M
P	Q	S	T	U
V	W	X	Y	Z

In case of emergency or doubt, a standard keyword is arranged. If it was not known whether the other side had or had not received the last message, or likely to make any mistake about it, the square was to be constructed on the keyword EQUINOX. To indicate that this was being done, the first group of the message was to be SCOOI. This precaution proved a wise one. Owing partly to the incompetence of the enemy, partly due to technical troubles, the emergency codeword has had to be used over and over again.

It will be clear to the expert that, in spite of the alternatives, the cipher does not present any very grave difficulties to the 'cracker'. This does not matter, so far as we were concerned, though it should have caused the enemy some anxiety, had he been alive to our wireless security precautions. Meanwhile, it was easy and quick to work, and free from possible ambiguities.

APPENDIX II

ALLIED ORDER-OF-BATTLE INVENTIONS

Between 1942 and 1944 'A' Force created a series of false military units with the intention of greatly exaggerating the strength of the Allied forces deployed in the Middle East. These fabricated units, which include battalions, regiments, divisions, crops and entire armies, supposedly possessed their own individual identifying insignia which aided specific observations and reports. Having been established earlier in the war, these fabricated components remained available for deception purposes throughout 1944.

1942	1st SAS Brigade
	2nd Indian Infantry Division
	8th Division
	10th Armoured Division
	12th Division
	27th, 38th, 39th, 101st Battalions Royal Tank Regiment
	15th Armoured Division
	74th Armoured Brigade

Seven infantry divisions, including two Indian, one New Zealand

25th Corps HQ

1943   Eight infantry divisions including two Polish and one Greek, three
armoured and one airborne

12th Army

14th Corps HQ

CHRONOLOGY

1939	September	snow becomes a double agent run by MI5
	November	Richard Stevens and Sigismund Payne Best are abducted at Venlo.
	December	Levi operates in Paris as a double agent for the Deuxième Bureau.
1940	June	Levi withdrawn from Paris.
	September	Levi visits the British embassy in Belgrade, then returns to Italy.
	October	Levi visits the British embassy in Belgrade for a second time.
	November	The ATSB is established in Istanbul.
1941	January	Levi is arrested in Istanbul.
		Tobruk is captured by the British.
	February	Levi arrives in Cairo.
		Rommel is posted to Libya.
	March	Simpson participates in the Lofoten raid.
		Rommel captures Benghazi.
	April	Levi leaves Palestine for Istanbul.
		Axis forces occupy Yugoslavia.

	May	Allied BATTLEAXE attack fails.
		German paratroops capture Crete.
	June	Levi leaves Istanbul for Rome.
		Ritter fails to infiltrate two spies into Egypt.
	July	CHEESE establishes radio link to Bari.
		Auckinleck replaces Wavell.
	August	Levi is arrested in Genoa.
	September	Nicossof recruits Piet.
	October	Levi is sentenced to five years' imprisonment.
	November	CRUSADER recaptures Tobruk.
	December	Italian HQ assessment of Allied forces seized.
1942	January	The Abwehr loses confidence in Nicossof.
	February	Levi is transferred to Lucera.
	March	Whiteley appointed 8th Army Chief of Staff.
	April	Plan FABRIC devised.
	May	Eppler and Sandstede arrive in Cairo.
	June	Torbuk captured by the Afrika Korps.
	July	Afrika Korps advance stopped at El Alamein.
		Eppler and Sandstede are arrested in Cairo.
	August	*U-372* is sunk off Haifa.
		Five German spies executed in Aleppo.
	September	Simpson completes SIME's CHEESE *Report*.
	October	Fackenheim parachuted into Palestine.
		Nicossof's nominee fails to bring money from Aleppo.
	November	TORCH landings in North Africa.
	December	MISANTHROPE's flat in Cairo is raided by the police.
1943	January	Nicossof joins OETA.
	March	T. A. Robertson critiques SIME's CHEESE *Report*.

	April	Dick White is briefed on CHEESE in Cairo.
	May	Simpson responds to MI5 criticism of SIME's CHEESE *Report*.
	August	The PASCHA network closes down.
	October	Levi is released from prison.
		Mayer is captured in Yugoslavia.
	December	Plan BIJOU identifies HMS *Indefatigable* in the Indian Ocean.
1944	January	The Vermehrens defect in Istanbul.
		CHEESE receives payment from the Abwehr.
		MARIE visits Nicossof in Alexandria.
	February	Hamburger defects in Istanbul.
		Levi writes to SIME from Italy.
	March	Levi arrives in Cairo and is interviewed by Robertson.
		Pope writes the history of the CHEESE case.
	April	The Greek navy mutinies in Alexandria.
		Cornelia Kapp defects in Istanbul.
	May	Plan JACOBITE expands CHEESE to Greece.
	June	Allied troops land in Normandy on D-Day.
	July	BLACKGUARD delivers transmitter to FATHER.
	August	Marwitz is interned in Turkey.
	October	ODYSSEY fails to produce transmitter in Athens.
1945	January	Kossiadis is arrested in Athens.
	February	CHEESE's final radio transmission.
	March	MI5 seeks to revive CHEESE.

BIBLIOGRAPHY

Andrew, Christopher, *Secret Service* (London: Heinemann, 1985)

— —, *The Defence of the Realm* (London: Penguin, 2009)

Bar-Zohar, Michael, *Arrows of the Almighty* (London: Macmillan, 1985)

Bower, Tom, *The Perfect English Spy* (London: Heinemann, 1995)

Chapman, Eddie, *The Real Eddie Chapman Story* (London: Library 33, 1956)

Crowdy, Terry, *Deceiving Hitler* (Oxford: Osprey, 2008)

Curry, Jack, *The Security Service 1909-1945: The Official History* (London: PRO, 1999)

Eppler, John, *Operation Condor*: *Rommel's Spy* (London: Frontline, 2013)

Farago, Ladislas, *Game of the Foxes* (New York: McKay & Co, 1972)

Haufler, Hervie, *The Spies Who Never Were* (New American Library, 2006)

Hesketh, Roger, *FORTITUDE: The D-Day Deception Campaign* (London: St Ermin's Press, 1999)

Hinsley, Sir Harry, *British Intelligence in the Second World War: Security and Counter-Intelligence* (London: HMSO, 1990)

Hoffmann and Campe, *Deckname Dr. Rantzau* (Tausend, 1972)

Holt, Thadeus, *The Deceivers* (London: Simon & Schuster, 2004)

Howard, Sir Michael, *British Intelligence in the Second World War: Vol. V: Strategic Deception* (London: HMSO, 1990)

— —, *Strategic Deception in the Second World War* (New York: W.W. Norton, 1996)

Kahn, David, *Hitler's Spies* (New York: Macmillan, 1968)

Kross, Peter, *The Encyclopedia of World War II Spies* (Fort Lee, NJ: Barricade Books, 2001)

Liddell, Guy, *The Guy Liddell Diaries* (London: Routledge, 2005)

Macintyre, Ben, *Agent Zigzag* (London: Bloomsbury, 2010)

— —, *Double Cross* (London: Bloomsbury, 2013)

Masterman, J.C., *The Double Cross System of the War of 1939-45* (Boston, Mass: Yale University Press, 1972)

Miller, Russell, *Codename Tricycle* (London: Pimlico, 2005)

Mosley, Leonard, *The Cat and the Mouse* (New York: Harper Bros, 1958)

Mure, David, *Master of Deception* (London: William Kimber, 1980)

— —, *Practise to Deceive* (London: William Kimber, 1977)

Owen, Frank, *The Eddie Chapman Story* (New York: Julian Messner, 1954)

Peis, Gunter, *The Mirror of Deception* (London: Weidenfeld & Nicolson, 1976)

Pincher, Chapman, *Traitors* (London: Sidgwick & Jackson, 1987)

Polmar, Norman, and Thomas Allen, *Spy Book* (New York: Random House, 2004)

Popov, Dusko, *Spy Counter Spy* (London: Weidenfeld & Nicolson, 1974)

Pujol, Juan with Nigel West, *Garbo* (London: Weidenfeld and Nicolson, 1985)

Ritter, Nikolaus, *Alias Dr Rantzau* (Hamburg: Hoffmann und Campe, 1972)

Sansom, A.W., *I Spied Spies* (London: George Harrap, 1965)

Simkins, Anthony, *British Intelligence in the Second World War* (London: HMSO, 1990)

Simmons, Mark, *The Rebecca Code: Rommel's Spy in North Africa and Operation Condo* (London: Spellmount, 2013)

Stephens, Robin, *Camp 020: MI5 and the Nazi Spies* (London: PRO, 2000)

Waller, John H., *The Unseen War in Europe* (London: I. B. Tauris, 1996)

West, Nigel, *MI5: British Security Service Operations 1909-45* (London: Bodley Head, 1981)

— —, *Seven Spies Who Changed The World* (London: Secker & Warburg, 1991)

Wighton, Charles, and Gunter Peis, *Hitler's Spies and Saboteurs* (New York: Henry Holt & Co, 1958)

INDEX

Alessi, Capt. 37

Alexander, Gen. Harold 112, 146–7, 150, 156

Alexandria 21, 25–6, 36, 44, 46–9, 73, 85, 90, 105, 111–12, 114, 116, 126–28, 132–3, 143–7, 150–52, 154, 158, 160–69, 182, 185, 196–8, 201–2, 211, 231, 275, 297

Alexandria Cotton Exchange 33

Algiers 54, 75, 79, 99, 191, 208

Allied Military Government for Occupied Territories (AMGOT) xiii, 213

Almasy, Count Laszlo 129, 134–7

ALT 281

Amanullah, King of Afghanistan 280

Amer, Ali 131

Amie Direct (AD)

Amer, Fatma 134

American Tank Destroyer Command 145

AMGOT, see Allied Military Government for Occupied Territories

Amt VI, 76

ANDREAS 89

Andrew, Christopher xxiv

Anglo-Turkish Security Bureau (ATSB) 77, 82, 195

ANKER 76

Annabella xvii, 5, 35, 37, 231–34, 251, 253

Aosta, Duke of 105

APOLLO 5

Apostolis 21

Arab Bureau 75

Arab Medical Congress 201

Arents, Henri (FATHER) 195

ARMANDO 5

ARMAVIN xvii, 86, 181–82

ARMEN 51, 116

Arrows of the Almighty (Michael Bar-Zohar) 277

ARTHUR 82

ARTIST, *see* Johnny Jensen

ASLAN 115

Astor, Viscount 192

Athens 5, 57

Atlantis 84

Auchinleck, Gen. Claude xxiv, 16, 38, 43, 107, 111–12, 114, 155

Australian 4 Special Wireless Section 128

Ayvazian, Joseph 195

Aziz 83

B1(b) 137, 274
    Head of, *see* Herbert Hart
    See also Helenus Milmo; Blanshard Stamp

B.2 114

B Division (MI5) 55

B Division (SIME) 74
    See also Intelligence Coordination and Collation Section; Interrogation Section; Investigation Section; Most Secret Material Section; Records Section

Bad Wildungen 282

Baheshy, Robert 103

Bakos, Louis 103

Baldwin, Oliver 11

Balkan Section (SIME, A Division) 74

BARCLAY 198–9

Barclay, Cecil 270

Bari xviii, 1, 2, 8, 14, 55–56, 79, 101, 167, 229, 296

Barnet 75

BARON 185–7

BARRER 96

Bar-Zohar, Michael 277

BATTLEAXE 107, 296

BBC 99–100

Eppler, Johannes xviii, 267, 274–77, 296
Eppler-Wallin, Sonia 132
Eritrea 23, 73, 75
Escape and Evasion Service (MI9) xiv, 257
Executive Administration (SIME, A Division) 74
Ezzat, Hassan 131, 133

FABRIC 110–11, 296
Fackenheim, Paul 77
Fadl, Mohsen 83
Fahmy, Hekmet 133
Farouk, King 171
FATHER, see Henri Arents
Federation of British Industry 77
Fekhe, Hassan el 96
Fellers, Col. Bonner F. 124–26
Festival Theatre, Cambridge 9
Festungskommandant Crete xxiv
Field Security Wing 24
First United States Army Group (FUSAG) 87, 285
FLESHPOTS xiv, 127
Foley, Frank 205
Force 133 79
Forte Braschi 273
FORTITUDE xxv, 205
Fortune Theatre 9
Free French 40, 124–5, 144, 154, 161
Fremde Heerc West 98, 285, 203, 278
Freyberg, Gen. Bernard 128
Funkbeobachterdienst (B-Dienst) 30
FUSAG, see First United States Army Group

GABBIE 193
Gafaar, Hassan 130, 133, 138
Gafaar, Husein, see Johannes Eppler

Gafaar, Johanna 132
Gafaar, Saleh 133
Gailani (TAN) 97
GALA xviii, 112–13
GALVESTON xiv, 70–71, 261
Galveston, Maj. (alias of Dudley Clarke) 105
Garbarino, Antonio 8
GARBO xxv, 288
Garvin, James 207
Gaulle, Charles de 146–7, 161
Geheimschreiber xxv
GEORGE, see Georges Khouri
GEORGES 279
Georgios Averof 21, 151
German Wireless Intercept Organisation, The (Tozer) 126
Gestapo xx, 81, 98, 100, 102, 112, 133, 224, 254, 271, 277
Gibraltar xxv, 44–5, 53, 73, 88, 92, 95, 99, 114, 116, 162–63
Giffey, C. K. O. B. (Frank) 192
GILBERT xviii, 54
Gloucester Hussars 167
GODSEND xviii, 184–87
Goebbels, Dr Josef 61
Golden Arrow (Dudley Clarke) 284
Gott, Gen. William 112, 147
Grandguillor, Capt. Pierre 285
GRANDIOSE xiv, 111
Graziani, Marshal Rodolfo 104
Greece, King of 147–8, 202
Greek Section (SIME) 22
GROWNUP xvii, 116–17
Guillement, Therese 133, 137
Guingand, Gen. Freddie de 16
GULL xviii, 174–75, 177
Gutentag, Arno 209

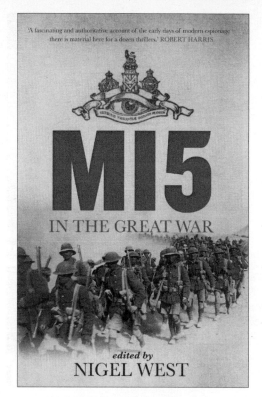

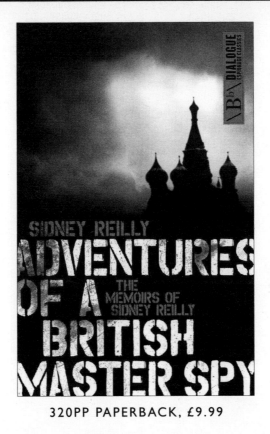

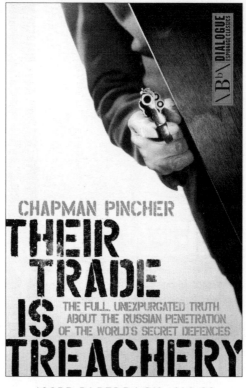

512PP PAPERBACK, £12.99

The British codebreakers at Bletchley Park are now believed to have shortened the duration of the Second World War by up to two years. During the dark days of 1941, as Britain stood almost alone against the Nazis, this remarkable achievement seemed impossible.

This extraordinary book, originally published as *Action This Day*, includes descriptions by some of Britain's foremost historians of the work of Bletchley Park, from the breaking of Enigma and other wartime codes and ciphers to the invention of modern computing and its influence on Cold War codebreaking. Crucially, it features personal reminiscences and very human stories of wartime codebreaking from former Bletchley Park codebreakers themselves. This edition includes new material from one of those who was there, making *The Bletchley Park Codebreakers* compulsive reading.

All royalties from this book will go to the Bletchley Park Trust.

— AVAILABLE FROM ALL GOOD BOOKSHOPS —